What Rosalind Likes

What Rosalind Likes

Pastoral, Gender, and the Founding of English Verse

PAUL J. HECHT

OXFORD
UNIVERSITY PRESS

OXFORD
UNIVERSITY PRESS

Great Clarendon Street, Oxford, OX2 6DP,
United Kingdom

Oxford University Press is a department of the University of Oxford.
It furthers the University's objective of excellence in research, scholarship,
and education by publishing worldwide. Oxford is a registered trade mark of
Oxford University Press in the UK and in certain other countries

© Paul J. Hecht 2022

The moral rights of the author have been asserted

Impression: 1

Published in the United States of America by Oxford University Press
198 Madison Avenue, New York, NY 10016, United States of America

British Library Cataloguing in Publication Data
Data available

Library of Congress Control Number: 2022930876

ISBN 978-0-19-285720-0

DOI: 10.1093/oso/9780192857200.001.0001

Printed and bound by
CPI Group (UK) Ltd, Croydon, CR0 4YY

For Heather

Acknowledgements

This book has been a long time coming and I owe debts of gratitude to many people, as well as several institutions; I am pleased to acknowledge a number of them here.

I have been lucky to have had wonderful teachers who encouraged my interests and obsessions. These include those who introduced me to poetry and literary possibilities: Ransom Griffin, David Sofield, William Pritchard, April Bernard, Caryl Phillips, Leslie Katz, Andrew Parker, and Karen Sanchez-Eppler. My studies continued with A. R. Ammons and Robert Morgan, and with Jonathan Culler, Reeve Parker, Roger Gilbert, Carol Kaske, and especially with Scott McMillin and Debra Fried. My dissertation advisor and lifelong mentor, Gordon Teskey, did his best to feed my desire to consume all of world literary history and theory; I am grateful for his patience and encouragement through the years. My knowledge of Roman poetry, such as it is, as well as shining examples to me of scholarship and devotion to teaching, I owe to the much-mourned Reginald Foster, and to Danuta Shanzer.

I am also grateful for generous and brilliant colleagues, many of whom have also been mentors in ways large and small. At Kalamazoo I met a supportive community of Spenserians and Sidneyans, including Anne Lake Prescott, Melissa E. Sanchez, Jeff Dolven, David Wilson-Okamura, Andrew Escobedo, Beth Quitslund, Ilona Bell, and Mary Ellen Lamb. At the Shakespeare Association I gained support from Timothy Billings, Kimberly Anne Coles, Stephen Guy-Bray, Richard Rambuss, Colleen Ruth Rosenfeld, Peter Holland, Russ McDonald, and Marion Wynne-Davies. My brief time in North Carolina gave me rich friendships with Louise Gossett, Allen Mandelbaum, Charles Ross, and Jeff Holdridge. I have benefitted enormously from the welcoming and encouraging community of the Chicago Area Renaissance Faculty Seminar, to whom I presented an early version of my work on Rosalind. I am particularly grateful to Richard Strier's benign leadership of this seminar, and the feedback from its rich and varied membership, including Bradin Cormack, William West, Jeff Masten, Suzanne Gossett, Michael Shapiro, Clark Gilpen, and Andrew Cutrofello. David Bevington was a frequent presence at the seminar, and the loss of his endless hospitality and energy I feel especially keenly. I am likewise grateful for the larger Chicagoland scholarly community, including Paula McQuade, Caterina Mongiat-Farina, Lara Crowley, Timothy Crowley, Timothy Harrison, David Simon, Megan Heffernan, and James Knapp.

A number of institutions have supported this work, including the Newberry Library, which gave me opportunities to try out ideas on Chicago area teachers, and also the opportunity to develop a digital exhibition. Much of my research depended on the University of Chicago's Regenstein Library with its splendid collections and expert staff. I am grateful to the Huntington Library for help in accessing the papers of Zoë Akins during the pandemic. Purdue University Northwest gave me supportive colleagues and supervisors, including particularly Michael Lynn, Colette Morrow, Angie Prinz, Liz Rodriguez, and Elaine Carey; I was also awarded a sabbatical leave that was crucial to the early drafting and development of the project, as well as consistent support and confidence in my research and writing in the years that followed. Fairleigh Dickinson University Press, and Rowman and Littlefield, gave me and my colleague J. B. Lethbridge a marvelous opportunity to press the limits of an essay collection in which a number of ideas for this project were in embryo. A conversation almost a decade ago with Jacqueline Norton of Oxford University Press gave me substantial encouragement through its long development. Since completing the manuscript, I have benefitted immensely from the expert guidance of Eleanor Collins and Karen Raith as well as Aimee Wright. I am also grateful for the many improvements to the text suggested by my project manager Hariharan Siva and copyeditor Rowena Anketell. I am especially grateful for the insightful and generous reports from my two readers for Oxford, one anonymous, and the other from Melissa E. Sanchez; the book is much improved through their detailed feedback and rich suggestions.

The book has also benefitted from many scholars whom I have never had the opportunity to meet but who, more and more, I realize have paved the way for my growth as a reader and writer. They include scholars in feminist and queer studies, who created those "studies" from whole cloth in the midst of skepticism, resentment, and outright resistance. Indeed, my growth as a scholar seems as much a gradual deepening and widening of my sense of those whose sacrifices and small victories have made this work possible.

I want to thank the students who participated in ten years of productions of early modern drama, especially Holly Trott, Aram Arden, Jeremy Harris, Eileen Long, Lillianna Pollnow, and Alexis Ulrich. My colleagues Jesse

Cohn, Bethany Lee, Sara Gerend, and Jason and Lilliana Curtis, made innumerable contributions as well. At an earlier stage for me were formative experiences with Shakespeare and Company, and Jonathan Epstein's marvelous sonnet workshops, as well as unforgettable experiences with Jeremy Lopez, Genevieve Love, and the casts of various non-Shakespearean drama projects in the early 2000s. I am also deeply grateful to Gerry Peters and the Canterbury Theatre as well as the Chicago arts community that supported our shows in Indiana with their experience, creativity, and generosity. In particular, I thank Rick Gilbert, Ariane Dolan, Rob Clearfield, Ada Palmer, and Lauren Schiller.

I have been lucky in friendship as well, with many who have provided mentorship too at various stages of this project and my career. Jake Adam York, my lost friend, is among those I most would like to give a copy of this book to provoke and bemuse him. Jeremy Lopez read a very early draft of a chapter and gave detailed advice and encouragement at several stages of its evolution. Matthew Harrison joined me in doing battle with the forces that prevent books from being written. Many conversations with Rachel Hile and Jeff Turco also kept me moving forward at various stages. And then there are my friends and extended family, including Donna Ng, Amber and Marlon Kuzmick, Paul and Cordelia Gover and Jasmine and my goddaughter Eleanor, Jonas Kellner, Tatyana Mamut, Joseph Braude, Will Hacker, Dina Bishara, Ron Corthell, Laura Bartolo, Susan Bussey, Emanuela Binello, and my sisters Suzanne Juhasz, Kathy Lawrence, my niece Alexandra Juhasz, my New Mexico family, Suzanne and David Fielding, Erin White and Lily Brooks. I know how much pleasure it would give my parents, Philip and Alcee, to see this work now entering the world, and I also have the keen pleasure of knowing that it would not much surprise them, such was their love and confidence. But my greatest debt I save for last, for my great love and partner, my wife Heather, who created with me the space for this book to be realized, and welcomed into our lives those who have given us endless love and support: Winnie, Franny, Agatha, Jeannie, Dasha, and Frankie. I dedicate this book to her.

Chapter 2, on Spenser, includes work that was originally published in two articles:

"Spenser Out of His Stanza." This article appeared in *Style* 39 (Fall 2005): 316–35. Copyright © 2005 The Pennsylvania State University Press. This article is used by permission of The Pennsylvania State University Press.

"Letters for the Dogs: Chasing Spenserian Alliteration." This article was published in *Spenser Studies* 25 (2010): 263–85. Copyright © The University of Chicago, https://doi.org/10.7756/spst.025.011.263-285.

Other previously published essays include starting points, and ideas and observations that have been expanded and developed throughout the book. These include the following:

"Receiving and Rendering: Notes on the Edited Shakespeare Page." This article was published in *Textual Cultures* 9, no. 1 (2014): 142–59. https://doi.org/10.14434/tc.v9i1.20118.

"Rosalind and Wroth: Tyranny and Domination." This essay first appeared in *Mary Wroth and Shakespeare*, edited by Marion Wynne-Davies and Paul Salzman, 115–24. New York: Routledge, 2014.

"Distortion, Aggression, and Sex in Mary Wroth's Sonnets." This article first appeared in *SEL Studies in English Literature 1500-1900* 53, no. 1 (2013): 91–115.

A Note on Texts

I have tried to quote from the most accessible versions of early modern and classical texts whenever possible. I have used Richard McCabe's edition of Spenser's shorter works (London: Penguin, 1999), and *The Norton Shakespeare* (3rd edn., 2016) except for *As You Like It*, where I have used Juliet Dusinberre's Arden edition (2006). With unmodernized texts (and with Spenser's deliberately archaic style) I have silently modernized u/v and i/j; in modernized editions I have silently supplied US spellings for British ones (e.g., "honor" for "honour").

Contents

1

Introduction

What Rosalind Likes

ORLANDO Good day and happiness dear Rosalind.
JAQUES Nay then, God b'wi' you an you talk in blank verse.
[*Exit.*]

As You Like It, 4.1.27–9

Shepherds devise she hateth as the snake.

The Shepheardes Calender, "Januarye," 65

Feeling the Fury

To be an expert is always to risk getting too close to the object of study, and to lose the ability to see it clearly and objectively. Can we imagine a theatergoer in the twenty-first century who, upon hearing an actor walk on stage and utter a line of iambic pentameter, gets up and walks out in disgust? What about hatred of pastoral poetry—that is *pastoral* poetry, not just poetry in general—hatred of the intensity described in that line from "Januarye"?[1] We still certainly feel hatred and feel disgust, but not about this: our world of endless punditry, of online comments and reviews leaves these matters to one side. Poetry, as such, exists in a highly circumscribed zone, such that one can make a joke like the one that showed up in the film *The Big Short*,

---

[1] I take "Shepherds devise" to encompass, among other things, "the creative projects of shepherds." Consulting the *Oxford English Dictionary* (*OED*) gives us usages contemporary to Spenser that include "A fanciful, ingenious, or witty writing or expression, a 'conceit'" (s.v. "device," 10); "Something artistically devised or framed; a fancifully conceived design or figure" (8); "The *manner* in which a thing is devised or framed; *design*" (1.b, my emphasis); and even "Will, pleasure, inclination, fancy, *desire*" (3.a, my emphasis again).

What Rosalind Likes. Paul J. Hecht, Oxford University Press.
© Paul J. Hecht (2022). DOI: 10.1093/oso/9780192857200.003.0001

namely that poetry is hated as much as an invitation to awake to the appalling and foundationless state of late capitalism: and nobody wants that.[2]

The mission of this book is to move closer to getting Shakespeare's Jaques joke, to a place where hearing a line of blank verse might elicit an unthinking "bye," having nothing to do with anything the line says, or where some "device" or devices—a certain kind of taste for alliteration for example— likewise can fill a listener with fury. This is not because this author wants to be more of a "hater," but because he wants poetry to matter now like it mattered then, because he wants the discussion to be, if not as intense now as it was then, then at least to have a connection to that intensity. Feeling the fury is necessary to feeling the joy.

I have selected one person with whom to pursue this mission, my guide into the world of high-stakes, charged and fraught Elizabethan aesthetics, and her name is Rosalind. It is she who does the hating in the second quotation, and she who is the object of the poetic greeting offered so innocently by Orlando in the first. Those two moments are tied to 1579 and about 1600 respectively, when the book and play in which they appear entered the world. And there is one more moment, in 1590, namely the publication of the popular book by Thomas Lodge upon which *As You Like It* was largely based. That was called *Rosalynde: Euphues' Golden Legacy*, connecting it loudly (in a pirated intellectual property kind of way) with the even more popular *Euphues* books by John Lyly of the previous decade.[3] Together, these three texts take us through twenty of the most consequential years in the history of English literature, and, with Spenser's book of pastoral lyrics and dialogues, Lodge's prose-verse romance, and Shakespeare's play, encompass the most consequential genres of that literature excepting only epic (and as we shall see, Spenser's Rosalind arguably touches on that genre too). What lines of development can such intense feelings about poetry in and surrounding this "Rosalind" display? This book explores how we might shed our expertise, our inability to experience this poetry freshly and rawly, as we devote ourselves to contemplating what Rosalind hates and what Rosalind likes.[4]

---

[2] *The Big Short*, directed by Adam McKay, screenplay by Adam McKay and Charles Randolph (2015). The line appears as a title on screen: "The truth is like poetry—and most people fucking hate poetry," and gets the credit "overheard in a Washington, D.C. bar by Michael Lewis." Lewis is the author of the book that inspired the film: *The Big Short: Inside the Doomsday Machine* (New York: Norton, 2010). The line quoted in the film does not appear in the book.

[3] The two originals were *Euphues: The Anatomy of Wit* (1578) and *Euphues and his England* (1580).

[4] Very few scholars have been interested in linking these three works; Clare Kinney is a notable exception, with an essay that explores what it means to see "Rosalind" as a woman reader

Where this leads me is to write a kind of technical history of "Rosalind," or a biography of poetry. By technical, I mean everything from large-scale questions about whether and how to use classical meters in English, or the nature of poetic ornament, to smaller-scale questions like how to prevent poems in stanzas from becoming boring and repetitive, or how much alliteration is too much—in every case investigating these questions on the basis of (often intemperate, exaggerating) cues from Rosalind and the voices that surround her in the texts themselves. By biography I mean the writing of life, how we move from the ephemeral Petrarchan shadow-Rosalind of *The Shepheardes Calender* to the Rosalind of *As You Like It*, and to some extent beyond, to the performances that inscribed the role in the public mind. Is that life—vivid, compelling, endlessly desirable—just some X factor of Shakespeare's genius that came like a bolt from the blue? This study presumes "no." I am postulating that the triumphant Shakespeare character at the end of this line of texts owes something to the development of English poetry in those twenty years. But what does she owe? And what kinds of exchanges take place between this fictive woman and the poetry that she both consumes and embodies? For of course she *is* poetry, "made" by words as much as she also tastes, tries on, and judges words.

In my attention to negative emotions, my interest in setting aside certain kinds of expertise, and my desire to press "technical history" and "biography" out of their standard uses, this project aligns with some broader impulses and questions about methodology across literary studies. While I am interested in, as Elizabeth S. Anker and Rita Felski put it, the "creative or generative force" of negative emotions, I tend more to think that my respect for Rosalind's scorn is the impetus for what could be understood as a kind of surface reading, where we take seriously indications in texts that have long been consigned to triviality.[5] But my use of "technical history" and "biography" against their respective grains points to the depths that I am interested in following out. For I am interested in feeling the technical texture of Rosalind, the materiality of rhythm and sound that inform her fictive life, and I am also interested in treating aspects of poetry that have been demoted to triviality with deeper respect, which may speak to its sensuous power, or

and writer across the three works. See Clare R. Kinney, "Feigning Female Faining: Spenser, Lodge, Shakespeare, and Rosalind," *Modern Philology* 95 (February 1998): 291–315.

[5] See Elizabeth S. Anker and Rita Felski, "Introduction," in *Critique and Postcritique*, ed. Elizabeth S. Anker and Rita Felski (Durham, NC and London: Duke University Press, 2017), 1–28, at 12.

4 WHAT ROSALIND LIKES

to an erotics of art, or an ethical stance toward art that parallels respect for humanity.[6]

I am also conscious of the fact that I am a man writing about a fictive woman in fictions created by men, and my destabilizing of terminology is also meant to keep me from becoming too comfortable in this role. With that said, the work of many literary scholars in feminist and queer studies has cleared a path for a project like this to unfold, and avoid, I hope, the kind of criticism that most prominently was argued by Elizabeth Harvey in her book of 1992, *Ventriloquized Voices*, as well as Marguerite Waller's review essay of 1987, "Academic Tootsie."[7] From that point of view, my project might seem destined to silence the voices of women and affirm or participate in misogyny, or, as Louis Montrose might warn, to express uncritical "infatuation" with Rosalind.[8] I would say that the path has been cleared to avoid such a destiny both in theory and methodology, as well as through new historical understandings. For example, Kathryn Schwarz's *What You Will* (2011) begins by stating its objective to "explore the ways in which predominately male-authored texts address the volition of women."[9] In supporting that project, Schwarz cites work by Valerie Traub noting that texts written by men could be "an intrinsic, indeed, constitutive part of women's lived experience," and by Dympna Callaghan on the "paradox of representation," that the nature of representation is such that its relationship to subjectivity is not limited by what Schwarz calls "the absence of 'actual' women."[10]

---

[6] Anker and Felski's overview highlights a number of these threads, from critics who replace a general attitude of suspicion and penetrative analysis with a commitment to "treating texts with respect, care and attention" ("Introduction," 16), to the continuing influence of Susan Sontag's call for an erotics rather than hermeneutics of art (see Sontag, *Against Interpretation and Other Essays* [New York: Farrar, Straus and Giroux, 1966]), to Jacques Rancière's arguments for the potential of "aesthetic dissensus" (17; see Rancière, *Dissensus: On Politics and Aesthetics*, trans. Seven Corcoran (New York: Continuum, 2010). Amber Jamilla Musser alerted me to a parallel, "intensive way of reading … with love" in the thought of Gilles Deleuze. See Amber Jamilla Musser, *Sensational Flesh: Race, Power, and Masochism*, Sexual Cultures (New York: New York University Press, 2014), 23, quoting Gilles Deleuze, "Letter to a Harsh Critic," in *Negotiations, 1972–1990*, trans. Martin Joughin (New York: Columbia University Press, 1995), 3–12.

[7] See Elizabeth D. Harvey, *Ventriloquized Voices: Feminist Theory and English Renaissance Texts* (London and New York: Routledge, 1992); and Marguerite Waller, "Academic Tootsie: The Denial of Difference and the Difference It Makes," *Diacritics* 17, no. 1 (1987): 2–20.

[8] See Louis Adrian Montrose, "'The Place of a Brother' in *As You Like It*: Social Process and Comic Form," *Shakespeare Quarterly* 32 (1981): 28–54, at 52.

[9] Kathryn Schwarz, *What You Will: Gender, Contract, and Shakespearean Social Space* (Philadelphia: University of Pennsylvania Press, 2011), 15.

[10] Valerie Traub, *The Renaissance of Lesbianism in Early Modern England* (Cambridge: Cambridge University Press, 2002), 21; Dympna Callaghan, *Shakespeare Without Women: Representing Gender and Race on the Renaissance Stage* (London: Routledge, 2000), 13; Schwarz, *What You Will*, 15.

As Schwarz summarizes, "the patriarchal enterprise is far less than the sum of its parts, and stories about feminine volition divulge a great deal about the strains and the breaks."[11] A great deal of pertinent new historical information has also become available since the early 1990s. As early as 2005, Phyllis Rackin, in *Shakespeare and Women*, was able to point out numerous complications to our understanding of the lives of women and aspects of Elizabethan patriarchal culture that had been taken for granted a few years earlier. These include new understanding of the importance of women (all kinds of women) in playgoing audiences, and the extent to which the prescriptions of conduct books are belied by facts on the ground, with respect, for example, to women's independence, participation and agency in marriage, and ownership of property. As Rackin notes, "while *As You Like It* is a fantasy, the female household that Rosalind and Celia establish in the forest had precedents in the very district where the theatre was located"—in that district, according to an essay published in 1997, "at least 16 percent of households were headed by a woman."[12] It changes things significantly to imagine that Rosalind was performing for people who could see themselves in her in this specific way, as well as people for whom the aesthetic success of what Shakespeare wrote would have mattered a great deal: for Shakespeare, we could argue, women *needed* to like Rosalind.

But in addition to tracing the development of Rosalind, one line of development that emerges here is that poetry gets better. This is an oddly contentious claim to make in the twenty-first century, that Spenser's poetry in *The Shepheardes Calender* is not as good as Shakespeare's in *As You Like It*. There are profound-seeming theoretical objections to such a claim (that aesthetic evaluation is a mask for ideology, or for class distinctions), but I think that the professional objections are likely more pertinent. Professional courtesy suggests that we do not compare authors or literature or poetry with significant scholarly followings in this way, at least not as part of a formal project. This isn't to say that there is not occasional griping about the *Calender* in particular to be heard even from devoted scholars of Spenser, but a position like Jeff Dolven's in his essay on Spenser's metrics in the Oxford *Handbook* of 2010 is more typical: "*Januarye* gives us Colin writing

[11] Schwarz, *What You Will*, 16.
[12] Phyllis Rackin, *Shakespeare and Women* (Oxford: Oxford University Press, 2005), 20. On p. 19, Rackin quotes Diana E. Henderson, "The Theater and Domestic Culture," in *A New History of Early English Drama*, ed. John D. Cox and David Scott Kastan (New York: Columbia University Press, 1997), 173–194, at 192.

in excellent pentameter and high rhetorical melancholy."[13] He then gives examples of the kinds of "neat" patterning that support his claim. The implication is that this is good poetry. But I am more inclined to agree with Rosalind's feeling toward Colin's poetry, which is to say "scorne"—as Colin puts it in "Januarye": "Shee deignes not my good will, but doth reprove, / And of my rurall musick holdeth scorne" (3–4). Where Dolven finds "neatness" I find verse effects that are stiff, contrived, and too obvious to elicit much pleasure. I want to pursue the sort of analysis that can lead one to feel Rosalind's "scorne," or at least to recognize the shortcomings of the poetry in the *Calender* with respect to the writing to which it sought to compare itself. Because this allows one then to feel the triumph of the writing that came after (including Spenser's later writing), and to pay attention to what makes that poetry succeed where this failed. And what we *can* appreciate about Spenser's art in the *Calender* is his willingness to allow Rosalind's view to enter the work itself. That, I will claim, is evidence of a profoundly experimental stance that is one of the greatest strengths of the *Calender*. To put it more bluntly, Spenser didn't know quite what he was doing, did not know how to match classical poetry in English as had been done in other languages, and didn't know more specific things—how to manage transitions between stanzas, how much alliteration was too much, how to manage some of the very effects that Dolven praises. But the book daringly explores possibilities, and, through Rosalind's negative evaluation, dares to consider its own failure, and responses to that failure. Which is to say that my entire approach to the book is based on listening to what Rosalind likes, and in this case, what she doesn't like one bit.

Virgil Problems

In order to provide a better sense of context in which to see what is wrong with poetry in 1579, it is useful to remind ourselves of what was right about it 1,500 years earlier, namely to turn to the pastoral poetry of Virgil, the Virgil of the *Eclogues*. Virgil is a presence for all three writers but for Spenser and Shakespeare this poetry is especially important.[14] There is a

---

[13] Jeff Dolven, "Spenser's Metrics," in *The Oxford Handbook of Edmund Spenser*, ed. Richard A. McCabe (Oxford: Oxford University Press, 2010), 397. The assumption is that the works of authors of scholarly interest are all interesting, all valuable.

[14] The importance of Virgil's *Eclogues* for *The Shepheardes Calender* is widely acknowledged. In arguing for a significant connection with *As You Like It*, I am more on my own, though

preconception in some quarters that, because it is pastoral, Virgil's *Eclogues* are less sophisticated than the *Georgics* and *Aeneid*. In fact, their influence on Western literature is based on remarkable achievements, achievements both of style and of content.[15] Stylistically, there is the merger of simplicity and plainness with the artfulness of Golden Age Latin poetry, which I will explore more closely below. And the *Eclogues* also deliver on major pastoral projects, demonstrating fellowship in suffering, and concord through song, through shared, joined expression of experience.[16] Looking at Virgil's technical and stylistic achievements helps to bring into relief the challenges English poets faced; and as it turns out, looking at the effects of translating Virgil's pastoral project into an English cultural context also highlights important aspects of the technical history of Rosalind, and what, in this context, can be called a feminist project; but first to the technical in the more ordinary sense.

Some of the most challenging aspects of Virgil's style to imitate in English emanate from features of the Latin language itself, and features of Augustan poetic and prose style. Latin is a case-based language without articles, which frequently goes without prepositions as well. Augustan Latin poetry, from the reign of Augustus (27 BCE–14 CE), and also known, from earlier philological traditions, as Golden Age poetry (spanning back to 70 BCE), is focused on symmetries and departures from symmetries, so an excellent line might have the verb in the center, and subject, object, and indirect object with associated adjectives distributed in concentric rings around it.[17] It is hard to

---

not entirely alone. For a useful recent discussion of Virgil's influence on and importance to Shakespeare, see Colin Burrow, *Shakespeare and Classical Antiquity*, Oxford Shakespeare Topics (Oxford: Oxford University Press, 2013), 51–91. Burrow develops an argument in the face of critics that have downplayed Virgil's importance, suggesting that Shakespeare's primary interest in Virgil relates to "the affective force of speech," as for example "the powerful influence of Aeneas's act of narrating on Dido" (56). While he writes at greater length of *Lucrece* and *Hamlet*, he notes that *As You Like It* is "the most eclogic of Shakespeare's plays" (55).

[15] Unlike Spenser, Virgil waited until he was almost 40 to publish these poems: they are not juvenilia. On the contrary, they show a fully formed poet, at home in his medium of un-rhymed dactylic hexameters—the same line he would use in all his published poetry, derived from Homer, and the basis for what we in English would eventually call "blank verse." David Scott Wilson-Okamura addresses the sense that the *Eclogues* were written in a "low style," as compared with the *Georgics* and *Aeneid*, but in an otherwise extremely illuminating discussion of the development of Spenser's style, I do not think he gives Spenser enough credit for also perceiving the density and sophistication of the *Eclogues*. See David Scott Wilson-Okamura, *Spenser's International Style* (Cambridge: Cambridge University Press, 2013), 20–4.

[16] In setting out this version of what pastoral delivers, I am very much influenced by the work of Paul Alpers in *What is Pastoral?* (Chicago: University of Chicago Press, 1996); see ch. 1, "Representative Anecdotes and Ideas of Pastoral," 8–43.

[17] For a wide-ranging exploration of such structures and effects, see L. P. Wilkinson, *Golden Latin Artistry* (Cambridge: Cambridge University Press, 1963).

make English do anything like this. Then there is the prosody. My view is that Roman poets were adept at working with both word-accent and quantity at once, and that the play of tension between these two, ordinarily resolved in the final two feet of every hexameter line, is one of the fundamental features of this poetry.[18] This as well is very hard to deal with in English, mostly since English is much less certain of what "quantity" is and how it works, whether rules can be applied to it, than was Latin and the Greek from which this system was derived. Spenser debated the issue with Gabriel Harvey in print, and did not come to a satisfying conclusion.[19]

But even setting to one side the knotty questions of translation and prosody, we can still access the beauty, range, and sophistication of Virgil's pastorals without a great deal of trouble, and without too heavy a dose of Latin. And we can do this at the same time as we explore examples of the non-stylistic pastoral achievements, of musical concord and fellowship in suffering. Virgil's opening eclogue is a dialogue, and has other qualities of a dramatic scene.[20] It features two strangers: a shepherd, Melibœus (who is essentially an internal refugee, forced to seek land following the displacement of people to make room for veterans of the civil war), wanders by the shepherd Tityrus, who has been granted an unappealing plot by Octavian, for which he is nonetheless eternally grateful to the extent of being worshipful (he refers to Octavian as "deus," and speaks of the continual sacrifices he makes in gratitude). The power of the poem emanates from the sympathy that the two men feel for one another, expressed both explicitly and through the music of the poem, through what becomes a kind of duet. This fellowship in suffering, sympathy, heightened and musical dialogue is most famously visible in the poem's ending in which, in a demonstration of the trust and good feeling that are the products of the poem, Tityrus offers Melibœus a

---

[18] There is ongoing controversy about this topic among scholars. T. V. F. Brogan and his colleagues note that the relevance of Latin word-accent in its meter is "the central unresolved question in the field." See T. V. F. Brogan, A. T. Cole, and L. Blumenfeld, "Classical Prosody," in *The Princeton Encyclopedia of Poetry and Poetics*, ed. Roland Greene et al. (4th edn., Princeton: Princeton University Press, 2012), 262.

[19] Or rather, he thought he did, but all later practice seems to show him dropping the claims for quantitative prosody that he makes here. For a brief, very cogent discussion, see Dolven, "Metrics," 395–6.

[20] Pastorals as Virgil inherited the form from Theocritus are both a lyric and a dialogic form, which is to say that pastorals often have more than one speaker, and to an extent can thus take on something approaching a dramatic scene. I know of no efforts to present Virgil's *Eclogues* as an evening of theater, but this does not seem beyond the realm of possibility—at a conference at Shakespeare's Globe in London in 2017, conferees were given much more of a sense of what this might be like, as actors staged excerpts from the *Calender* and other works by Spenser in the Sam Wanamaker Playhouse.

place to spend the night, and the simple refreshments (apples, chestnuts, cheese) that are on hand. As night descends, with its "vespertinal" quality,[21] these two are not alone, and the forces that determine their existence and that of their flocks, and which can become so quickly malevolent, are for this evening, kept at bay.

> et iam summa procul villarum culmina fumant
> maioresque cadunt altis de montibus umbrae.
>
> (82–3)

> And already in the distance, the tops of houses smoke,
> And shadows from the tallest mountains loom.[22]

That makes for the first eclogue's famous ending, but it is another moment, earlier in the poem, that provides a better indication of the combination of song and fellowship that the poem offers. This is the moment when Melibœus, though he has never previously met Tityrus, provides a narrative that fills in what happened when Tityrus made his pilgrimage to Rome. Melibœus sings of Amaryllis, the woman, we are led to imagine, that Tityrus had been singing of as Melibœus first approached. Now he picks up the tune, and sings, not of his own suffering, nor of Tityrus's, but of the loneliness of the people Tityrus left behind, the crops and the landscape itself.

> Mirabar, quid maesta deos, Amarylli, vocares,
> cui pendere sua patereris in arbore poma:
> Tityrus hinc aberat. ipsae te, Tityre, pinus,
> ipsi te fontes, ipsa haec arbusta vocabant.
>
> (36–9)

> I wondered why, Amaryllis, you called up sadly to the gods,
> And for whom you allowed the fruit to hang on trees;
> Tityrus had abandoned you. For you, Tityrus, the pines,
> For you the fountains, for you these fields called out.

---

[21] The term is Erwin Panofsky's, a quality which he also ventured to call Virgil's special and "most personal" achievement, in *Meaning in the Visual Arts* (Chicago: University of Chicago Press, 1955), 300.

[22] The text is from *Eclogues, Georgics, Aeneid I–VI*, trans. H. Rushton Fairclough, vol. 63, Loeb Classical Library (Cambridge, MA: Harvard University Press, 1999). The translation is mine. Subsequent quotations are from this text.

From just these lines, a reader would be forgiven for thinking that Amaryllis is present in the scene and that Melibœus knows her. But she never speaks, and Tityrus himself never addresses her. It seems more likely that this is a further extension of the poetic sympathy that Melibœus displays, to sympathize with the Amaryllis that pined for the absent Tityrus, and sympathize indeed with the inanimate objects, the nature that poetry in its mythological imaginings always yearns, with Orpheus, to touch. And likewise, even if you don't know a word of Latin, we can agree on a few things: Virgil's verse shows off its sophistication in a number of ways. Its lines are not end-stopped, but pauses (just look at the commas) are continuously variable.[23] The first line, addressed to Amaryllis, puts us into this space of sympathetic memory, but does so in the somewhat halting manner of naturalistic speech; the second is a line of poetry if we ever saw one, with the main verb "patereris" in the center, with prepositional phrase "in sua arbore" (on its tree) split and arrayed around it, and main object "poma" (fruit) at the end, with the verb it controls, "pendere" (to hang), at the start.

cui	pendere	sua	patereris	in arbore	poma
for whom	to hang	their→	you left	on **their** tree	the fruit

That's Latin poetry. What is also Latin poetry is to follow that complexity with simplicity, plainness, and compression—which is exactly what happens next: "Tityrus hinc aberat" (Tityrus had left)—a simple explanation for what comes before, but also a half-line with a very strong stopping point, before the sentence that starts up next and, with its repeated "ipsa"s, stretches over to the next line. We have lyrical complexity, plainness and simplicity, and naturalistic speech, and the ability to move effortlessly among these.

We also have sound patterns, some of which require a more detailed analysis of rhythm, of quantity and accent, but even without those and again, without any Latin at all, one can perceive the strong alliteration of that same concentrically constructed, lyrical line:

cui **p**endere sua **p**atereris in arbore **p**oma:

This is unrhymed poetry, but, as we will explore in more detail in chapter 2, alliteration is a key poetic ornament for Spenser and Elizabethan poets generally—and also the object of considerable debate and concern.

---

[23] The commas are not Virgil's of course—the codices that transmit Virgil's work do not even contain spaces between words.

Such a simple and lowly sound effect is not one popularly associated with Virgil, but there it is.

So what do I claim from these observations? Fundamentally I claim that Elizabethans were good enough Latinists and sensitive enough poets that their reverence for Virgil was not blind, but was founded on detailed appreciation of the effects and techniques that Virgil wove together in his poetry, including the supposedly plain and humble pastoral.[24] I further claim that they could appreciate the simple power of what Melibœus does here: not just sympathizing with a stranger's suffering, but being ready to sing, movingly, of that suffering on the spot, to give it weight and reality and also to lift it aesthetically, to turn it into something beautiful. A dual comfort then: speaking, acknowledging, witnessing this past grief, and doing so with an eloquence and lyricism that make the grief both more poignant and more easily borne. And this is all the more moving because it comes unbidden, is offered entirely for free, although in the end Tityrus reaches for tangibles to reward, or perhaps simply to acknowledge that as much as one would like to be sustained by the giving and receiving of poetry, poets have bodies that must be sustained by more than praise. This concord, this interplay, this giving and receiving is the aesthetic and moral economy that Virgil's pastoral makes available to Elizabethans and which, I want to show, my three authors gradually mine more and more deeply.

Problems with Sex and Aesthetics

But if Virgil's pastorals in this view set a standard or a lofty goal for what English poetry might accomplish, a telos for the "biography" of poetic development that is one half of this project, what do they offer for the understanding of the development of Rosalind, or more broadly the development of feminine identity or what I earlier called the feminist project of this study? The obvious element is the frank and unpejorative portrayal of the homoerotic, the homoerotic as unproblematically substitutable for the heteroerotic, and the fundamental question that this poses to Christian heterosexual culture. Christian Europe abominated sodomy but the Renaissance celebrated classical learning and culture that often sets homoerotic

---

[24] I am also suggesting that the rather more narrow view of how Elizabethans read and heard Latin verse established by Derek Attridge may be ripe to be challenged. See Derek Attridge, *Well-Weighed Syllables: Elizabethan Verse in Classical Metres* (Cambridge: Cambridge University Press, 1974).

relations above heteroerotic ones—this all the way back to such founding texts as the *Iliad*, where Achilles' main-act rage is over the death not of his slave-girlfriend Briseis but his long-term lover Patroclus, and where Plato's *Symposium* argues for the superiority of love between men and boys over commonplace heterosexual congress, however pleasing and useful. Virgil's pastorals present this vexing difficulty of cultural inheritance in the second poem of the sequence, as Corydon "burns" for a slave boy Alexis, who is the favorite of the master, and therefore sexually inaccessible to another retainer like Corydon. The young man sings his unrequited longing, not to a woman but a boy. And furthermore this gains some sharpness from the fact that the poem Virgil is imitating from Theocritus is heterosexual, though also cross-species—as the cyclops Polyphemus pines for the sea nymph Galatea.[25]

Built into the classical poetic tradition that feeds directly into pastoral is thus an extraordinary equivalence or substitutability between male erotic passion for women and boys. Christian culture condemned this, made laws against it, and yet a similar dynamic of substitutability was especially prominent in Elizabethan England, and nowhere more so than on the Elizabethan stage—that could not, generally, tolerate women performing, and preferred instead to have boys in their roles. This substitutability will gradually be more and more exploited in the history and development of Rosalind, which tracks with the development of Elizabethan drama, and the increasing complexity of cross-dressing plots. What seems to be lacking in Virgil at least, and more widely in classical literary culture, is pervasive anxiety about these matters, or at least anything comparable to Christian anxiety.[26] Not only

---

[25] The reading of Eclogue 2 as displaying sexual passion between two males appears to have been general in Elizabethan England, even as it was possible to ignore this. Jonathan Goldberg discusses an asexual, pedagogical interpretation of the poem that appears in Erasmus's *De Ratione Studii*; this in Goldberg's *Sodometries: Renaissance Texts, Modern Sexualities* (Stanford, CA: Stanford University Press, 1992), 66. But Goldberg also notes a famous quotation attributed to Christopher Marlowe by Thomas Kyd, which has received renewed interest in the wake of the convergence of queer theory and theology known as "queer theology." Marlowe, Kyd alleged, "wold report St John to be our saviour Christes Alexis." This in "Kyd's Unsigned Note to Puckering," in *The Life of Marlowe and the Tragedy of Dido Queen of Carthage*, ed. C. F. Tucker Brooke (London: Methuen, 1930), 107; quoted in Richard Rambuss, "The Straightest Story Ever Told," *GLQ: A Journal of Gay and Lesbian Studies* 17, no. 4 (2011): 543–73, at 563.

[26] This not to say that versions of European Christian anxieties about sexuality and gender are not to be found in the classical world: one of the most famous is also Virgil's, namely the affair between Aeneas and Dido. But in Elizabethan England, we never seem free of such dynamics. In important volumes, Stephen Guy-Bray analyzes pastoral, Virgil, and homoeroticism with a considerably different focus from mine. This study partially diverges from this work, in deemphasizing, with Alpers, the nostalgic and elegiac frameworks for understanding pastoral, and also diverges in its greater focus on women. See Stephen Guy-Bray, *Homoerotic Space:*

do the *Eclogues* lack the slightest sense that a love like Corydon's might be shameful, they lack a sense that erotic passion generally should shame the one who feels the passion, as much as it can cause pain. For Elizabethans, *amor* toward anyone, or indeed anything, risks emasculation, risks sinfulness, risks a descent into uncontrolled appetites that are all associated with the feminine.[27] Thus when we get to Spenser's closest version of the Tityrus–Meliboeus dynamic in the *Calender*, the Meliboeus figure is acutely feminized by his economic misfortune. There is no indication of anything comparable for Virgil's Meliboeus.

Let me set out my logic: if to be in Meliboeus's position in Eclogue 1 is to be a man shamefully feminized, then to embrace and support such a man is to resist that shaming. And if it is shamefully feminine to sing at all, to sing in sympathy for another's suffering, then to celebrate such sympathetic eloquence is to resist that shaming. And both acts of resistance I would call feminist, in the sense that to resist the shaming of what is feminized in a patriarchal culture is to resist patriarchy. Which is to say that such feminism might not have existed for Virgil, for the *Eclogues*, but when translated into the realm of anti-aesthetic anti-feminist Elizabethan culture, a feminism can come into being.

So in fact the act of translating Virgilian pastoral into Elizabethan England yields more complications than just the problem of homoerotic or pederastic desire (or "disorderly love" as E.K. refers to it[28]); the translation generates complex gender and gendering dynamics that engulf the speakers, and also engulf the aesthetic project of writing poetry that "does Virgil in English." This leads me to claim, broadly, that tracing the history of "Rosalind" through these texts, and tracing the development and improvement of English poetry, can be called a feminist project. Where in Virgil to be a refugee can simply be to be down on one's luck, for Elizabethans to be a refugee is to be emasculated and feminized. And that is also the effect, bizarrely, of aesthetic *success*, and *working* to achieve aesthetic success. To be involved in an aesthetic project, say, attempting to raise the standard of poetry in English, is likewise to be emasculated and feminized. I will discuss

---

The Poetics of Loss in Renaissance Literature (Toronto: University of Toronto Press, 2002) and *Loving in Verse: Poetic Influence as Erotic* (Toronto: University of Toronto Press, 2006). And see Alpers, *What Is Pastoral?*, 8–43.

[27] I don't believe that this point is particularly controversial, but it does require more development, which it receives in chapters 2 and 3, especially the latter, where I explore, following Kimberly Anne Coles's work on the subject, the religious backdrop to Elizabethan attacks on aesthetic productions and pastimes of various sorts.

[28] In the Shepheardes Calender, note to "Januarye" line 59, p. 39.

this below with respect to Ben Jonson's first major stage success, *Every Man In His Humour*, a play contemporary with *As You Like It* which provides some clarifying corroboration of the sexual and aesthetic dynamics I see in Shakespeare and elsewhere. Even in 1600, even with two decades of the Elizabethan High Renaissance under the culture's collective belt, there is extraordinary sexual tension swirling around aesthetic matters. But the larger claim is that Rosalind's development across the texts, the way she develops complexity, agency, the way, in Lodge, she begins to explore all manner of social and political and religious topics, and intervene (sometimes by virtue of her daring cross-dressing) in a variety of relationships in a way that can easily be seen as consonant with freedom and possibility, is a parallel development to the wrestling with aesthetic challenges that each author takes on. Rosalind's feminine freedom and agency develops in parallel and sometimes in overlap with poetic development that is detailed, technical, geeky, and also in conflict with Elizabethan and Western hang-ups about art, sexuality, gender, and politics, hang-ups which I would summarize under the banner of problems with sex and aesthetics.

I have elsewhere explored the basis for a study of this kind, a study with a dual concern for sex and aesthetics in early modern British literature.[29] The basis is arguably "presentist" too, because for various reasons, studies of aesthetic matters, like poetic rhythm and stanza structure, have tended to go on quite separately from matters of gender and sexuality. Building a book around the three literary Rosalinds that appeared between 1579 and 1600 resists that separation and compartmentalization, and highlights what for Elizabethans was not easily separated. Once one begins to observe this, examples proliferate, including both within the diagetic frame of *The Shepheardes Calender* and in its surrounding "apparatus," as I will explore in chapter 2. In chapter 3, I explore more deeply the broader Elizabethan conversation about the nature and health of the culture, including the well-known intervention (anti-aesthetic diatribe) by Stephen Gosson of 1579, *The Schoole of Abuse*, to which Lodge made the first published response. Chapter 3 also builds on Kimberly Anne Coles's work linking Gosson's arguments to those visible in writings of Calvin and Augustine, showing how aesthetic disputes overlapped with disputes about sexual morality and religious practice that form fault lines of Reformation and

---

[29] Paul J. Hecht, "Queer/Ordinary: Thinking Spenserian Sex and Aesthetics," in *Spenser in the Moment*, ed. Paul J. Hecht and J. B. Lethbridge (Madison, NJ: Fairleigh Dickinson University Press, 2015), 159–68.

Counter-Reformation conflict. As Coles aptly writes, Gosson's position was "that poetry was essentially an un-Christian activity" and that the larger view to be found in common between Augustine and Calvin, was that "form inevitably distracts from content."[30] This led Calvin, for example, to wonder whether it was a good idea to translate the Psalms into anything other than prose, suspicious that "poetry," considered as a set of formal enhancements or ornaments to holy and truthful "content," could only cause trouble.

But how far can one go with this linking of aesthetics and "sex"? Could reading a poem be as much of a sensuously enveloping experience as having sex? Could it be as socially and politically overdetermined or fraught? Putting the question so bluntly crosses contemporary taboos, certainly insomuch as to cite intercourse itself, or in any case some version of direct genital stimulation, "the act itself," or some version thereof, as opposed to something like "erotic experience," seems a little rude. Because as much as anglophone academia is typically identified with progressive thinking on gender and sexuality, there is a strong sense of category error to suggest that literary art, or an experience of that art, might be compared with sex "itself." But such comparison, and its implicit conflation of categories of pleasures and experience, does not misstate the nature of Elizabethan suspicions and anxieties about poetry, which mirror religious anxieties and suspicions of pleasures of all kinds, including sexual pleasure, including musical pleasure, including pleasure in the sound of words, that operate at the level of "earthly" form, in rhythms that speak to and move the body, and are therefore bodily. And sex can hardly be left out because "fornication" is so central to Christian morality full stop, and the uncomfortable evocation of sex acts themselves does work within this moral and argumentative framework. Rosalind highlights this, and provides a special focus and angle on these topics. She is a woman who is the object of seductive poetry, which she resists, or condemns because, perhaps, she is too sophisticated for it, or perhaps to assert sexual agency. She gradually, across the works in this study, develops a potent voice, intervening in sexual and political struggles, participating in her own sexual and political destiny, and finally appearing as a radiant, mostly feminine (which is to say queerly feminine), embodiment of Elizabethan concerns about art. And yet she is a powerful counterargument to their views, as she asserts a compelling ethical point of view even as she seduces men and women around her.

---

[30] Kimberly Anne Coles, *Religion, Reform, and Women's Writing in Early Modern England* (Cambridge: Cambridge University Press, 2008), 94.

Active and Passive Art

I think there is plentiful evidence in the texts and contemporary materials to support the dual approach to aesthetics and sexuality that I take with respect to Rosalind in this project. But I have also found support for the approach in affinities between theorists of aesthetics and of gender and sexuality. Particularly influential have been Theodor Adorno and Leo Bersani. And so I want to give here a brief introduction to the aspects of their work that I have found illuminating for the Rosalind books, and the cultural situation of the late sixteenth century, as well as crosscurrents between their thinking that took place, it is safe to say, quite independently. That is, I sketch briefly some ways that Frankfurt School aesthetic theory (mostly focused on eighteenth- and nineteenth-century cultural objects) comes into conversation with American queer theory from the 1980s.

A set of terms that particularly concentrates aesthetic and technical issues and issues of gender, sexuality, and social status is the active and the passive. In chapter 2 on Spenser, where Rosalind's presence is the most limited, I argue that Spenser adopts a "passive poetics" (which, again, in the context of Elizabethan sexual politics, is also a feminist poetics). Not only does Shakespeare's poetics seem highly active in comparison with Spenser's, but one can present Rosalind's "technical biography" as of a woman (starting position passive, silent) gradually becoming less passive, more active, gaining agency, autonomy. Since this happens with the aid of cross-dressing, it is easy to see this trajectory as entailing a takeover of qualities reserved for and by men. And furthermore, the version of feminism that this would seem to support is one where women essentially abandon their oppressed social position and stage a takeover of the role of oppressor. That women could then be in jeopardy of also acquiring negative aspects of the power they have acquired—i.e., tyranny, domination—is not one that is lost on the writers and works considered here. Indeed, I will argue in chapter 4 that a sense of doubt about the implications of such a takeover is involved in a climactic moment in *As You Like It* that is also a climactic moment for the study as a whole. But the texts that we deal with here also complicate things in a different way, both in aesthetic and in more overtly social and political terms. In brief, they question whether passivity is always bad, and whether a progressive politics might, instead of rejecting passivity, reframe it positively, and likewise that a more capacious aesthetics might see a special power in a passive poetics inaccessible to an active.

I am conscious that some influential scholars of early modern literature have mobilized the active and the passive in ways that are different from what I am attempting here. Melissa E. Sanchez's *Erotic Subjects* (2011) is a significant example of this. Sanchez builds this study of literary works from Sidney to Milton on the twin backgrounds of Foxean hagiography and Petrarchan poetry, both of which contain surprising reversals of expectations contained in the active–passive binary. Sanchez notes that "for Foxe, mildness and constancy, virtues traditionally encouraged in women, are constitutive of 'true manhood,'" and thus "the abject, feminized figure of the martyr … becomes a model to which the virtuous male subject ought to aspire."[31] Similarly, Sanchez emphasizes that the "abjection" associated with Petrarchan male devotion "is not free of aggression."[32] Sanchez's work is an apt caveat on any claim of uniformity or stasis in Elizabethan and Jacobean culture with respect to these very broad terms. Nonetheless, with Adorno and Bersani I believe I can bring into focus a constellation of aesthetics, sexuality, and gender that is particular to the situation of the Rosalinds.[33]

I will discuss Adorno first. I take Adorno's versions of "good passivity" from essays he wrote on the poet Joseph von Eichendorff (1788–1857) and the composer Franz Schubert (1797–1828). In both cases, his work is partly defensive, as against the claims of more "active" artists—in Eichendorff's case, Stefan George (1868–1933) provides a good example; in Schubert's, the rival is much more obvious and ubiquitous, namely Ludwig van Beethoven (1770–1827). In both cases Adorno is interested in how aesthetic "weakness"—working with old, tired pieces of harmony and melody, for example, or language and imagery that is in danger of being called hackneyed and clichéd—can nonetheless result in aesthetic success. What does he see as aesthetic success? In a word, the answer would be philosophy. Art that works, for Adorno, is art that thinks, that thinks through the intimidating impediments to thought that characterize the modern world.[34] Students of poststructuralist theory might most easily understand this in

---

[31] Melissa E. Sanchez, *Erotic Subjects: The Sexuality of Politics in Early Modern Literature* (New York: Oxford University Press, 2011), 17.

[32] Sanchez, *Erotic Subjects*, 19.

[33] By putting them in the plural, I mean to embrace the instability of significance and identity, of subjectivity and form, that follow from my focus on the figure of Rosalind. This is to say that while my overall project benefits from thinking together figures that have not been entertained at this length for their unifying qualities, the inconsistencies and fluidities around them are positive values for this book.

[34] I owe much of my sense of Adorno's aesthetics to the work of Simon Jarvis and Shierry Weber Nicholsen. For Jarvis, see "Art, Truth, and Ideology," in *Adorno: A Critical Introduction* (New York: Routledge, 1998), 90–123. For Nicholsen, see below on *Geräusch*.

terms of ideology, say, Louis Althusser's ideological state apparatuses, or Pierre Bourdieu's Marxist critique of aesthetic appreciation. In either case, what seems like ideology-busting potential in art turns out to be nothing of the sort, turns out merely to reinforce existing structures and patterns. For Adorno a "passive" approach to aesthetic materials produces something like a back door around the well-defended frontal approaches to, say, Kafka's "law." By "loosening" the grip on aesthetic materials, by introducing "distance" from words, sounds, these artists can allow a deeper sense, a sense-beneath-sense, or what Adorno refers to as *Geräusch*, a sort of noise or "rustling," to emerge.[35] This is not, that is to say, passivity as virtuous fortitude in the face of suffering extolled by Foxe; nor is it the passive aggression of the Petrarchan lover. I explore this in much more detail in chapter 2, in the context of the passive poetics I argue Spenser develops in the *Calender* and beyond. For now I want to make the point that while there is a decided lack of explicit reference to gender and sexuality in Adorno's writings on these matters, in the context of early twentieth-century German-speaking culture—in Vienna, in particular—one cannot but read such claims as a rebuke to thinkers like the appalling Otto Weininger (1880–1903), in whose misogynistic and anti-Semitic book *Sex and Character* (1903), thinkers of such reputation as Wittgenstein found matters of interest at the time.[36] For this strain of gendered, misogynist thinking has been around a long time in the West, and it suggests that to be weak is to be feminine and to be feminine is to be weak, and if we do not want civilization to collapse, we must promote the masculine and the active and keep "woman" in check, whether actual women, or any quality, any inclination that (contra Foxe) can be judged womanly.

I read Spenser, at least in the *Calender* and later texts and moments associated with Rosalind, to be attempting a project like this, and to be aware that it is resisting gender politics that are in the air at the time, are indeed expressed in the very packaging materials of the book.[37] But in advancing a passivity that does not balk at being called feminine, what does Spenser's

[35] My attention to *Geräusch* builds on the work of Shierry Weber Nicholsen; see "Language: Its Murmurings, Its Darkness, and Its Silver Rib," in *Exact Imagination, Late Work: On Adorno's Aesthetics* (Cambridge, MA: MIT Press, 1997), 59–102.

[36] Wittgenstein's interest, along with that of James Joyce and Arnold Schoenberg, is noted by Alex Ross in *The Rest Is Noise: Listening to the Twentieth Century* (New York: Farrar, Straus and Giroux, 2007), 41.

[37] As I will discuss in chapter 2, the introductory writings supplied by "E.K." make claims for the masculine superiority of the poetry, while simultaneously presenting the unnamed author as a sort of debutante hoping to attract the attentions of the reading public.

work say about the development of the more active Rosalind in Lodge and Shakespeare? What does his work say about the development of a woman as not only chief judge of poetry but also chief poetic creation, beguiling audiences, indeed, "seducing" them, in that way we speak of stars winning over the unlimited allegiance, the love of audiences, of readers?

I am interested in Adorno's defense of a passive aesthetic, or rather his arguments for what a passive aesthetic can accomplish that an active one cannot. It is only by circumstantial evidence that I can tie such an argument to "feminism" by simply noting how it flies in the face of a contemporary misogynist point of view like Weininger's. But it also seems useful to approach similar material from an overtly sexual point of view, and that is why I want to turn now to Leo Bersani. Bersani entered the heated anglophone discussion of gender and sexuality in the 1980s that is also known as the "sex wars" with a provocative response to prominent feminist theory and theorists of the time. To Catharine MacKinnon and Andrea Dworkin's critique of straight heterosexuality, and depictions of hierarchy and masochistic pleasure in pornography, Bersani responded by saying that MacKinnon and Dworkin had got the facts right but their interpretation wrong. To pick up at a dramatic point in his argument, take this:

> Phallocentrism is exactly that: not primarily the denial of power to women (although it has obviously also led to that, everywhere and at all times), but above all the denial of the *value* of powerlessness in both men and women. I don't mean the value of gentleness, or nonaggressiveness, or even of passivity, but rather of a more radical disintegration and humiliation of the self.[38]

This is a sample of the way he dismantles not the analyses, but the ethical and political conclusions of MacKinnon and Dworkin, as he argues that this "radical disintegration and humiliation of the self" is why sex is valuable, and furthermore, as Janet Halley summarizes the move, "phallocentrism is a social calamity because it blocks *men's* access to the 'humiliation of the self' *enjoyed* by women."[39] What is left is to call this thinking feminist, and call it part of a recuperative project for the benefit of women—that rather than finding the peculiar subordination associated with heterosexuality to be a political oppression that must be thrown off (literally), this might be

[38] Leo Bersani, "Is the Rectum a Grave?," *October* 43 (1987): 217.
[39] Janet Halley, *Split Decisions: How and Why to Take a Break from Feminism* (Princeton: Princeton University Press, 2006), 155.

embraced for what it does.[40] And what it does I would like to link to what Adorno finds in the much less violent scene of "rustling," where nonetheless a "radical disintegration" occurs, that has effects that I think are comparable to those Bersani argues non-"pastoral" sex is capable of—and "pastoral" is a word he uses surprisingly often.

The implication for the technical history of Rosalind is that as she gradually gains dimensions of thought and action through Lodge and into Shakespeare, we need be wary not only of a straightforward appropriation of masculine qualities of dominance and tyranny, but also of other losses inherent in the growth of active subject-hood, losses that parallel the growth of increasingly active, increasingly anti-pastoral poetry. For Rosalind, this danger may be intellectual as much as anything: that it is more difficult to penetrate occluded social structures, ideology, the way the world works, from a position of active engagement, management, running things—this taking us back to Adorno's *Geräusch*: not something you can hear when you are doing all the talking.

To put it another way, Bersani's largely pejorative sense of "pastoral" highlights what becomes a central question for Rosalind: how much does her freedom rely on usurping patriarchal power in a way that might approach revenge fantasy? As Rosalind finds the pastoral landscape amenable to feminist exploration, critiques of structures of Western thought and its moral and religious underpinnings, how does her development align itself with or against the art of mutual sympathy and selfless singing that defines Virgil's pastorals? And for the writers of Rosalind, do they seek a poetry that can take readers by the throat, an art that dominates, that arrests and energizes, or one that passively awaits readers?

All of this is to suggest that the shedding of expertise I am advocating might not just expose aesthetic or technical debates at a level of intensity to

---

[40] While Halley's project does not argue for this explicitly, advocating as it does for the positive potential of "splits" between feminism and queer theory, other feminists and queer feminists and queer feminists of color have continued to address Bersani's observations in service of a queer feminism that can answer them. Lynne Huffer's *Are the Lips a Grave?* (New York: Columbia University Press, 2013) builds a response to Bersani into its title, as it attempts to envision a new version of "convergence" that does not paper over areas of divergence and disagreement. The work of Amber Jamilla Musser is particularly relevant in that it in part proceeds from the observation that while Bersani aims for universality in his observation, the subject "is most easily legible in these accounts as a gay white male." She then attempts to remedy that fault through accounts of masochism and "brown jouissance" that work to develop theories of particularly racialized queer femininity, mostly through engagements with work by living artists and writers of the last century. See Amber Jamilla Musser, *Sensational Flesh: Race, Power, and Masochism* (New York: New York University Press, 2014), 18; and *Sensual Excess: Queer Femininity and Brown Jouissance* (New York: New York University Press, 2018).

which we are unused, but that, following Rosalind's fury, we might also make our way to political and sexual thinking that has a radical intensity for us right now. Thus our biography of poetry and technical history of Rosalind might produce payoffs as potentially forceful on both sides—both sides of the disciplinary gap between aesthetics and gender, and on both sides of the gap between the early modern and the present.

Burning Verses

I want to end with a scene of exuberant elitism and cultural machismo, the finale of the first, "Italian" version of Ben Jonson's *Every Man In His Humour*.[41] *Every Man* displays, from the opposite end of the developmental period chronicled in this book, the sexual tensions and gender trouble that continue to be associated with aesthetic questions, with the definition and production of poetry, and also displays an attempt at a forceful, direct solution to these problems—banging on the front door of the Law, as it were. It also displays, in its revision history, an acknowledgment that this frontal assault did not in fact do the job, that however well Jonson was able to evoke a hothouse atmosphere of aesthetic and sexual tension, intense disagreement and condemnation, fury and joy, he was not able to sew up these tensions through a long blank verse speech, through a speech that tells us what poetry "really is."

In this scene, in what would become the trademark Jonson style, all of the plots and cons that have developed during the play are unraveled, and justice is dispensed. The most prominent justice concerns poetry, poetry which has been a major source of conflict from the beginning, when a crabby patriarch (whom tradition indicates Shakespeare might have played, a tradition to which modern editors give little credence[42]) inveighs against the evils of poetry, and urges his son to avoid it. This man does not have much of an argument, but the rest of the play supplies much more. Poetry is effeminate, and effeminacy is associated with failed male gender performance, and homosexuality, especially passive homosexuality. Within the first minutes of the play we are presented with a letter between Elizabethan bros

[41] The play was first performed in 1598 and the first quarto version, set in Italy, was published in 1601. See David Bevington, "Introduction," in Jonson, *Every Man In His Humour, Quarto Version*, in *The Cambridge Edition of the Works of Ben Jonson*, ed. Bevington, vol. 1 (Cambridge University Press, 2012), 113.
[42] Bevington, "Introduction," 113, 114.

that jokingly suggests that the most poetically inclined and sophisticated of the characters, Lorenzo Jr., is a "passive partner in homosexual anal intercourse" with Apollo ("'Sblood, I doubt Apollo hath got thee to be his ingle, that thou comest not abroad to visit thine old friends" [1.1.129–31]).[43] The play's chief poetaster, Matheo, is likewise presented as someone who has fantasy relations with women to whom he writes poems, but really wants to spend his time geeking out on Kyd with a man whose legs he admires ("That boot becomes your leg passing well, sir, methinks" [1.3.123]). If the patriarch isn't willing to go quite so far in shaming his son by reference to effeminacy and sodomy, the boorish and bellicose Giuliano surely is, associating poetry and such like "toys," with "tricks," which is to say, bawdry, fornication, prostitution.

The ending, then, attempts to meet these criticisms, prejudices, associations, and carve out a role for poetry that is both worthy and manly. The way this unfolds bears a closer look. Chief are two figures, Doctor Clement, a "magistrate" whose learning and kindly disposition are trumpeted by his name, and Lorenzo Jr., the same object of paternal care and friendly gay-shaming mentioned above. In earlier scenes, as Matheo recited verses, Lorenzo and his friend Prospero provided a running commentary lampooning the poetry and the proceedings. Here, Doctor Clement, sorting his way through the various gulls and misfits, finds his way to Matheo, and upon being informed by the clever servant character that he is "an author," proceeds to display a couple of instances of verse parody before examining some extracts from the author's pockets. The first is the start of Samuel Daniel's *Delia* sequence, and the second a line from a ballad—both identified as such in the dialogue. After hearing the snatch of ballad, the boor Giuliano asks scornfully "call you this poetry?" and suddenly we realize that the whole scene—which as it happens has been in prose when we are not extemporizing verses or reading from Matheo's stocking stores—has teed us up for this moment.[44] Lorenzo Jr. replies in blank verse:

> Poetry? Nay, then call blasphemy religion,
> Call devils angels and sin piety;
> Let all things be preposterously transchanged.

> (5.3.253–5)

---

[43] The clinical language is the *OED*'s, s.v. "ingle," n. 2, 1. The definition also connects the word with "catamite," and thence, via its etymology, with none other than Ganymede. The Jonson is quoted, here and through the remainder of the chapter, from *Every Man In*, ed. Bevington.

[44] This aligns the moment with one in *As You Like It*, namely the shift into blank verse following the revelation of Orlando's identity after defeating the duke's champion. See chapter 4, "Mark how the tyrant writes."

I hope to demonstrate over the course of this study just how characteristic a moment like this is through the late sixteenth century, where, like
Rosalind condemning Colin's verses, the condemnation gradually seeks to
embody the replacement of what it condemns, attempts to interpose itself
as the phoenix upon the ashes of what it burns—what will be done literally to Matheo's verses shortly after this speech commences. This is an odd
kind of performative: demonstrating a replacement simultaneously with the
destruction of what it replaces.

And what does manly, confident verse, replacing the effeminate travesties
of Matheo, sound like? Let's listen again, and note how it rhythmically gets
itself going:[45]

/ x \ x   \   x / x / x / x
Poetry? Nay, then call blasphemy religion,

\   / x / x   \   \ / x /
Call devils angels and sin piety;

\ / \   / x / x \ x   /
Let all things be preposterously transchanged.

By "gets itself going" I mean the halting rhythm of the first syllables of the
first line, leading up to the more metrical, steadier "blasphemy religion," and
in the next line "devils angels" and "piety" as places of relative rhythmic in-
sistence owing to their polysyllabic, set-stress structure. But the third line
has the solidity of the near-spondaic monosyllables "let all things be" before the forceful polysyllabics (including the compression of "terous" into
"trous") "preposterously transchanged." It also gains power from its mar-
shaling of opposites, those same polysyllables having the force of antithesis,
until, again, the final preposterous punch. So what then: a poetry that vis-
ibly, audibly wrestles linguistic materials into metrical alignment? This in
contrast with the "excellent" and "neat" patterning praised by Dolven in
"Januarye"?

After a baiting comment from his father about "how abjectly your poetry
is ranked / In general opinion" (258–9), Lorenzo continues:

---

[45] My rhythmic notation is a hybrid of a few common practices, with "x" denoting lack of
emphasis or accent, "/" a full accent or stress, and "\" something in between those two.

Opinion? Oh, God, let gross opinion
Sink and be damned as deep as Barathrum!
If it may stand with your most wished content,
I can refel opinion and approve
The state of poesy, such as it is,
Blessèd, eternal, and most true divine.
Indeed, if you will look on poesy
As she appears in many—poor and lame,
Patched up in remnants and old worn rags,
Half-starved for want of her peculiar food,
Sacred invention—then I must confirm
Both your conceit and censure of her merit.
But view her in her glorious ornaments,
Attirèd in the majesty of art,
Set high in spirit with the precious taste
Of sweet philosophy, and, which is most,
Crowned with the rich traditions of a soul
That hates to have her dignity profaned
With any relish of an earthly thought:
Oh, then, how proud a presence doth she bear!
Then is she like herself, fit to be seen
Of none but grave and consecrated eyes.
Nor is it any blemish to her fame
That such lean, ignorant, and blasted wits,
Such brainless gulls, should utter their stol'n wares
With such applauses in our vulgar ears,
Or that their slubbered lines have current pass
From the fat judgments of the multitude,
But that this barren and infected age
Should set no difference 'twixt these empty spirits
And a true poet—than which reverend name
Nothing can more adorn humanity.

(260–91)

As will be a running theme of this study, Lorenzo's defense of poetry is startlingly religious and startlingly sexual. Where we have just been judging poetry through what can only be understood as connoisseurship and education—enough to be able to get Clement's classical fart joke[46] —suddenly here the basis for evaluation is looking on the *woman* that poetry "is." In this vision, the woman poetry may be cherished or abused—but these days she is mostly abused, given ill treatment that makes her "poor and lame"—lame being a reference to bad poetic rhythm that *is* common to *As You Like It*.[47] And moreover, "patched up in remnants and old worn rags," she is almost unrecognizable, and seems to lack "merit" and deserve "censure." Lorenzo's fantasy of reversing all of this nourishes her with "her peculiar food," but the rest is all about the extreme makeover. She is stripped of her patches and rags, and "attired in the majesty of art," "in her glorious ornaments," and then other things are done to her: she is "set high in spirit," "crowned with the rich traditions of a soul / That hates to have her dignity profaned / With any relish of an earthly thought"—a crowning that wipes away the memory of that homeless half-starved tramp and makes a lady of her, a "proud presence." But curiously as she leaves behind the "barren and infected age" that brought her to such a sorry state, and becomes "like herself," she also becomes almost impossible to see, or at least only "fit to be seen" by an audience almost as refined as she is. And as such she has grown so proud that she "hates to have her dignity profaned / With any relish of an earthly thought." And we might ask at this point, then what good is she? She no longer has anything to do with the earth, she is so glorious that we cannot even look upon her—she seems like Astrea returned to heaven. Moreover, how does this speech play on the Globe stage in front of a mixed audience, rather than the law courts audience of Jonson's first playwriting effort? It seems decidedly more edgy than Hamlet's colloquy with the players about what fails to please "the million."[48]

But more important than any of these observations is the observation of what happened next, in the sequence of events that led to the revised, "English" version of the play that appeared nearly twenty years later in Jonson's folio of 1616. In that version, this speech was cut. Why? My theory is that Jonson had a revised view of his youthful directness in his later years, even if that directness was given voice in a young man already in the first version balanced by a less intemperate older man. But if we can agree that Jonson felt

---

[46] "Mount thee, my Phlegon muse, and testify / How Saturn, sitting in an ebon cloud, / Disrobed his *podex*, white as ivory, / And through the welkin thundered all aloud" (219–22).

[47] See discussion of the "false gallop" the verse Rosalind's friends find attached to trees in act 3, scene 2, and chapter 4, "Devising sports."

[48] *Hamlet*, 2.2.360.

this strongly about this topic—and I know of no reason to doubt that—then why hold back? Because, even though the entire play may have been working to create this moment, when we get to sweep away the inferior and ridiculous (though entertaining) rhetoric of the gulls and hear the real thing, it still is not the moment to come out and say what that real thing is. It grates, it does not clarify, does not persuade. *Or*, Jonson perceived that the argument itself was flawed, that the inclination to "heavenly" poetry, however understandable after feeling mired in ignorance and tawdry, travestied copies of what wasn't very good to begin with, is not right, is a false response.[49]

Furthermore, Jonson tries to "answer" the concentrated agglomeration of Elizabethan-Christian anxieties about art and sex with a vision of female purity, a young man's idealization of femininity without earthly identity, without a mortal body, or if there is one, quite hidden from view by "ornaments," by "art" in this sense of the artificial, the ornate, and the exterior. But this is also clearly an erotic vision, a young male poet's vision of poetry that focuses his erotic and aesthetic desires into one. Such a vision is arguably what motivates Colin Clout in Spenser's *Shepheardes Calender*, and receives its first rebuke from a Rosalind who is unwilling to play such a role. And as I will argue, Colin Clout, disappointed by the "earthly" Rosalind, ultimately conjures a heavenly one atop Mount Acidale, in a fleeting vision of aesthetic and erotic consummation. But the Rosalind that develops through Lodge and Shakespeare is very different—and of course no one ever calls her "poetry." And yet, as I have already indicated, it seems quite possible in Shakespeare's time that a "character" like Rosalind could very well stand in for "what makes poetry valuable," or "the highest achievement of imaginative literature." It is then her "life," as we can understand and describe it, that is the most potent argument for "poetry." And instead of men arguing over what ornaments look best on which kind of line, Rosalind is gradually accorded more and more agency to make such determinations herself. And that is the evolution that I wish to follow here. As we shall see, there is no easy way to be sure whether her lock on this art is more secure when she is engaging supple blank verse to expose the ridiculousness of erotic conventions, of pastoral Petrarchism, or when she is rendering a blistering critique of poetry in prose, or when she steps out of character and calls attention to the anatomical gender of the boy playing her.

---

[49] After all, Jonson's art surely tells us, if nothing else, of the necessity of idiocy for its success. As the judgment of the ages has been clear, his art literally cannot live without it. *Macbeth* is imaginable without the Porter: his is an art that does not need low humor to succeed. Jonson needed it.

My thesis in a sentence: because Elizabethans conflated sex and aesthetics, their writing projects could simultaneously address both. So the charge that verbal music effeminizes could be addressed through an exploration of that effect, through thematizing the effeminization effected by art within a fictive world. We see this in a variety of Rosalind-related projects through these three texts. The Spenserian project, which is to embrace the passive, effeminized role of the rejected lover, and sink into it, plumbing its depths. The Lodge project: looking to the feminine, the erotic, and the aesthetic to find "concord" for divisions at the family, religious, and political levels: along the way, Rosalind as a figure who argues against misogyny, fear of art, and also engages a surprisingly subversive, queer reading of central aspects of Christianity. The Shakespeare project: a "rematch" between the Spenserian poet and Rosalind. Rosalind as less religiously critical than Lodge's Rosalind, but in all other ways, raising the level of the critical game immensely. And thus, Rosalind as "star," and as vehicle of progressive politics.

My highest aim in this project is an ethical one. Can one argue that poetic development could be as important as political development? Could art have as much of a call on our attention as—a life? Could we see poetic development as intertwined with a political project, an equity project, some kind of feminism? For some readers, mixing areas of inquiry like this may seem impertinent or unnecessary, and I expect they will either read no further, or, if I am lucky, test their views on the chapters that follow.

But let me explain a little further. "Rosalind" represents one of the deepest ways that people connect with art. It is no exaggeration to say that we can fall in love with Rosalind, and when we are in love, there is no end to which we will not go to defend her. But how much does this astonishing capacity, to be able to love a fiction, a congregation of few thousand-odd words, depend on the poetry that underlies it and surrounds it, and all the development of that art of making that preceded it, especially the last decades prior to it? This study argues that this is worth thinking about. And furthermore, if our love for Rosalind extends to political work she is capable of doing, the space she may clear for freer, more brilliant, more hilarious and penetrating, more indomitable women to follow in her footsteps, how much is that space also a function of the poetic evolution that leads to her? This study then accords the possibility that the stakes for what makes one set of sounds work better than another in a line of pentameter might be those stakes, the capacity for art to do work in the world, this specific, living, political, imaginative work. This is the version of aesthetics that I am pursuing.

2

Spenser's Rosalind

Flawed Poetry and Feminist Experiments

The Shepheardes Calender was a productive failure.[1] We should take seriously Rosalind's scornful condemnation, as a way of registering just
how far short Spenser in 1579 was falling before his poetic ideals—Virgil,
yes, but also more proximate exemplars in the French poet Clément
Marot (1496–1554) and the Italian neo-Latin poet Baptista Mantuanus
(1447–1516). So in terms of our biography of poetry, we begin by exploring
some of the "shepherds devises" that are worthy of scorn, evidence of, on
the one hand, Spenser's upstart experimentalism, and on the other, that he
didn't really know what he was doing, did not know how to find adequate responses to the potent effects he perceived, particularly in classical verse. But
he was searching. In chapter 1, I pointed to two areas where I believed this
could be shown: in the management of stanzas, and specifically transitions
between stanzas, and in the management of alliteration. In the first case I will
demonstrate a clear development and improvement of Spenser's technique,
visible if one compares stanzaic verse in the *Calender* to later poems written
in stanzas. With alliteration the progression is more difficult to demonstrate, but I explore what kinds of effects Spenser seemed to be pursuing,
even if it is doubtful that he achieved what he pursued. So we will see one

---

[1] This is, to put it mildly, a minority view in Spenser criticism. But with that said, the *Calender* drew, alongside praise, censure for its "old rustic language," as early as Sidney's *Defence*.
Another notable naysayer was C. S. Lewis, who found the book "rather dull." Among prominent recent critics, the one closest to this overt skepticism is Harry Berger, Jr., who praised
the *Calender* but argued that it was heavily satiric, filled with bad poetry that Spenser was
deliberately writing to send up pastoral. I sometimes agree with his criticisms, but am unable to agree with his claims for Spenser's "squint" consciousness of the flaws he identifies.
See Sir Philip Sidney, *Sir Philip Sidney*, ed. Katherine Duncan-Jones (Oxford: Oxford University Press, 1989), 242; C. S. Lewis, *English Literature in the Sixteenth Century Excluding
Drama* (Oxford: Clarendon Press, 1954), 363; Harry Berger, Jr., *Revisionary Play: Studies in the
Spenserian Dynamics* (Berkeley and Los Angeles: University of California Press, 1988), 277.

What Rosalind Likes. Paul J. Hecht, Oxford University Press.
© Paul J. Hecht (2022). DOI: 10.1093/oso/9780192857200.003.0002

trait of poetry that grew through Spenser's own poetic biography, and another that remained fixed, for better or worse, as a component of Spenser's style.

These fairly technical exertions will I hope enable readers to get closer to Rosalind's fury, in the sense of her disappointment and disgust with bad art, and set us up to appreciate the rest of our journey through Lodge and Shakespeare. But I also indicated in chapter 1 that by focusing on Rosalind I am specifically trying to resist the isolation of technical, formal concerns in poetry from dynamics from which they were never, in early modern culture, isolated. The second half of the chapter then provides a technical prehistory of Rosalind, which I have also called the feminist project of the *Calender*. This is a project that opens up in the space of Rosalind's rejection and condemnation of Colin Clout, where the book meditates on responses to the effeminization and emasculation elicited by sexual and aesthetic rejection. The most productive form of this meditation I find in the oddest, queerest corner of the *Calender*, the eclogue entitled "September." Here I argue that Spenser gives us a radically experimental version of the object of Rosalind's scorn, in which "effeminization" is taken as far as changing the gender of pronouns, and the poem's protagonist, Diggon, is figured as a woman, pregnant as the result of a rape. From this pronominal and metaphorical cross-dressing, the eclogue dramatizes a search for poetic language that goes in the opposite direction from Spenser's avatar Colin, which is to say a search for plainness and unvarnished truth, digging into the depths of a corrupt and exploitative world.[2]

My discussion of the *Calender* concludes with the most hopeful moments in the book, where we explore passivity in ways that resonate with aesthetic theory which Theodor Adorno formulated around poetry and music very distant from Spenser, but struggling with similar forces. This passivity in the face of condemnation is offered as a potential way both out of political and religious struggle, and out of patriarchy and the tyranny of men over women. In both cases, the feminist project defends, sympathizes with, and supports figures who are shamefully feminized and emasculated. To

[2] I have lately been struck by the resonance of this motion with recent developments around surface reading and postcriticism, which treat skeptically terms like "digging down" or "excavation." See e.g. Rita Felski, *The Limits of Critique* (Chicago: University of Chicago Press, 2015), 1–13, and ch. 2, "Digging Down and Standing Back"; also see Elizabeth S. Anker and Rita Felski, "Introduction," in *Critique and Postcritique*, ed. Elizabeth S. Anker and Rita Felski (Durham, NC and London: Duke University Press, 2017), 1–28. I return to this topic in the section on "September," "Badde is the best," below. See also chapter 1, "Feeling the Fury."

be clear, it is the *Calender*'s Rosalind who is doing the shaming, but the test the book takes on is whether there can be a response to this shaming that does not lead to misogyny or the reassertion of patriarchal tyranny. In the final phase of the chapter, following out the reappearances of the *Calender*'s characters in two late Spenser poems, the story becomes more bleak, as we see Colin Clout pursuing, at best, a form of Petrarchan sublimation of Rosalind. What this means is that while I do argue that we can see technical flaws and shortcomings in the *Calender*'s poetry, and thus gain a more vivid sense of both Spenser's poetic development and the development of poetry in the late sixteenth century in England, using Rosalind's condemnation as a window into the development of Spenser's feminism does not finally show much in the way of development: instead, with respect to Rosalind (and I am not asserting this for Spenser's works as a whole) the *Calender* is the place where the most potent questions about the overlap between gender, social status, sexuality, and power are explored, with the most radically experimental spirit. We will have to wait for Lodge and Shakespeare to see substantial advances beyond Spenser's experiments as we follow out the technical history of Rosalind.

In sum, we begin the biography of poetry by looking at poetic problems that were later solved by Spenser, poetic problems that disappeared into the weave of Spenser's style, and some intriguingly feminist responses to the situation of aesthetic and sexual rejection that comes here in the form of Rosalind's ringing denunciation of Colin Clout.

Bad Spenser, What Rosalind Hates

Static stanzas

In chapter 1, I noted some aspects of Virgil's style in the *Eclogues*, including that while from a distance, the *Eclogues* look formally unidimensional—they are all written in unrhymed dactylic hexameter—closer inspection reveals other kinds of formal complexity and variety, such that within just a few lines, Virgil can move between elaborately patterned and ornamented speech and remarkable plainness and compression. It is this kind of variety of motion where we can see another significant technical impediment to the success of the *Calender*, and it is important not just because variety is a universal aesthetic good, a principle which at least has to contend with various kinds of aesthetic minimalism, but because it is necessary for characterization, for writing speeches that sound like people might actually say them—because no one who wants an audience to remain engaged speaks in repetitive units that all unfold in the same predictable fashion, and no actual person who is not a robot speaks that way either. What becomes apparent when one pays attention to stanza structure in the *Calender* is that the more complex stanza forms are suffering from exactly that problem: it is as though Spenser has found a few consistent ways to "solve" the demands of rhyme and rhythm, and he too often sticks with those methods in a way that can suck energy and life out of the poems. In particular there is a kind of stasis in stanza writing that appears in the *Calender*, and a lack of connection and propulsion between stanzas that has been identified as a problem in world literary history, especially when there is so little propelling things from one stanza to the next that it becomes possible to change their order without having much effect on the poem.[3]

In "June," for example, there is a repetitive quality to the stanzas, because the ways that sense unfolds within them seems limited. The ways that sense is passed from one stanza to the next are likewise constrained, leading to the possibility of interchangeability, and a lack of concatenation or linking between stanzas.[4] Motion between stanzas also conforms to a predictable and narrow set of possible choices. The lack of rhythmic variety at the end of stanzas seems one contributing factor: especially in "June," stanzas end with cadences so similar that it begins to sound something like the end-refrain from the "November" elegy or the *Prothalamion*.[5] The last two lines of four out of the first six stanzas in "June" are rhythmically nearly identical:

> The Bramble bush, where Byrds of every kynde
> To the waters fall their tunes attemper right.
>
> (7–8)

---

[3] Ernst Häublein notes "the danger of extreme *stasis* and monotony" in what he calls "exchangeable" stanzas. See Häublein, *The Stanza* (London: Methuen, 1978), 90.

[4] Concatenation is, I hardly need add, the technical term. See the article by T. V. F Brogan and I. D. Copestake, s.v. "concatenation," in *The Princeton Encyclopedia of Poetry and Poetics*, ed. Roland Greene et al. (4th edn., Princeton: Princeton University Press, 2012), 288–9.

[5] "November" uses "O heauie herse," "O carefull verse" around a variable line in between to end its stanzas; *Prothalamion*'s famous stanza tag is "Sweet *Themmes* run softlie, till I end my Song."

> Will pype and daunce, when *Phoebe* shineth bright:
> Such pierlesse pleasures have we in these places.
>
> (31–2)

> (As garments doen, which wexen old above)
> And draweth newe delightes with hoary heares.
>
> (39–40)

> And losse of her, whose love as lyfe I wayd,
> Those weary wanton toyes away did wype.
>
> (47–8)

The other two simply invert the order, placing a caesura after the fourth syllable in the last, rather than the penultimate line.

> And angry Gods pursue from coste to coste,
> Can nowhere fynd, to shroude my lucklesse pate.
>
> (15–16)

> Here no night Ravens lodge more black then pitche,
> Nor elvish ghosts, nor gastly owles doe flee.
>
> (23–4)

This repetitiveness prevents the buildup of periods, of breath or sense units larger than a stanza, as beginning readers, not picking up on the links between sentences, end each one with an identical drop of the voice. There are few other strategies visible in the *Calender* for carrying readers from one stanza to the next. Significant nouns or phrases do not tend to get picked up between stanzas, and grammatical subjects are mostly isolated in single stanzas. As a result, it is possible to reverse the position of stanzas at two places in "June," without significantly disrupting the progress of the poem (stanzas 7 and 8, and 9 and 10).

These issues evaporate in the formal space of the non-stanzaic poems. In the debate between youth and age in "Februrarie," for example, speeches unfold unpredictably, making use of a continuously changing approach to the pattern of the couplet—sometimes sense aligns with the two-line structure, but just as often, three-line sense groups create syncopations. Observe this dialogue leading up to the "tale of Tityrus" that Thenot tells the youthful shepherd Cuddie in order to demonstrate the folly of youth:

THENOT	But shall I tel thee a tale of truth,
	Which I cond of *Tityrus* in my youth,
	Keeping his sheepe on the hils of Kent?
CUDDIE	To nought more *Thenot*, my mind is bent,
	Then to heare novells of his devise:
	They bene so well thewed, and so wise,
	What ever that good old man bespake.
THENOT	Many meete tales of youth did he make,
	And some of love, and some of chevalrie:
	But none fitter then this to applie.
	Now listen a while, and hearken the end.

(91–101)

The dialogue at the start is split across a rhyming couplet, and forms a group of three lines as against the couplet's inclination to pairs. Splitting speakers across couplets also happens as we shift back to Thenot, as we get another syntactic group of three lines, followed by a line that stands on its own as a sentence. The effect of these small, unpredictable changes is to avoid the predictable patterns of the stanzas, and make this sound more like actual people talking.

The Faerie Queene displays none of these problems. Instead, what is on display everywhere in *The Faerie Queene* is a combination of elaborate stanza and continuous change in the way lines and sense units are grouped—a synthesis of the syncopations and unpredictable unfolding of "Februarie" and similar poems, and the constraints of "June." For a generically comparable moment in *The Faerie Queene*, we can look at the pastoral section of book 6. The beginning of Meliboe's speech to Calidore in canto 9, for example, is, like "June" and "November," a speech that forms part of a pastoral dialogue, and so seems a reasonable point at which to touch down for a comparison. Here Meliboe tries to explain the happiness for which Calidore has just declared his envy:[6]

> Surely my sonne (then answer'd he againe)
>   If happie, then it is in this intent,
>   That having small, yet doe I not complaine
>   Of want, ne wish for more it to augment
>   But doe my selfe, with that I have, content;

[6] My text for *The Faerie Queene* is Edmund Spenser, *The Faerie Queene*, ed. A. C. Hamilton (2nd edn., Harlow, England: Longman, 2001).

> So taught of nature, which doth litle need
> Of forreine helpes to lifes due nourishment:
> The fields my food, my flocke my rayment breed;
> No better doe I weare, no better doe I feed.
>
> Therefore I doe not any one envy,
>   Nor am envyde of any one therefore;
>   They that have much, feare much to loose thereby,
>   And store of cares doth follow riches store.
>   The litle that I have, growes dayly more
>   Without my care, but onely to attend it;
>   My lambes doe every year increase their score,
>   And my flockes father daily doth amend it.
> What have I, but to praise th'Almighty, that doth send it?
>   (6.9.20–21)

Within the stanzas, we can note the enjambed lines, coupled with a wider variety of caesuras. Here, for example, a separation of verb from its direct object, and a caesura after the second syllable of the next line: "yet doe I not complaine / Of want." Mirroring that caesura, and partly echoing it, the main verb of the next clause is delayed to the very last two syllables of the next line:

> yet doe I not complaine
> Of want, ne wish for more it to augment
> But doe my selfe, with that I have, content;

"Little need / Of forreine helpes" also seems beyond the spectrum of enjambment allowed in "June" or "November."

Between the stanzas there is an extraordinary mirroring of two two-line chiasmic structures, creating a double chiasmus as a concatenation:

A	B	B	A
The fields my **food**, my flocke my **rayment** breed; / No better do I **weare**, no better doe I **feed**.			
Therefore I doe not	any one **envy**, /	Nor am **envyde** of any one **therefore**;	

A little later in the same speech we can see two stanzas in which the second picks up the object of the last line of the previous stanza ("such vainenesse"), and also delays the arrival of the main clause of the sentence until the fifth line:

The time was once, in my first prime of yeares,
>   When pride of youth forth pricked my desire,
>   That I disdain'd amongst mine equall peares
>   To follow sheepe, and shepheards base attire:
>   For further fortune then I would inquire.
>   And leaving home, to roiall court I sought;
>   Where I did sell my selfe for yearely hire,
>   And in the Princes gardin daily wrought:
> There I beeld such vainenesse, as I never thought.

With sight whereof soone cloyd, and long deluded
>   With idle hopes, which them doe entertaine,
>   After I had ten yeares my selfe excluded
>   From native home, and spent my youth in vaine,
>   I gan my follies to my selfe to plaine,
>   And this sweet peace, whose lacke did then appeare.
>   Tho backe returning to my sheepe againe,
>   I from thenceforth have learn'd to love more deare
> This lowly quiet life, which I inherite here.

(stanzas 24–25)

In the *Calender*, it would be much more likely for the object to be dropped, and for the grammatical subject of the new stanza to appear forthwith.

I have been trying to play fair with the *Calender*. If one leaves the arena of the pastoral conversation, the contrast becomes far more pronounced, for example, in this early description of Errour:

And as she lay upon the durtie ground,
>   Her huge long taile her den all overspred
>   Yet was in knots and many boughtes upwound,
>   Pointed with mortall sting. Of her there bred,
>   A thousand yong ones, which she dayly fed,
>   Sucking upon her poisnous dugs, eachone
>   Of sundrie shapes, yet all ill favored:
>   Soone as that uncouth light upon them shone,
> Into her mouth they crept, and suddain all were gone.

(1.1.15)

A new sentence beginning midline, a strong enjambment off of an eight-syllable hemistich, two violent initial inversions ("Pointed," "Sucking"), the entire description coming to an end in line 7, with an entirely separate action following—it's a different universe altogether.

Likewise, one does not have to look far in *The Faerie Queene* to find a much greater variety of ways in which sense is divided within stanzas. This is Despair at the beginning of his six-stanza speech to the Red Cross Knight:

> Is not his deed, what ever thing is donne,
> In heaven and earth?
> did not he all create
> To die againe?
> all ends that was begonne.
>
> Their times in his eternall booke of fate
> Are written sure, and have their certain date.
>
> Who then can strive with strong necessitie,
> That holds the world in his still chaunging state,
> Or shunne the death ordaynd by destinie?
>
> When houre of death is come, let none aske whence, nor why.
>
> The lenger life, I wote the greater sin,
> The greater sin, the greater punishment:
>
> All those great battels, which thou boasts to win,
> Through strife, and bloud-shed, and avengement,
> Now praysd, hereafter deare thou shalt repent:
>
> For life must life, and blood must blood repay.
>
> Is not enough thy evill life forespent?
>
> For he, that once hath missed the right way,
> The further he doth goe, the further he doth stray.
>   (1.9.42–43)

Compared with the way sense is organized in the stanzas of "June" and "November," the impression here is of constant and continually evolving variety. Just as important, and more difficult to demonstrate, is the sense that stanzas are never constructed in isolation, that these irregular patterns are not simply irregular for irregularity's sake, but are rather responding to one another, and thus building up ever larger, more complex patterns on top of those in specific stanzas. William Empson described this sense of the stanza, that it "may be broken up into a variety of metrical forms, and the ways in which it is successively broken up are fitted into enormous patterns."[7] And furthermore, "every use of the stanza includes all these uses in the reader's apprehension of it."[8] That very non-statistical claim by Empson is one that has continued to be quoted admiringly by Spenser scholars, but none to my knowledge have noted how ill the observations fit the stanzaic writing in the *Calender*.[9] *The Faerie Queene* may be "unflaggingly regular" in its deployment of Spenser's personal stanza, but in terms of its strategies for creating motion within and between stanzas, it is worlds away from the stiff, repetitive, sometimes nearly immobile stanza writing of the *Calender*.

What I hope to have demonstrated is that when Spenser wrote in stanzas at the time of the *Calender*, his writing was stiffer and more repetitive, such that it threatened to deprive the reader of a sense of forward motion. But does the book display awareness of this flaw, such that we can bring this dimension of poetry plausibly under the canopy of Rosalind's condemnation of "devise"? There is some tenuous evidence of this. In the *Epistle* that prefaces the *Calender*, written by the commentator known only as E.K., we find this claim: "what in most English wryters useth to be loose, and as it were ungyrt, in this Authour is well grounded, finely framed, and strongly trussed up together" (p. 28). Could "fineness" of "framing" refer to tidy, self-contained stanzas? Could strong trussing-up mean allowing only a small set of enjambment and caesura patterns? Could what this reader's ear longs for in flexibility and unpredictable units of sense and their unfolding in the twenty-first century (and finds in *The Faerie Queene*) have been to E.K.'s ears in 1579 threateningly chaotic and wild? And could it be that one explanation of Spenser's poor handling of stanza form, his excessive stiffness, is that he was overly worried about writing in a way that could be described as "loose" or "ungyrt"? And of course now that I have introduced this language I have

[7] William Empson, *Seven Types of Ambiguity* (13th edn., New York: New Directions, 1947), 33.
[8] Empson, *Seven Types of Ambiguity*, 34.
[9] Both Kenneth Gross and Jeff Dolven, for example, refer admiringly to Empson's comments on the stanza in articles they published in 2004: Kenneth Gross, "Shapes of Time: On the Spenserian Stanza," *Spenser Studies* 19 (2004): 29; Jeff Dolven, "The Method of Spenser's Stanza," *Spenser Studies* 19 (2004): 20.

opened up the possibility of a sexual dimension to this discussion of style, because "loose" and "ungyrt" are both suggestive of sexual looseness, openness to erotic temptation; those valences are given much more support by the place where E.K. goes immediately following that sentence:

In regard whereof, I scorne and spue out the rakehellye route of our ragged rymers (for so themselves use to hunt the letter) which without learning boste, without judgement jangle, without reason rage and fome, as if some instinct of Poeticall spirite had newly ravished them above the meanenesse of common capacitie. And being in the midest of all their bravery, sodenly eyther for want of matter, or of ryme, or having forgotten theyr former conceipt, they seeme to be so pained and travelied in theyr remembrance, as it were a woman in childebirth or as that same Pythia, when the traunce came upon her.

Os rabidum fera corda domans &c.

(p. 28)[10]

From a general lack of "looseness," we suddenly receive this furious excursus on alliteration and effeminization, furious recalling a negative version of the Platonic *furor poeticus* as an unmanning, a womanly submission of reason before the demands of the body, comparable to labor pains or the ecstasy of an oracular Sybil.[11]

---

[10] The Latin is from *Aeneid* 6.80, describing how the spirit of Phoebus Apollo must work to master her "frenzied mouth" and "fierce spirit." E.K.'s point seems to be to recall the ecstasy associated with being an amenuensis, but it is also odd in that it pauses on a moment when the Sibyl is on the point of being brought under the control of the divine spirit: her thrashing seems to indicate not a feminine descent into the sensuous or the bodily, but rather the struggle of her reason *against* divine possession. For the translation of this passage, I have drawn on Virgil, *Eclogues, Georgics, Aeneid I–VI*, trans. H. Rushton Fairclough, vol. 63, Loeb Classical Library (Cambridge, MA: Harvard University Press, 1999), and also *The Yale Edition of the Shorter Poems of Edmund Spenser*, ed. William A. Oram et al. (New Haven: Yale University Press, 1989), 17.

[11] Both positive and negative meanings of the theory of the poet's divine frenzy can be found in the *Calender*. The second, positive sense, appears in the "argument" to "October," under the Platonic name "enthusiasmos," which E.K. glosses as "celestial inspiration." Ernst Robert Curtius points out that the two have a common origin in Plato's *Phaedrus*, in *European Literature in the Latin Middle Ages*, trans. Willard R. Trask (Princeton: Princeton University 1953), 474–5. Raphael Falco gives an overview of the changing understandings of the term in his article on "furor poeticus" in *The Princeton Encyclopedia of Poetry and Poetics*, ed. Greene, Cushman, and Cavanagh, 531–3. For a recent extended discussion of Plato and Spenser, including poetic fury, see Kenneth Borris, *Visionary Spenser and the Poetics of Early Modern Platonism* (Oxford: Oxford University Press, 2017), e.g., 38–44.

And so it has become apparent that the first stage in our biography of poetry—my effort as much as possible to isolate technical flaws in the poetic performance of the *Calender*, and sharpen our sense of them through comparison with Virgil and later Spenser—has also found its way into the shadow of Rosalind's sexual condemnation of Colin Clout: what was at stake for Spenser in exploring a variety of stanza patterns, and moving between more open and metrically loose poems in couplets, and highly articulated stanza forms with multiple demands on syllable counts and rhyme, was not just the project of making his way to become the Spenser of the Spenserian stanza, with its happy synthesis of qualities we see at both ends of the formal spectrum in the *Calender*. It seems quite possible that, just as for Colin Clout, Spenser's masculinity was at stake as well. Because there seems little question of the sexual stakes of "hunting the letter" as E.K. describes it above; with that in mind it is time to turn to the next technical basis of possible complaint about the *Calender*, namely that it just hunts the letter way too much.

Chasing the letter

Alliteration in the poetry of the late sixteenth century could have been a habit, something left over from oral and popular traditions that are visible in *Beowulf* and *Piers Plowman*. But for Spenser I want to argue that it had a higher purpose, that he took this traditional and popular attribute of English poetry and saw the potential for achieving an aspect of Latin poetic style otherwise nearly shut off to English poets. In the face of the inability to fashion lines concentrically in symmetrical structures tied together grammatically by word-endings in a case-based language, he developed the ability to achieve similar results through the like sounds of word-beginnings, which is to say, alliteration. What this theory gives us is a reason that Spenser might have struggled with alliteration that is quite different from the struggle with stanza writing we just explored. Because the obvious way to avoid fury like that articulated by E.K. above, to avoid the sexual as well as technical vulnerabilities of over-alliterating, was simply to do it less. But Spenser did not do that, and the frequency of alliteration indeed stays fairly constant across his entire corpus of poetry. I want to explore here the idea that in the *Calender* this was part of a higher ambition for the lowly figure of speech.

I provided one example of the kinds of symmetries I mean in Virgil's pastorals in chapter 1; here is one more example to focus our sense of things, the very first line of Virgil's first eclogue:

Tityre tu patulae recubans sub tegmine fagi

"Tityrus," whose dual identity in the *Calender* as Virgil and Chaucer we will return to at length, is "lying under the shade" with the verb and prepositional phrase in the center of the line, surrounded by what gives that shade, the genitive phrase, "of the broad-spreading [*patulae*] beech [*fagi*]."

Tityre tu	patulae	recubans	sub tegmine	fagi
Tityrus, you		lying		
			under the shade	
	of the broad-spreading			beech

This play of syntactic suspension through the predictable unfolding rhythm of the line is everywhere in Augustan verse. Spenser's alliterations can produce patterns in sound that are similar to and reminiscent of Latin syntactic patterns.

But before we focus specifically on the patterns that bear that resemblance most, let us examine "ordinary" alliteration, alliteration in the weave of the cloth for the *Calender*. Here are the first two stanzas of "Januarye":

> A shepeheards boye (no better doe him call)
> when Winters wastful spight was almost spent,
> All in a sunneshine day, as did befall,
> Led forth his flock, that had bene long ypent.
> So faynt they woxe, and feeble in the folde,
> That now unnethes their feete could them uphold.
>
> All as the Sheepe, such was the shepeheards looke,
> For pale and wanne he was, (alas the while,)
> May seeme he lovd, or els some care he tooke:
> Well couth he tune his pipe, and frame his stile.
> Tho to a hill his faynting flocke he ledde,
> And thus him playnd, the while his shepe there fedde.
>
> (1–12)

The first thing to comment on is frequency: the average seems to be about one instance of alliteration per line. The first line has "boye" and "better"; the third "day" and "did"; the fourth, "forth," and "flock"; and more "f" in the next, "faynt," "feeble," and "folde." In lines where alliteration is not obvious, closer inspection reveals more: "now" and "unnethes," in line 6; "seeme" and "some" in line 9; and "tune" and "stile" in the next. In the lines without

obvious alliteration, it seems only to have withdrawn slightly, not disappeared. Between lines with obvious alliteration, single words can also carry
on the alliteration of a previous line—this is the case with "feete" in line 6.
A look at any other stanza in the poem, and, in fact, any other stanza in the
Calender will reveal the same: alliteration at this level of about one instance
per line is constant.[12] But alliteration, in groups of two, three, or more, does
not obviously get us very close to the kinds of word associations and group-
ings created by Latin poetic syntax. To find that we have to look more closely.
The second line of "Januarye" takes us part of the way. Observe how this line
alliterates two letters, "w" and "s," in clusters on the left and right of the line:

> when **W**inters **w**a**s**tful **s**pight was almo**s**t **s**pent

A similar pattern appears in the Alexandrine at the end of the poem:

> **Wh**ose **h**anging **h**eads did seeme his **c**arefull **c**ase to weepe
> (79)

In addition to these clusters, alliteration also appears in chiasmic patterns,
and here we arrive at something that starts to look demonstrably Virgilian:

> Wherein the **b**yrds **w**ere **w**ont to **b**uild their **b**owre
> (32)

That kind of concentric pattern is visually and aurally reminiscent of
Virgil, even as the pattern emerges from entirely different linguistic elements. And the level of complexity we can find does not end there. Consider
this line:

> A thousand sithes I curse that carefull hower (49)
> th   th   th
>   s   s   s
>   c   c
>   r   r   r

"Th" and "c" make up the primary alliterated consonants, but I have also
pointed out the patterning of "s" and "r," which are less audible. This is a

---

[12] This claim is based on an analysis of alliteration in the entire *Calender*.

critical point: whereas past discussions of alliteration generally wall it off from other kinds of sound patterns—assonance, rhyme—to my mind there is no reason to make such hard divisions.[13] And opening our ears in this way allows patterns of this richness and complexity to emerge around alliteration, despite its associations with stylistic simplicity and plainness, on the one hand, or debauchery, decadence, and looseness on the other. The result with a line above is an internal organization that, when analyzed this way, yields a structure that looks similar to the syntactic unfolding of "Tityrus tu patulae ..."

Sometimes also assonance or internal rhyme can function in concert with alliteration to produce similar braiding:

```
You naked trees, whose shady leaves are lost (31)
                              l            l
         trees              leaves
              s      s          s
         t                              t
```

The successive layers here represent ever less noticeable patterns.

And of course there is no reason to limit our awareness of such patterns to the level of the line, even as examples like those above display most clearly the resemblance to the syntactic patterns of Latin verse. As internal rhymes can create a kind of sonic patterning within the line that is similar to alliteration, so too can patterns within lines be extended across lines through end-rhymes, and vice versa. A reasonably straightforward example of this occurs in "Maye" when a collection of hard "c" sounds is extended to the second line of a couplet through the end-rhyme:

> Tho creeping close behind the Wickets clinck,
> Prevelie he peeped out through a chinck.
>
> (251–2)

At the beginning of "Januarye" there is a slightly more complex structure linking lines. Here we find a letter that is in the same metrical position as one of the "f" words in the previous line.

---

[13] For an example of a study that maintains these divisions, see Percy G. Adams, *Graces of Harmony: Alliteration, Assonance, and Consonance in Eighteenth-Century British Poetry* (Athens: University of Georgia Press, 1977).

> So *f*aynt they woxe, and *fee*ble in the *f*olde,
> That now unnethes their *fee*te could them uphold.
>
> (5–6)

Since these words also share a vowel, this comes close to creating a miniature quatrain:

> So faynt they woxe, and fee-
> ble in the folde,
> That now unnethes their feete
> could them uphold.

Once one begins to listen for such patterns, they become more and more apparent, but at the same time, there is no requirement to hear or see them, or address them as a reader: there is a fundamental difference between the kinds of patterns that Spenser is able to create with alliteration and allied sounds, and the syntactic patterns of Virgil. Virgil's writing creates unavoidable intellectual tension through the separation of syntactic elements: the sensitive Latin reader hears a syntactic element—an adjective in the genitive case modifying an unknown noun—and holds that element in suspension until a noun in the appropriate case comes along. To that tension is added the tension and release of the unfolding poetic rhythm, the particular expression in spondees and dactyls of the hexameter line. And if you are of my party in the reading of Latin poetry, to that you also add the standard accent of Latin prose, sometimes in conflict with poetic rhythm, almost always aligned in the last two feet. Spenser's alliterative patterns mirror some of the symmetries of Latin verse, and when analyzed as I have been doing, they create diagrams of comparable complexity. But they do not impose the multiple layers of intellectual and aesthetic tension of Latin poetry; they remain, effectively, optional for readers.[14]

And furthermore, when Spenser's writing *does* connect sound patterns with sense, the result tends to be, if anything, less complex, less tense, less demanding. Take the alliteration that is involved in the chiastic figures of syntax that are among the most prominent stylistic features of "Januarye."

---

[14] It may effectively be optional for most readers of Latin too; one should note an important difference between English literary study and Latin relative to performance: I write of various layers of interlocking tensions involved in reading Latin poetry, but for many competent and accomplished teachers and students of Latin, only some such tensions would be felt—as the poetry is "unlocked" with a focus on revealing its sense and much less on achieving a performance of the poetry where all these elements, or even some of them, are negotiated simultaneously.

Colin's lament begins with alliteration between "pitie" and "payne," and in the next line, when the statement is rephrased as a question, those words are inverted, but the sonic pattern remains almost the same:

> Ye Gods of love, that pitie lovers payne,
> (If any gods the paine of lovers pitie:)
>   (13–14)

The other words repeated from the first line are kept in the same order ("gods," and "lovers"). The two lines have a very close sonic profile, even as Spenser has changed the syntax and order in forming a question. But the result is also arguably as repetitive as it is sonically adroit, and certainly creates little tension. A similar use of sound occurs not across two lines but rather within two single lines in a row, where alliteration emphasizes the punning symmetry that Spenser creates through the use of the inverted syntax of the interrogative:

> I love thilke lasse, (alas why doe I love?)
> And am forlorne, (alas why am I lorne?)
>   (61–2)

At another moment, alliteration shows up in one of Colin's comparisons:

> Thou weake, I wanne: thou leane, I quite forlorne:
>   (47)

The pattern is like many others in the poem, but here sonic likeness suddenly aligns with the likeness Colin is suggesting exists between him and his flock, and so produces alliterative emphasis for a logical structure of the kind so common in Lyly and which, as we will see, also seems to be most amenable to the *Calender*'s E.K. Notice too that "weake" and "leane" share a vowel sound, and both apply to the flock. So the logical pattern, with letters standing for Colin and the flock, and subscript numbers for the attributes they share might look something like this:

$$a_1 \text{ is like } b_1, \text{ and } a_2 \text{ is like } b_2$$

Alliteration, then, lines up with the numbers (1 with "w" and 2 with "l") while a single vowel sound is assigned to "a" (though not to "b"). But again, if anything, these structures seem less interesting, less remarkable than the earlier patterns of alliteration we examined. As Spenser connects sound and sense, tension seems to flow out of the verse rather than the opposite. At least in the earlier examples, one had to work to perceive the sonic patterns independent of sense. Here, Spenser is creating symmetries and patterns reminiscent of Latin verse, but simplified, and sound is in some cases further emphasizing what are already pretty straightforward structures to begin with—the result risks overkill.

However, in writing this way Spenser seems to be coming closest to the deployment of alliteration that E.K. authorizes, even, indeed, as E.K. condemns effeminate poets who give themselves over too much to alliteration. In that same passage of condemnation discussed at the end of the previous section, we hear E.K. condemn those who "without judgement iangle, without reason rage," and indeed throughout his writing in the *Calender*, E.K. displays alliteration as a proper accompaniment of critical prose. But the emphasis is on accompaniment, on highlighting logical groups and argumentative structures. At least, it usually is; E.K. also, remarkably, both criticizes alliteration in his endnotes and praises it, but not in a way that, as far as I can tell, leads to any systematic understanding of how much alliteration is too much, and when alliteration—or the musical component of poetry more generally—is allowed to please independently of sense. In his commentary on "October," he alternatively praises and criticizes these two lines: "For lofty love doth loath a lowly eye" (96) and "To feede youths fancie, and the flocking fry" (14). Can you tell which? It isn't easy, since both alliterate at pretty much the same level of density, with four or five instances of either "l" or "f." And yet one receives praise and the other criticism, from the commentator whose ostensible purpose is to promote the excellence of the poet's premiere: "Frye) is a bold Metaphore, forced from the spawning fishes. for the multitude of young fish be called the frye" (p. 133)—where "forced" seems a deliberate word choice that echoes the alliteration of the line he is glossing; but in contrast, "For lofty love) I think this playing with the letter to be rather a fault then a figure, aswel in our English tongue, as it hath bene alwayes in the Latin, called Cacozelon" (p. 134). Fair enough. But if, in terms of alliterative frequency, the "loudness" of the effect, it seems impossible to deduce E.K.'s line between good and bad zeal, he does make clear enough where he can find no fault in the figure, and that is highlighting an antithesis like "fault" and "figure" in his gloss. That isn't playing: that is making a distinction, thinking, and using sound to highlight the thought.

We have seen then how the "homely" and simple figure of alliteration can participate in patterning that is not at all simple, and might be beautiful and complex in the way that Virgilian syntactic symmetries are beautiful. We have also seen how there is potential for trouble along the same lines, as Spenser moves to align sound and sense. That is, however, just the beginning of the trouble. How much alliteration is too much? What happens when alliteration is overutilized? Down at this technical level of analysis, it is easy to see how alliteration might cause problems with information management, both in the sense that these patterns might be too subtle to perceive, require too much effort of attention *away* from sense, and also that, if the patterns are too forceful, they might distract from what the poem is saying by becoming glaringly unsubtle. Thus it appears that alliteration was at best an imperfect vehicle as Spenser pursued an answer to the complex sonic patterns regularly deployed in Virgil. This did not, however, lead him to abandon alliteration altogether, or even to lessen its frequency. If we analyze alliteration in Spenser's later works, we find that poetic development in this case seems to mean learning better to integrate the elements of his preferred style into a more seamless performance.

Colin comes home

Alliteration is still present in Spenser's later poetry, very much so in *The Faerie Queene*, and at a level of frequency comparable to the *Calender*. And indeed it may be that the two formal qualities I have examined so far—the division and management of sense units across lines and through the schemes of stanzas, and the sonic patterning of alliteration—may be connected in that creating a more supple poetry that avoids repetition and stiffness also eases attention on alliteration patterns that are otherwise more conspicuous. But there is one more location in Spenser's poetry that we can hardly overlook if we are interested in the extent to which these problems with Spenser's "devise" in the *Calender*, these potential provokers of Rosalind's "scorne," are problems that Spenser outgrew or solved. That location is the late pastoral poem *Colin Clout's Come Home Againe*.[15] The Virgilian longings of the *Calender* are placed front and center as *Colin Clout's Come Home Againe* begins, including the identification of Colin Clout, in the opening lines, as "The shepheards boy (best knowen by that name) / That after *Tityrus* first

---

[15] The poem was first published in a quarto dated 1595, but includes a dedication dated 1591. For a discussion of the complexities of dating this poem and assessing its textual situation, see Elizabeth Chaghafi, "Spenser and Book History," in *Spenser in the Moment*, ed. Paul J. Hecht and J. B. Lethbridge (Madison, NJ: Fairleigh Dickinson University Press, 2015), 67–99.

sung his lay." The identification with Tityrus, we will recall, is dual: Tityrus is both what early modern writers took to be the pastoral pen name of Virgil and a name for Chaucer, something first imputed to him within the pastoral world of the *Calender*.[16] To write after Tityrus, then, is to write after the best classical and vernacular poetic models.

The alignment does not end there. Virgil's first eclogue is an encounter between a shepherd exiled from his lands, searching for a place to bring his flock (displaced by soldiers relocated after the end of the civil war), and Tityrus, a somewhat luckier shepherd who made his way to Rome and requested dispensation to keep his not very good parcel of land. That trip to the capital is what Spenser picks up in *Colin Clout's Come Home Againe*, expanding and riffing on the moment of special lyric power in Virgil's poem that we already examined in chapter 1, where the exiled shepherd Melibœus, despite having just met Tityrus for the first time, adds a section, like a new verse of a song, to the unfolding lyric dialogue describing how Tityrus's love Amaryllis must have mourned his absence, and furthermore

> Tityrus hinc aberat. ipsae te, Tityre, pinus,
> ipsi te fontes, ipsa haec arbusta vocabant.
> (38–9)
> Tityrus had abandoned you. For you, Tityrus, the pines,
> For you the fountains, for you these fields called out.

Stepping into the role of Melibœus is Hobbinol, that thwarted lover of Colin Clout, the description of whose love provoked E.K., in "Januarye," so eagerly to assure us that this was no "disorderly" love.[17] Hobbinol here proclaims himself "of many greatest crosse" (18) and then goes on in a Virgilian vein:

> Whilest thou wast hence, all dead in dole did lye:
> The woods were heard to waile full many a sythe,
> And all their birds with silence to complaine:

---

[16] The identification of Tityrus with Virgil was a commonplace in the ancient world, and came to early modern readers principally though commentaries; Servius makes the connection on line 1 of Eclogue 1; for Servius see e.g. Wendell Clausen, *A Commentary on Virgil Eclogues* (Oxford: Oxford University Press, 1994), 32. The standard edition of Servius remains that of Georg Thilo and Hermann Hagen (Leipzig: Teubner, 1881–7); for the *Eclogues*, see vol. 3, pt. 1. Spenser refers to Chaucer as Tityrus, in the voice of Colin Clout, in "June," 81, reinforced by a note by E.K. (p. 93).

[17] Note to "Januarye" line 59, p. 39. See chapter 1, "Problems with Sex and Aesthetics" for the first discussion of this phrase.

> The fields with faded flowers did seeme to mourne,
> And all their flocks from feeding to refraine:
> The running waters wept for thy returne,
> And all their fish with languor did lament:
> But now both woods and fields, and floods revive,
> Sith thou art come, their cause of merriment,
> That us late dead, hast made again alive
>
> (22–31)

As usual with comparisons of English and Latin verse, structures in the Latin seem to take many more words and syllables to play out in English, if we can even assert a direct link. But note how much Virgil's poetry too indulges in alliterative pattern and repetition—"ipsae te, Tityre, pinus, / ipsi te fontes, ipsa haec arbusta vocabant." The repetition and variation of three versions of "ipsa" is only the most obvious pattern, that picks up the "p" of "pinus," as well as two "b" sounds. There are lesser patterns of "s" and "t" as well. To this we might compare this alliterative pattern across two lines: "The fields with faded flowers did seeme to mourne / And all their flocks from feeding to refraine." While it is difficult to say how this avoids being "bad" alliteration, it clearly avoids the kind of intensity that drew the implicit admiration of E.K.—"To feede youthes fancie, and the flocking fry." And yet there is "flock" and "feed" in the second line. What makes this subtle difference in deployment of word sounds seem so significant, the *Colin Clout's Come Home Againe* lines fluid and professional, the *Calender* line oddly disjointed and jarring? To be sure, the resting area of "did seeme to mourne" takes pressure off of the intensity of the pattern. But beyond that, it seems as though aspects of rhythm of syllabic "weight" are coming into play:

x   /   /   / x

To feede youthes fancie

"Youthes" is surely a heavy word to put on an off-beat. Here is the remainder of the line:

\   x   /   x   /

and the flocking fry

I give that "and" a middling accent advisedly, but the line clearly has trouble recovering from the spondaic first half—something of a "stuttering effect" which might be punk rock, or might be not-very-good poetry writing.[18] In any case,

> The fields with flowers did seeme to mourne

seems the work of a poet at peace with using minor words to pace out a line of iambic pentameter. That "did" is utterly rhythm-supporting, but how easily it fits in after the retarding weight of "flowers," presumably a disyllable slightly smeared into a monosyllable.

To turn from pastoral-lyrical mellifluousness, we can contrast that Virgilian passage with the *Colin Clout's Come Home Againe* Spenser when he wants to conjure force and violence, as here when the river Mulla's mountain father Mole exacts his revenge on Bregog, the clever river who so subtly seduced, married, and consummated his marriage without the permission of the father:

> Who wondrous wroth for that so foule despight
> In great avenge did roll downe from his hill
> Huge mightie stones, the which encumber might
> His passage, and his water-courses spill.
>
> (148–51)

Again we can see a willingness to accelerate lines with unnecessary "did"s as in "In greate avenge did roll," or the "the" of "the which encumber might." That fluency makes variations, here placed right on their signifiers, seem to deliver rhythmic and sonic hits with perfect accuracy:

> \ / x / x /
> Who wondrous wroth for that

and

> / / x / x /
> Huge mightie stones, the which

The first works by sonic patterns of "w" as well as rhythmic slowing, and the second a more overt spondaic opening that makes the first part of the line almost grind to a halt, before skipping ahead on the already highlighted unnecessary "the."

---

[18] For more on punk rock as a useful concept for reading early modern lyric, see chapter 5, on Wroth's sonnets.

What Spenser seems to have learned is, more or less, how to loosen up. Lilting lines that move a reader along prepare the way for variations to be more noticeable and effective. Spenser has increased his rhythmic and dynamic range as a poet. How did Spenser improve technically as a poet in his later writing? At the level of poetic rhythm and sound management, with an eye on Virgil, he did it like this.

Radical Passivity

It is not clear at all, however, that any of these improvements would have impressed Rosalind, because "shepheardes devise" is not narrowly technical, and Rosalind's scorne is not limited to Colin's poetry *qua* poetry. Similarly, the difficulties of doing Virgilian pastoral in English are not limited to those generated by qualities of the Latin language or Golden Age prosody. Indeed, the whole arc of *The Shepheardes Calender* can be seen as a response to the crisis of masculinity and sexuality provoked by trying to do poetry at all in 1579, a crisis emblematized by Colin's physical collapse at the end of the first poem in the book, as well as by his sinking into death at the end of the last. And as I indicated at the outset of the chapter, unlike the technical problems I spotlighted above, there is much less evidence that this suite of issues with gender and sexuality are resolved or grown out of in Spenser's later poetry.

To begin our discussion, I want to look not at Colin Clout, but at a minor and less-discussed shepherd. He looks less minor, however, if our attention is focused on the problems with sexuality and gender that are generated by the translation of Virgilian pastoral into English. As it turns out, this obscure shepherd is very much another Melibœus figure, and in many ways this eclogue, "September," is the most direct imitation of the dramatic content of Virgil's first eclogue.[19] But as I argued in chapter 1, the circumstances of translation from Virgil's Rome into Elizabethan England mean that the Melibœus figure is feminized by his economic position.[20] As with other poems in the *Calender* that attack corruption, Spenser makes significant use here of the Italian neo-Latin poet Mantuan, who was lionized by

---

[19] The connection to Virgil has been noted in the past. See McCabe's headnote to "September," which remains an excellent summary scholarship tracing the influences and likely topical references of the poem (pp. 553–4).

[20] See chapter 1, "Problems with Sex and Aesthetics."

Elizabethans for criticizing corruption in the Catholic Church.[21] But the radical experimentalism of the style of the poem is all Spenser's own, and scholars have struggled both to explicate it and explain its purpose. Next to the style of Virgil in particular, it looks almost hallucinatory. In my reading the poem's radically experimental style comes into focus from the position to which Rosalind condemns Colin Clout at the outset of the *Calender*: a man shamefully feminized, for whom eloquence itself may deepen his plight. Diggon Davie, the Meliboeus figure in this poem, makes no pretense to the heights that Colin has scaled prior to his downfall; on the contrary, he seems, with his name, to be more intent on digging than soaring. We have been considering ways that Spenser might have been struggling and at times failing in the writing of the *Calender*. In "September," we will examine a poem that embraces failure and searches its depths, that shears away all that pretends to make poetry beautiful or illuminating or reflective. If Rosalind will condemn "shepherds device," then here is a new device that inverts the values of the old: a poetry harsh, brash, and raw.

Badde is the best

The peculiar radical experimentalism of this poem arrives right at the start, as Spenser abandons more subtle ways of registering the effeminization of his Meliboeus figure. Diggon Davie is feminized in "September" in the very first line of the eclogue, but not through any more or less subtle comparison with women, but rather simply by calling him "her." The strange dialect of "September," prominent enough at the time to merit an explanatory note from E.K. at the head of its glosses, has been identified by scholars as Welsh-influenced, perhaps meant to help knowing readers identify Diggon Davie as Richard Davies, bishop of Saint David's, and an associate of the reformer Archbishop Grindal (praised under the transparent pseudonym "Algrind" in "Julye").[22] But this seems inadequate to explain what we read in the opening lines of the poem.

---

[21] Mantuan is how the English referred to Baptista Mantuanus (1447–1516), a Carmelite monk. "September" draws principally on Mantuan's ninth eclogue. See Baptista Mantuanus, *Adulescentia*, trans. Lee Piepho (New York: Garland Publishing, 1989).

[22] For the identification of Diggon, see John N. King, *Spenser's Poetry and the Reformation Tradition* (Princeton: Princeton University Press, 1990), 25. One strain of recent criticism has aligned Diggon more closely with exiles and refugees: this is the case with Catherine Nicholson's treatment of Diggon, in which she argues that "errancy has marked his speech," in the chapter on "Pastoral in Exile" in her book *Uncommon Tongues: Eloquence and Eccentricity in the English*

HOBBINOL   Diggon Davie, I bidde her god day:
           Or Diggon her is, or I missaye.
DIGGON   Her was her, while it was daye light,
           But now her is a most wretched wight.

Readers of the *Calender* up to this point will be thrown by the "her," and not because they won't be ready to read it as other than a feminine pronoun. As it appears in the glossary of McCabe's edition of the *Shorter Poems*, "her" is ordinarily used for "their" throughout the *Calender* and elsewhere in Spenser's works. But that makes no sense here. McCabe instead supplies a special note for the usage in "September," namely "him," which McCabe identifies as "a Welsh usage" (p. 554, note to line 1). But that gloss hardly deals with the awkwardness of these opening lines, where "her" is made to stand for "him," as well as, in lines 2 and 3 "it," or "he": "Or Diggon *it* is," "*It* was him" or, perhaps, "*He* was him." And it also doesn't explain why such a Welsh usage would appear in the speech of Hobbinol, who hasn't been traveling in foreign lands but is instead one of the main supporting characters of the *Calender*—Colin's disappointed would-be lover and, according to E.K., the shepherd who stands in for Gabriel Harvey.[23] It may seem impossibly unsubtle of Spenser to use such a device to suggest that Diggon has been feminized by his travels and experiences. But in the larger context of the eclogue that considers the relative advantages of such qualities as discursive flatness and darkness, such unsubtlety becomes more plausible. As Diggon is shortly urged to speak plainly about his suffering, so the poem adopts a startlingly direct way of emphasizing the gendering that this suffering has caused.

Only slightly less direct is the way Diggon's travels are figured as a pregnancy. Hobbinol notes that it has been "thrise three Moones" since he "saw thy head last" (19, 20). E.K. helpfully does the math in his note: "nine monethes" (p. 125, note to 20). Other language in Hobbinol's request for Diggon to tell him of his travels plays on the notion of a figural pregnancy: he can see that Diggon is in possession of "a burdenous smart" (16); he urges him to disburden himself, to give birth to his sorrows: "eche thing imparted is more eath to beare" (17). Similar punning can be heard in Hobbinol's description of Diggon's travels, that "thou hast measured much grownd" (21), where it

Renaissance (Philadelphia: University of Pennsylvania Press, 2014), 115. Syrithe Pugh also emphasizes this aspect of Diggon while connecting the *Calender* to Ovid's calendric *Fasti* as well as his poetry-of-exile, the *Tristia*, in *Spenser and Ovid* (Burlington, VT: Ashgate, 2005), 12–41.
    [23] The identification is made in E.K.'s note to line 176 of "September."

is possible to see him "grown" and his pregnant belly of sorrow recalling the "world rounde" of the next line. That language emphasizes the inverted nature of this pregnancy: what has grown is his sufferings, their impact on his sense of himself, his loss of his sense of himself, while his body has become emaciated. To be feminized in this way is to be rendered powerless, relieved of agency and of possessions (as in his flock, which has apparently starved to death). And such a figural or inverted pregnancy also suggests pregnancy as a result of rape, which emphasizes lack of female agency in the extreme, while also serving as a powerful metaphor for repressed trauma.

As we saw in the *Epistle*, E.K. included "a woman in childbirth" (p. 28)[24] as an example of the effeminizing lack of agency he saw on display in England's poets held rapt by their love of alliteration. There he seemed to play upon the vulnerability of the female body—susceptible to rape, susceptible to pregnancy, which finally exacts the labor of birth. It is possible for women to have no agency at any stage of this process, and that is the passivity that E.K. emphasizes, and which Diggon's figural pregnancy likewise seems to highlight.[25] We should also note, in an anticipatory vein, that this inversion offers Rosalind the possibility of the role of impregnator. For her condemnation of Colin Clout is very much an expression of agency, and it effeminizes him and puts him in a position comparable to that of Diggon Davie, even if we never call Colin "her" or figure his suffering that follows as an unwanted pregnancy. And yet, the *Calender*'s whole structure is not entirely unsuggestive of this: twelve months, not nine, but still, that is the period it takes for Rosalind's condemnation to reach the culmination of "December," namely Colin's death. (And September *is* month 9 following the crisis of "Januarye.")

Understanding Diggon's figural pregnancy as the result of a rape is also encouraged by the hyper-masculinized form of his oppressors, specifically two references to bulls. In the first case, he identifies the dominant players in the economy to which he traveled as people who carry themselves with excessive pride:

> They looken bigge as Bulls, that bene bate,
> And bearen the cragge so stiffe and so state,
> As cocke on his dunghill, crowing cranck.
>
> (44–6)

---

[24] Quoted above, "Static stanzas."
[25] See also discussions of Wroth, and Dora Jordan's early career, in chapter 5.

That is, they look like roosters strutting about except that roosters don't capture the physical intimidation of bulls. But both are known for pride, willingness to fight and dominate other males and groups of females. Diggon returns to the bull later in the poem, in a memorable passage in which he struggles to cut to the heart of the corrupt economy he has experienced:

> But they that shooten neerest the pricke,
> Sayne, other the fat from their beards doen lick.
> For bigge Bulles *of Basan* brace hem about,
> That with theyr hornes butten the more stoute:
> But the leane soules treaden under foote.
> And to seeke redresse mought little boote:
> For liker bene they to pluck away more,
> Then ought of the gotten good to restore.
>
> (122–9)

I will return before long to the larger context of this passage, in which Diggon is attempting to summon extreme plainness and directness of speech after (as he understands it) he is criticized by Hobbinol for being too murky. But if he doesn't find his way to clarity here, he does find his way to sexual language and imagery. "The pricke" can be the bull's eye of an archery target, but it is also a phallic term;[26] "the fat from their beards doen lick" is a proverbial expression "for appropriating the profits of someone else's labours",[27] but in its proximity to "pricke" it is hard to deny its sexual allusiveness, even in the intimacy and homoeroticism of the literal image—of one man licking the fat (grease? pieces of actual fat?) from another's beard.

Then we arrive at the bulls. Commentators (not E.K.) have noted that "bigge Bulles *of Basan*" alludes to the moment in Psalm 22 in which the speaker, in the King James Version, finds that "Many bulls have compassed me: strong bulls of Bashan have beset me round" (12). However, in the Psalm, the bulls take their place with lions, and later, dogs, all of whom seem to threaten to kill and devour. What happens in "September" is different, the bulls again representing, not hostile or homicidal forces, but

[26] See e.g. Shakespeare, Sonnet 20, line 13: "But since she pricked thee out for women's pleasure," and *OED*, s.v. "prick, n." I. 12. b.

[27] The gloss is McCabe's, p. 556. McCabe also notes that Spenser uses a very similar form of the expression in the *Mother Hubberds Tale*, lines 77–8: "Whilst others always have before me stept, / And from my beard the fat away have swept."

dominant figures within a corrupt economy. And quite unlike the Bible, the sexual imagery continues here, as the bulls "butten" the more stout, butting being a euphemism for intercourse, at least in Boccaccio.[28] Again, the image promotes a sense that those who benefit from the corrupt economy carry themselves with a dominance that is specifically sexual, intimidating and harassing those that might resist them, and when that fails, treading them underfoot.

The sexual imagery, the feminizing of pronouns, and the burden of accumulated suffering-as-pregnancy all support the sense that his experience at the hands of these bulls has been comparable to a rape, both in terms of non-sexual rapine, having his goods and his sense of himself as a productive citizen forcibly stripped from him, and in terms of being violated and impregnated with a corrosive sense of worthlessness and inutility, as well as a comprehensive sense of cynicism that will emerge more fully as we continue to explore his discourse in the next section: that the world is utterly without merit, that all hierarchies of power, wealth, and social status are based on nothing but force and self-serving lies. These qualities link Diggon with victims of actual sexual violence, with ravished women, even if the poem is not quite ready to make this explicit.

All of this effeminizing, sexualizing imagery and wordplay serves vastly to amplify what in chapter 1 I argued was already here as a result of the translation of the situation of Virgil's first eclogue to the Elizabethan landscape. It is one thing to suggest that Colin Clout is effeminized by his sexual rejection by Rosalind, or by her aesthetic rejection, or by the enterprise of poetry or art-creation altogether. It is quite another to open up "effeminization" to include a suite of qualities endured by women who are the victims of violence including sexual violence. And as I suggested in chapter 1, this amplification and embrace of what in E.K.'s language is strong but also easily overlooked, creates the opportunity for a feminist project in response. That is, if we can see Diggon as having common currency, through his social and economic position, with the worst abuses of patriarchy perpetrated on women, we have the basis for common cause, where Diggon's victimhood, his figural rape and pregnancy, make him into something like an "honorary woman"—an honorary woman who is welcomed to the resistance, that is.

---

[28] See *Decameron*, Day 2, Story 7, in which Alatiel, in bed with Pericone, is described as "avendo mai davanti saputo con che corno gli uomini cozzano"—this from the edition by Cesare Segre (Milan: Mursia, 1966), 133—and in translation, "she had no conception of the kind of horn that men do their butting with," Giovanni Boccaccio, *The Decameron*, trans. G. H. McWilliam (2nd edn., New York: Penguin, 1995), 130.

Let me be clear, that I do not want to be glib in my characterization of Diggon (or of feminism). Having brought into focus the dynamics around Diggon's effeminizing I am also struck by how we might also see Diggon in other terms. For example, reading with Amber Jamilla Musser, I might foreground the "weight" of Diggon's suffering as aligned with "flesh," linking, for example, the plight of women and racialized others, including, of course, the victims of slavery.[29] The aggressive figuration of women and Blacks as bodies, inferior via Descartes from minds, and then further reduced to flesh, Musser reads as "part of the equation of blackness with depersonalization and nonsubjectivity."[30] And yet, she also finds flesh, with its "fraught position within studies of difference" as "a territory ripe for reclamation."[31] And Musser is also alive to "networks of affinity between … the illegal alien and the queer," and this is another way that Diggon's particular constellation of othering and queering could lead.[32] Reading with Juana María Rodríguez might foreground both of those qualities in Diggon, pressing us to see him not as simply effeminized, but as stigmatized for his non-cis-gendering, or language that labels him as foreign or disabled, in which case it might be more pressing to work to imagine for him (if that continues to be the appropriate pronoun) ways of reversing or flipping the significations of what is stigmatized, or, in exactly that state, imagining a sexuality. Yet Rodríguez also notes, "despite the undoing of a category such as 'woman,' that formation—as an undifferentiated, socially authorized, and juridically legitimated form of identification, and as an embodied and performatively articulated mode of being in the world—continues to exert a powerful political and affective shadow."[33] Thus I remain most inclined to take Diggon's effeminizing in the poem as expanding the realm of women's persecution in patriarchy to encompass a White male economic migrant, and then to imagine resistance from this point.

And what is the nature of that resistance for Diggon? It looks to be a search for a style, which begins as a search for a narrative style adequate to the corruption and pathology he must penetrate, and then also seems a search for a style of thinking and finally a style of living. At two moments in "September," Hobbinol's skeptical response to Diggon becomes as explicitly

---

[29] Amber Jamilla Musser, *Sensational Flesh: Race, Power, and Masochism* (New York: New York University Press, 2014), 19.

[30] Musser, *Sensational Flesh*, 20.

[31] Musser, *Sensational Flesh*, 20.

[32] Musser, *Sensational Flesh*, 19.

[33] Juana María Rodríguez, *Sexual Futures, Queer Gestures, and Other Latina Longings* (New York: New York University Press, 2014), 23.

focused on style as anything in the *Calender*. Here is the first such moment, after Diggon's first effort to describe the practices of the shepherds he has encountered in his travels:

> Diggon, I praye thee speake not so dirke.
> Such myster saying me seemeth to mirke.
>
> (102–3)

After this, Diggon launches into the speech that includes the "Bulles *of Basan*" quoted above; it begins this way:

> Then playnely to speak of shepheards most what,
> Badde is the best (this english is flatt.)
>
> (104–5)

At the conclusion of this speech, Hobbinol revises his criticism: "Nowe Diggon, I see thou speakest to plaine" (136), but Hobbinol is not reversing himself. Rather, it seems that this discussion of plainness has turned out not to be very plain. In an effort to escape his feminized position, Diggon is trying to lever himself to a position of clarity and rhetorical control, to speak of the ills of the world in a fashion that penetrates their disguises and makes them plain. He thus interprets Hobbinol's complaint about the "dark" and the "murky" to say that he isn't going far enough. This provokes the remarkable line, "Badde is the best (this english is flatt.)," which in four words concentrates Diggon's view that the whole ethical hierarchy of the world is upside-down, and then comments, perhaps to Hobbinol, or perhaps to himself—is that plain enough for you?

But the continuation of Hobbinol's response after the "to plaine" line clarifies that this is not what he was getting at:

> Nowe Diggon, I see thou speakest to plaine:
> Better it were, a little to fayne,
> And cleanly cover, that cannot be cured.
> Such il, as is forced, mought nedes be endured.
>
> (136–9)

That is, Hobbinol is not objecting to a lack of plainness and clarity, or a lack of critical penetration on Diggon's part. On the contrary, he seems to think that Diggon is going too far, speaking of evils, darkness, from which there is no escape, so they had better not be spoken of at all. Hobbinol's criticism is hard to accept at face value because, as it turns out, other than the "Badde is the best" line, it is very difficult to call the two speeches Hobbinol is responding to excessively plain. The first makes use of the standard pastoral-satirical connection between clergy and shepherds to criticize, harshly, various corruptions of the Church; the second moves further into economic and political territory: the "Bulles" Diggon speaks of are not obviously church figures, but instead seem to be simply the powerful: oligarchs who make a joke of societal institutions and the rule of law, gather all good to themselves and crush anyone who opposes them.

I say "seem" because it is really very hard to be sure, such are the layers of figuration that Diggon uses in his search for plainness and clarity. The speech is a series of reports of hearsay, of what various unspecified groups, "they," *say* is at the heart of the world's evil. The report about the "Bulles" comes from those who Diggon says "shooten nearest the pricke" (122)—and when Diggon narrates this most central insight into evil, he doesn't name names; instead he uses the figure of bulls. In the lines that follow it seems as though that figuration, that anti-personification of actors who are presumably people, is layered with an additional figure, of the quagmire:

> For they [presumably the "Bulles"] bene like foule wagmoires
> overgrast,
> That if thy galage once sticketh fast,
> The more to wind it out thou doest swinck,
> Thou mought ay deeper and deeper sinck.
> Yet better leave of with a little losse,
> Then by much wrestling to leese the grosse.
>
> (130–5)

Diggon's digging into the world's ills, his search for utter flatness and plainness, "leaves off" at this point, where critical thought seems to have revealed an endless abyss: no matter how far down one goes attempting to cast light on the evil, or to cut into the pathology, there is always more, and eventually one is sucked in never to be heard from again.

We might conclude from this that Diggon's effort to claim a plain style of critical penetration as a way to escape his position of feminized victimhood has failed. But "September" is not yet over. Though Hobbinol does not point it out, one clear way in which Diggon's speech has failed thus far is in its lack of specificity and personal connection. Though he purports to be narrating his travels, his speeches have so far lacked any element of the personal travel narrative, and instead have trafficked in broad statements about institutions:

the Church, and the political and economic state of ordinary people. As it turns out, we never do get such a personal narrative, but we do at least get more of a narrative, namely the tale of Roffy, his sheepdog Lowder, and an extraordinarily resourceful wolf. Thus as Diggon seems on the verge of sinking inextricably into layers of critical figuration he manages to find his way to a narrative—one still focused very much on the evils of the world, but also one that leads from questions of discursive and narrative style finally to lifestyle.

The story of Roffy and Lowder engages Hobbinol much more so than anything Diggon has said previously: it tells a story, with characters good and ill, and it has a connection (Roffy) to Hobbinol's beloved Colin. But at the end of the narrative Diggon and Hobbinol once more find themselves at odds. Having learned of wolves that can mimic a shepherd's voice, Hobbinol asks how such evil can be perceived and avoided. Diggon says this:

> How, but with heede and watchfulnesse,
> Forstallen hem of their wilinesse?
> For thy with shepherd sittes not playe,
> Or sleepe, as some doen, all the long day:
> But ever liggen in watch and ward,
> From soddein force theyr flocks for to gard.
>
> (230–5)

If we want an example of such a shepherd, Diggon has already provided one in Roffy, and beyond him a mythological ideal: "For Roffy is wise, and as Argus eyed" (203). We will return to Argus momentarily. For now I simply want to observe that, despite Roffy's reputation, and Argus's status as ideal shepherd in the community of the *Calender*, as well as the other reasons that such a straight and watchful style of living might appeal to Diggon, Hobbinol once more unceremoniously rejects it:

> Ah Diggon, thilke same rule were too straight,
> All the cold season to wach and waite.
> We bene of fleshe, men as other bee.
> Why should we be bound to such miseree?
> What ever thing lacketh chaungeable rest,
> Mought needes decay, when it is at best.
>
> (236–41)

This is the definitive rejection of what Diggon offers in the way of poetic narrative or wisdom; in response, Diggon admits that the whole discursive exercise has done him no good, and that he has no idea how to proceed. To that, Hobbinol finally offers his "vetchy bed" and the eclogue comes to its Virgilian close. The language of this speech is, however, legible as an intellectualized version of Hobbinol's first, more visceral reaction to Diggon's poetry and thinking. To set up this reaction to Diggon's first attempt to explain what has happened to himself and his flock, it is useful to review a few of Hobbinol's reactions to other poetry he hears in the *Calender*. For example, in his response to Colin Clout complaining of Rosalind in "June," Hobbinol exclaims, "*Colin*, to heare thy rymes and roundelays ... I more delight, then larke in Sommer dayes" (49, 51); and later, "O carefull *Colin*, I lament thy case, / Thy teares would make the hardest flint to flowe" (113–14). To Diggon's first extended speech, he says this: "Diggon, I am so stiffe, and so stanck, / That uneth may I stand any more" (47–8). He then suggests that they move out of the wind before continuing.

These reactions make a mockery of E.K.'s confident assertions about sentences and style "strongly trussed up together": more is required of language than this, and likewise more is required of life than this and, indeed, of manhood or sexuality. The stanza experiments of the *Calender* show that the imposition of this kind of order on poetic language does not necessarily yield the desired results, and can instead make for fatiguing stiffness. "September," like the speech-based line grouping I explored in "Februarie," looks in many ways like an experiment in the other direction, opening up poetic form to accommodate speech and thought in a continuously variable manner. But as Hobbinol complains, there can be a "stiffness" that emerges from too much looseness as well. Lack of form requires increasing amounts of cognitive energy to render comprehensible, to know where one is and where one is going. And at a less formal level, a desire for discursive "plainness" can also run into something like stiffness too. "Bad is the best" may well be the plainest way of summarizing the world that Diggon has encountered, but doesn't cast much light on anything. And there is a definite threat of recursiveness or circularity within all of these binary or axial ways of thinking, that as he digs deepest, trying his hardest to penetrate to the truth of things, his metaphors become more and more layered, as though layers of sedimentation are closing above him the farther he digs.

But to return to the opening move of this study, can we ask at this point: is Diggon's poetry "bad" too? Or is "September"? I have suggested that it is a kind of inversion of Virgil's first eclogue. I will now go ahead and say that as a radical experiment, as a poem that thematizes and explores failure, and as a poem that in particular goes far and deep in exploring the sexual dynamics of its situation, of the dangers of effeminacy, there is a lot to celebrate here. This is not to say that the character Diggon escapes his initial position as a result of his experiments, his plumbing of the depths and his search for a style: particularly because of the lack of sympathy he receives from Hobbinol (who is more inclined to recoil in horror), he seems to have advanced little from the aggressive figuration of rape victim with which the poem began.

But in other ways, we can see Diggon's efforts as connecting to the stylistic, technical grounds of activity that we explored in the first half of the chapter. Rather than avoiding emasculating, feminizing dynamics in the translation of iconic Virgilian pastoral, this poem embraces them. And as well, the poem explores stylistic responses to the criticisms that surround and threaten its style at a more global level. Poetic ornamentation and musicality as exemplified by alliteration come under severe scrutiny from within and without the *Calender*. E.K. makes strident claims that the poet he introduces avoids at all cost the feminizing, irrational, bodily seductions of letter-chasing. Diggon, feminized and emasculated in the extreme, explores what a poem of extreme plainness, denuded of all ornament, shorn of all pretense to musical pleasure, might sound and look like. And where E.K. champions the "trussing up" of what is "ungirt" in other writers, Diggon explores the extreme of the untrussed, the unpredictably unfolding, hyper-metaphorical rant, and finds that this leads to "stiffness" in a listener who feels unmoored and at sea. This is why I see Diggon and the poem as fundamentally connected to the frame I am advancing for the book as a whole: Diggon is one of a number of figures who parallels and reflects Colin Clout, and Diggon's experiments, and the entire experiment of "September," is legible as a response to Rosalind's scorn.

Passive poetics

For the remainder of the chapter I want to step back from the extreme of "September" and explore the possibility of other responses to Rosalind's condemnation, other ways that *Calender* experiments with not escaping from the sexual dynamics of its cultural and historical moment. I also want to track the *Calender*'s movement toward some of the less technical virtues of Virgilian pastoral, in particular the concept of concord, which in chapter 1 we explored as a musical-cognitive concept, whereby one of the things that pastoral dialogue might do is to resolve conflict musically, with two speakers finding their way to sympathetic speech, bridging the gap between them sonically. For all its experimentalism, that is not something that seems to emerge from "September," but there are other places where it might. To approach possible positive examples of passive poetics, I first need to fill in one more important negative example, from "October," and expand our sense of the way the *Calender* engages the myth of Argus. As we shall see, while this myth appears negatively in "October," its presentation lays the groundwork for how we can see positive reworkings of its elements.

In "September," Diggon references Argus as a shepherdly ideal, a shepherd infinitely vigilant, who never rests, and sees threats in all directions at once. Hobbinol shoots that down as a plausible lifestyle, but the reference is of further interest. That is because there are other references to Argus in the *Calender*, and also because Diggon leaves out some quite pertinent parts of the story of this creature. Argus shows up in "Julye" as a figure of sexual virtue, but otherwise not too differently from his appearance in "September." But in "October," the eclogue most explicitly concerned with poetry writing and the life of the artist, we get a look at Argus from quite a different perspective within the myth. "October" concerns a young poet-shepherd, Cuddie, who had appeared earlier in "Februarie" and "August," as well as an older shepherd, Piers, who had appeared in "Maye." Cuddie in this dialogue is in a straightforwardly parallel position to Colin Clout and Diggon in that he is in despair and has stopped writing. Piers attempts to cheer him up and offer promising ways forward for his writing. At one point, Cuddie compares himself to the peacock, suggesting that the praise the peacock receives for his beautiful plumage is empty, does not give him anything to sustain himself on, and similarly, human society praises artists but fails to attend to their basic needs in order to support their art.

The connection to Argus is through the peacock's feathers, which Cuddie calls "bright *Argus* blazing eye" (32), directing us to the tail end of the myth. For, as it is told most prominently in Ovid's *Metamorphoses* (1.624–722), Argus turns out not to be quite such an ideal shepherd as he is set by Juno to guard what is formerly the beautiful girl and is now the beautiful heifer Io. Ovid's Argus has a hundred eyes, and some can sleep while others are awake, but exposed to Mercury's sleep-inducing singing—telling the story of Pan and Syrinx and the origins of pastoral music—all his eyes eventually close, allowing Mercury to behead him. But

Juno intervenes and transfers the seeing eyes to the feathers of Juno's bird, the peacock. So in addition to being symbols, for Cuddie, of how approval of artistic beauty, aesthetic production—with the eyes now taking a position parallel to artistic products, or in Cuddie's case, poems—comes with no guarantee of subsistence for the artist, they are also symbols of a strange version of aesthetic passivity, whereby ornaments are figured as what was once concentrated usefulness, the eyes that were the instruments of Argus's vigilance, the source of his towering virtue. In death, they are merely beautiful.

In this way Cuddie links himself to Diggon while further undercutting the ideal of vigilant wakefulness that Diggon espoused. In the context of other things Cuddie says, his Argus reference also looks like a shot at the ideal of Christian sexual virtue with which Argus is also associated, specifically in "Julye." Argus represents a failure of the desire to be infinitely vigilant, "always on," but he also represents a specific failure to protect beauty from Eros, to ensure sexual virtue through vigilance and the threat of force. In other ways in "October" a similar attitude seems to pick up on suggestions that E.K. has made about Spenser's sexual virtue as a poet and threats to that virtue. Right at the start of the *Epistle*, E.K. compares Spenser to Cressida using the language of Pandarus, and then gives us this hopeful fantasy of Spenser's literary career: "But I dout not, so soone as his name shall come into the knowledg of men, and his worthines be sounded in the tromp of fame, but that he shall be not only kiste, but also beloved of all, embraced of the most, and wondred at of the best" (p. 25). It is hard not to see this in light of the vision of Cressida's joint sexual ownership among the Greeks at the end of Shakespeare's furious telling of the story, which for E.K. of course would be coming from Chaucer. But the point for us is that E.K. envisions literary success as sexual promiscuity. Cuddie, at his lowest point, having reviewed literary history and found himself in a period of hopeless decadence, has a parallel, if overtly negative vision:

> And if that any buddes of Poesie,
> Yet of the old stocke gan to shoote agayne:
> Or it mens follies mote be forst to fayne,
> And rolle with rest in rymes of rybaudrye:
> Or as it sprong, it wither must agayne:
> Tom Piper makes us better melodie.
>
> (73–78)

Cuddie imagines as his only path forward, that is, a kind of populist effeminacy, and an explicit embrace of the vision of loose, effeminate, "ragged rymers" (p. 28) that so exercised E.K. in the *Epistle*.

But does the *Calender* also investigate any more positive versions of a passive response? It may be that the book contemplates another way to frame or interpret a kind of sinking into sounds of like letters. Not in this case as a sinking into corporeal femininity, not as the abandonment of reason, nor yet as an expression of stylistic control, of intricacy, either in service of logic (as E.K. would like) or in imitation of the refinement and artificiality of Virgil (when he writes in this mode), but rather a passivity and sinking before sound that might show a path beyond some of the most vexing conflicts of Spenser's time. In "Maye," the allegorical machinery of the plants-at-war in "Februarie" has been set aside, and we contemplate directly the great religious and political schism of early modern England, between Protestants and Catholics. F. W. Brownlow has argued that we should reject E.K.'s straightforward designation of Palinode in the "Maye" eclogue as a Catholic priest, but nonetheless, we see in their disagreement the grounds for violent conflict and the potential for civil war.[34] The moment I want to look at is one where Palinode asks whether their differences—differences "among shepherds"—are really so severe, and Piers responds that yes, they are:

PALINODE   And sooth to sayne, nought seemeth sike strife,
              That shepheardes so witen ech others life,
              And layen her faults the world beforne,
              The while their foes done eache of hem scorne.
              Let none mislike of that may not be mended:
              So conteck soone by concord mought be ended.
PIERS   Shepheard, I list none accordaunce make
              With shepheard, that does the right way forsake.
              And of the twaine, if choice were to me,
              Had lever my foe, then my freend he be.
              For what concord han light and darke sam?
              Or what peace has the Lion with the Lambe?
                                                    (158–69)

---

[34] See F. W. Brownlow, "The British Church in *The Shepheardes Calender*," *Spenser Studies* 23 (2008): 3.

This passage addresses the large-scale possibility or lack of possibility for "concord," for reconciliation between hardened, entrenched views, for synthesis where only antithesis seems imaginable. But in the play of alliteration within and across their speeches—I am thinking particularly of the extension of the alliteration of "m" and "c" from one speech to the next—we might perceive the glimmer of a sort of "concord" that betrays both speakers in their impasse, language organizing itself into sonorities not heard by the speakers, but which suggest reconciliation that they might pursue if they could. This is certainly different from the sympathetic singing of Melibœus in Virgil's first eclogue, but it also seems allied in some ways. At one level, the effect seems metatheatrical, a "loosening"—to use Theodor Adorno's language—of the structure of the narrative, the solidity of the speakers, the illusion of separate subjectivities, comparable to informing a character that he is a character, or to go even farther, to informing these characters that they are constituted from nothing but characters, have no distinct identity beyond language (something that eventually the "character" of Rosalind will do "herself" in *As You Like It*).

This is thus how Spenserian alliteration approaches an Adornian aesthetic effect that he names with the German *Geräusch*, noise, or "rustling," as of trees. This comes into focus in Adorno's essay on the poet Joseph von Eichendorff (1788–1857). Adorno speaks of the "distance from meaning" in Eichendorff's use of language, which imitates the distance from meaning in the unknowable language of the rustling of leaves; the poetry "thereby expresses an estrangement which no thought, only pure sound can bridge."[35] We approach here reconciliation of the division between words and things, with all the implications of historical estrangement and decay that Adorno sees associated with that division. Such a reconciliation, in Spenser, takes up actually opposed voices, subjects, characters, into which the poet has divided himself in imitation of the world's divisions. Adorno also makes a remarkable claim for the poet's passivity in achieving this. He quotes a Brecht poem about Lao Tse and the power of "soft water" to cut through stone in time:

> The soft water with its movement: that is the descending flow of language, the direction it flows of its own accord, but the poet's power is the power to be weak, the power not to resist the descending flow of language rather than the power to control it. It is as defenseless against the accusation of triviality

---

[35] Theodor W. Adorno, "In Memory of Eichendorff," in *Notes to Literature*, Vol. 1, ed. Rolf Tiedemann, trans. Shierry Weber Nicholsen (New York: Columbia University Press, 1991), 69.

as the elements are; but what it succeeds in doing—washing words away from their circumscribed meanings and causing them to light up when they come in contact with one another—demonstrates the pedantic poverty of such objections.[36]

Adorno is speaking at the end there of the simplicity and derivativeness of Eichendorff's images, his "devices," which critics take aim at, but he might as well have been speaking of the apparent triviality of alliterative patterns, or the sense of feminine weakness attributed to those who seem too in love with or beholden to them. The sense that the poet might achieve power by being weak, by giving in to "the descending flow of language" also connects with Elizabethan anxieties about letter-chasing and passivity that so concern E.K at the start of the book, and Cuddie in "October." But the sound patterns throughout the *Calender* that we have seen sampled above indicate that Spenser was indeed ready to "allow" sound to flow around meaning independently, and Adorno indicates the enormous potential to be found in that letting-go. More directly, "the power to be weak" is a formulation that takes on directly the championing of order, governance, control, and vigilance that so characterize the aesthetics, the economics, and the gender politics of figures in the *Calender* like E.K. and Thenot, and show themselves influencing Colin, Diggon, and Cuddie. "The power to be weak" is a response to Rosalind's rejection and aesthetic condemnation: not to take revenge on her, and not to collapse into despair, but to explore the possibilities of a different kind of letting-go.

I want to argue that we see this version of Colin Clout most clearly in the final eclogue, "December," and here another, parallel aesthetic analysis by Adorno helps bring the elements I am interested in into better focus. Adorno's arguments concerning Eichendorff's passivity are formed in contrast with his analysis of another German poet, Stefan George, whose poetry he finds "active" in almost every sense in which Eichendorff is passive. But a nearer example for anglophone readers will most likely be the contrast Adorno draws, in an early essay, between the composers Schubert and Beethoven. Beethoven occupies George's position in this comparison, as the incessantly active and restless shaper of his works. Schubert, Adorno suggests, might be understood as comparatively passive, indeed, using what he calls "dead" materials. He writes of Schubert's music in this essay as a

---

[36] Adorno, "In Memory of Eichendorff," 70.

landscape that avoids "the spontaneous unity of a person";[37] instead he describes it this way:

> The stream, the mill and the black winter wasteland, stretching out time-lessly in the twilight of the mock suns as if in a dream, are the signs of the Schubertian landscape, and dried flowers its sad ornaments.[38]

This particular description, though intended for Schubert's music generally, is centered on Schubert's two great song cycles, *Winterreise* (*Winter Journey*) and *Die Schöne Müllerin* (*The Pretty Miller's Daughter*), which explains why the pastoral imagery happens to be so resonant with the *Calender*. But let me put next to this a telling moment from "December":

> The fragrant flowres, that in my garden grewe,
> Bene withered, as they had bene gathered long.
> Theyr rootes bene dryed up for lacke of dewe,
> Yet dewed with teares they han be ever among.
>> Ah who has wrought my *Rosalind* this spight
>> To spil the flowres, that should her girlond dight?
>>> (109–14)

The winter landscape is the landscape that begins and ends the *Calender*, and in this passage Colin Clout can easily be read as writing about his own po-ems, the poems presented in the *Calender*, as "dead flowers," in the language that was so current in the 1570s. Adorno suggests that Schubert assembles dead components into his compositions in order, for one thing, to cheat death. Rather than writing "fresh" and innovative melodies, rather than cre-ating a new musical vocabulary, he works with what is not only not fresh, but what is antiquated, musty. And rather than assembling this in the manner of a "living entity" he places it within a "crystalline" structure.

As it has actuated the language of death, this version of passivity in Adorno comes even closer to the mythological theorizing of the Argus story, in which the ornaments that beautify the peacock's feathers are at one level sublimated instruments of vigilance, but at another are dead eyes, now

---

[37] Theodor W. Adorno, "Schubert," in *Night Music: Essays on Music 1928–1962*, ed. Rolf Tiedemann, trans. Wieland Hoban (London: Seagull Books, 2009), 20.
[38] Adorno, "Schubert," 30–1.

inspiring admiration rather than admiring. But the Argus cycle of irony, loss, and consolation we have already found to be more of a description of something in which various shepherds of the *Calender* have been trapped, rather than a path away from the situations in which Colin, Diggon, and Cuddie find themselves. Can we see at the end of the *Calender*, among its dead flowers and within a sinking toward an "adieu" to Rosalind just at the point of Colin's death, glimpses of a passivity that aligns with Adorno and escapes the closed circle offered by the Argus myth? But escape to where?

We need to note that between the two Adorno essays I am drawing from, the famously elusive philosopher is speaking of "passivity" in quite different ways. With Eichendorff the crucial sense seems to be in the letting-go, for example, setting up sonic patterns and then allowing them to carry us away from semantic content, negatively as noise, positively as the "rustling" of which Adorno speaks. At other times Adorno's passivity seems to mean "lack of conspicuous subjectivity," or a sense of an active, shaping or governing intelligence ordering the elements of the poems, elements which themselves often seem flat, clichéd, and ineffective. So the releasing here is pushed back to the selection of narrative components: rather than inventing fresh materials, hackneyed materials are deliberately chosen.

We have already seen, with respect to the localized kinds of strife that appear in the *Calender* (e.g., between "youth" and "elde" in "Februrarie") and the larger struggles that it more carefully addresses—Catholic and Protestant—that an Adornian aesthetic passivity, passivity of "power," might be intuited through Spenser's attraction to aesthetic elements for their own sake—that what people like E.K. and Rosalind are ready to condemn as precious and effeminate, disordered, self-indulgent ribaldry, might in fact offer a path to "concord" amidst these vexing, seemingly impossible-to-resolve conflicts. But does this version of passivity also offer a path forward for someone like Diggon Davie? So far the answer seems to be "no," since in applying Adorno's version of passivity we are really not looking at characters and their lives, but rather the whispering beneath their voices, the hints from their surroundings, the voice of the landscape murmuring beneath their speech.

But in "December" there is one more possibility to consider. "December" is a very odd poem, we should note, in its relationship to one of Spenser's principal sources for the *Calender*, namely the pastorals of Clément Marot. The E.K. headnote to "November" acknowledges Marot's presence behind the poem, but "December" does not, even as it is in many places a close translation.[39] The reason for the lack of connection may have to do with the way Spenser finally turns Marot's poem in a very different direction: Marot's original ends with a celebration of his patronage from the king, and ends happily. Colin, as we know, gives up on everything and heads toward death. But in one passage we hear of a portion of Colin's life that we have not heard of before:

> Then as the springe gives place to elder time,
> And bringeth forth the fruite of sommers pryde:
> Also my age now passed youngthly pryme,
> To thinges of ryper reason selfe applied.
>> And learnd of lighter timber cotes to frame,
>> Such as might save my sheepe and me fro shame.
>
> To make fine cages for the Nightingale,
> And Baskets of bulrushes was my wont:
> Who to entrappe the fish in winding sale
> Was better seene, or hurtful beastes to hont?
>> I learned als the signes of heaven to ken,
>> How *Phoebe* fayles, where *Venus* sittes and when.
>
> And tryed time yet taught me greater thinges,
> The sodain rysing of the raging seas:
> The soothe of byrds by beating of their wings,
> The power of herbs, both which can hurt and ease:
>> And which be wont tenrage the restlesse sheepe,
>> And which be wont to worke eternall sleepe.
>
>> (73–90)

In this section we glimpse a phase of Colin's life where neither self-pity, nor nostalgia for better times with better poetry and better patrons, nor desire for revenge on Rosalind or those she loves, seem to take precedence for him. Instead Colin seems to acquire wisdom, wisdom which seems to have the quality of "natural philosophy," which is to say that he becomes something of a scientist. The final version of passivity seems to be observation, learning, and human modesty before "greater things" than human affairs. Rather than

---

[39] The relationship of "December" to Marot's "Eglogue au Roy" is well known; for a detailed comparison, see Owen J. Reamer, "Spenser's Debt to Marot—Re-Examined," *Texas Studies in Literature and Language* 10 (Winter 1969): 504–27.

being consumed with his position of power and sexuality, with his status as a poet or his acceptance or rejection as a suitor, rather than letting Rosalind's judgment immerse him in never-ending despair, in this passage Colin seems to turn not away from the world but toward it, in a larger sense, devoting himself not to upward striving or sexual achievement, but to learning, both to make himself a better steward of his sheep, and for its inherent joy and pleasure: "the soothe of byrds" indeed.

Late Rosalinds

In that part of "December" some readers might wonder if we are seeing a basis for a feminist project of the kind I alluded to in chapter 1. Could Colin, or perhaps Spenser, recognize this productive and positive response to Elizabethan hang-ups about sex and aesthetics? Could we take someone effeminized by love or love of art, and find a way of defanging those charges, within, perhaps, a framework of inquiry outside of concerns for hierarchy and status? To imagine, even further, the basis for a community where knowledge and inquiry are the common objectives, and sex and status lose their force? Alas, we get little hint of this in the vein of Spenser's writings that continues to follow the characters and concerns of Colin and Rosalind (and to consider this in the larger body of Spenser's work is a project outside the scope of this book). Instead, in the latter part of *Colin Clout's Come Home Againe* that concerns Colin and Rosalind, and in the scene with Colin Clout on Mount Acidale in book 6 of *The Faerie Queene*, we see more fitful longings to escape the situation Rosalind has created, which never themselves escape either blaming Rosalind for the audacity of wishing to be the agent of her own sexual destiny, or metamorphosing her into a "divine creature" that he seems doomed to try to conjure for the rest of his days.

The latter part of *Colin Clout's Come Home Againe* concerns love—first love in the court from which he has just come, and then a larger view of love with a Lucretian cast, love as the power by which all things "Be ever drawne together into one" (845). This extolling speech on love is greeted with great warmth by the shepherdess Melissa, who notes that "all wemen are thy debtors found, / That doest their bountie still so much commend" (901–2). We might be forgiven for seeing this as egomaniacal self-praise (by Spenser) if it were not for the quick rejoinder from Hobbinol that "ill … they him requite" (891) and that the one to whom he has devoted himself has returned his love "with scorne and foule despite" (893). Even though what comes immediately after is a defense of Rosalind by the shepherdess Lucida, it seems important that this version of Rosalind aligns precisely with the one we saw in "Janurye": nothing, it seems, has mitigated the ferocity of this Rosalind, at least in the mind of Hobbinol.

But Lucida's defense is worth quoting at greater length:

> Indeed (said *Lucid*) I have often heard
> Faire *Rosalind* of divers fowly blamed:
> For being to that swaine too cruell hard,
> That her bright glorie else hath much defamed.
> But who can tell what cause had that faire Mayd
> To use him so that used her so well:
> Or who with blame can justly her upbrayd,
> For loving not? for who can love compell?
>
> (907–14)

Who indeed? This is a remarkable statement of good sense: Lucida's suggestion that we have no real insight into Rosalind's thinking is surely tonic—we really know Rosalind hardly at all, and Lucida's speech suggests that Rosalind is also outside of the social circle of the shepherdesses that have gathered to greet Colin. And Lucida also brings to bear a sense of justice with respect to wooing and being wooed: it is unjust to "upbraid" Rosalind for "loving not," and presumably we can extend that doctrine to any woman, or indeed anyone—since everyone would fall under the open question "who can love compell?"[40] It is a remarkable, remarkably "lucid" statement of privacy and freedom, and that as much as people (like Colin) find themselves enslaved by love, there is a contrary sense that to love or not is a profound human right. And while Lucida does not make a big deal out of it, claiming such a right for a "faire Mayd" is also a remarkable commitment to erotic gender equity, for the right of women to choose their own sexual destinies as much as men have the right to woo them.

But it is a fleeting moment. The speech not over, Lucida then continues in very different terms:

---

[40] For a discussion of the topic in *The Faerie Queene*, see Melissa E. Sanchez, *Erotic Subjects: The Sexuality of Politics in Early Modern Literature* (Oxford: Oxford University Press, 2011), ch. 3, "Tyrannous Seduction," 57–85.

And sooth to say, it is foolhardie thing,
Rashly to wyten creatures so divine,
For demigods they be and first did spring
From heaven, though graft in frailnesse feminine.
And well I wote, that oft I heard it spoken,
How one that fairest *Helene* did revile,
Through judgement of the Gods to been ywroken
Lost both his eyes and so remaynd long while,
Till he recanted had his wicked rimes,
And made amends to her with treble praise:
Beware therefore, ye groomes, I read betimes,
How rashly blame of *Rosalind* ye raise.

(915–26)

The latter part of this refers to the ancient lyric poet Stesichorus, and the story of divine punishment associated with him. But much more troubling is the genealogy of Rosalind that precedes it, which seems to undo several things. The genealogy manages to be both flattering and condescending, as with one hand Lucida gives—imputing divinity or demideity to her—and with the other takes away: that this divinity is "graft in frailnesse feminine." So to the extent that Rosalind is divine she is worthy to avoid being rashly "wyten," but then again to the extent that she is female, that her (unsexed?) divinity is grafted to a female body, it is accordingly "fraile," an adjective that implies not only physical but also moral weakness, indeed the whole range of suspicion of women that Lucida had until this point had seemed to shun. And not the least of the damage she does is to her own female voice, since we must wonder whether she sees Rosalind as categorically different from herself, whether she is happy to accuse herself of the same frailty, or indeed whether Lucida's coherence as a "she," as a coherent voice and fictional personage, is slipping. What underlies this strange assertion of divinity with a caveat of feminine frailty? Is it that she wants to praise Rosalind for being divine but sees it as sacrilegious to overlook her embodiment in flesh, and is feminine flesh particularly frail morally or physically, or is the engendering in any way, any physical form necessarily "frail" as all flesh is frail?[41] The frailness of course could lead us to think that if Rosalind behaves badly, it isn't her divine nature but her feminine frailty that excuses her cruelty and

---

[41] The famous reference is Isaiah 40:6, and KJV's rendering, "all flesh is grass."

injustice. How different that is from the assertion of freedom and agency in the first part of the speech.

But in any case, Lucida effectively gives Colin a new choice for how to think about Rosalind in the final moments of this poem, a choice that was not supplied in the *Calender*; to wit, whether to think of Rosalind as a "faire Mayd" who cannot be compelled to love, and whose motives for not loving cannot be questioned, for whom both the choice to love (if it is a choice) and the reason to love or not to love are rights reserved to her and to all people; or, to think of her as divine and frail, heavenly and inscrutable, and locked into a mortal form that is likewise inscrutable in its frailty. Two ways of shutting down criticism, of silencing the anti-Rosalind agitators, but two ways with extraordinarily different implications for modern readers. Lucida makes us feel the possibility of Colin accepting Rosalind's right not to love him, that it is no wrong from her. But she does not, I think, do as any pastoral therapist would suggest and tell him to "move on." This acceptance would not necessitate Colin abandoning his love: if he wishes to hold on to it and try to sublimate it or nurture its potential for Platonic uplift, well, that is his right too. If she has the right not to love him, then surely he has the right to love or not to love her. But in this choice, his love is capacious enough to make room for her independence and agency and freedom.

Sadly this is not the choice he makes, not the direction in which his thinking goes. Instead his speech begins by condemning his fellow shepherds for criticizing a "thing celestiall," an inauspicious appellation. The speech that follows asserts her singularity and difference from ordinary people:

> For she is not like as the other crew
> Of shepherds daughters which emongst you bee,
> But of divine regard and heavenly hew,
> Excelling all that ever ye did see.
>
> (931–4)

He then asserts that it stood to reason that she "scorned a thing so base"— "thing" again, but this time referring to himself, who should never have "lookt so hie" as her. This is followed by two lines that take on a special significance in the light of what we have seen earlier in this chapter:

> So hie her thoughts as she her selfe have place,
> And loth each lowly thing with loftie eie.
>
> (937–8)

Colin seems to have no sense that to "loth each lowly thing with loftie eie" might be legible as not heavenly at all, but rather as proud and arrogant.[42] But there is more at work here, as we come vanishingly close to the sonic profile of this line:

> For lofty love doth loath a lowly eye

—the line, that is, that E.K. condemned for "hunting the letter"—a line that E.K. felt was so clothed in such feminine frailness as to drag it into ornamental effeminacy, rolling with the ribald rymers. It is a potent irony: just as Colin asserts his inability to meet Rosalind on her heavenly plane of existence, his prosody echoes the material frailty that had been so much in dispute in the *Calender*, and which, up to this point in *Colin Clout's Come Home Againe*, he seemed to have soared beyond. Is this Cacozelon, reaching too high and then falling to earth? Stridency at a moment of maximum expressiveness? Bathos? At the very least it feels like, if not an undoing of the technical development from *The Shepheardes Calender*, then an ironic echo of which Colin seems unaware.

So far Rosalind's divinity has been deployed either to distance her from "the other crew," or to emphasize the tension between her divinity and her mortal feminine form. In Lucida's view the divinity is highly classical, calling Rosalind a "demigod" and comparing her with Helen. The start of Colin's speech refers to her "divine regard and heavenly hew" but does less to localize the divinity. And then in the second half of the speech a new religious term is introduced, "grace," which is indeed the refrain of the speech, invoked three times in what is effectively the closing flourish of the poem.

> Yet so much grace let her vouchsafe to grant
> To simple swaine, sith her I may not love:
> Yet that I may her honour paravant,
> And praise her worth, though far my wit above.
> Such grace shall be some guerdon for the griefe,
> And long affliction which I have endured:
> Such grace sometimes shall give me some reliefe,
> And ease of paine which cannot be recured.

---

[42] Compare this with the lofty contempt for the sublunary that Lorenzo Jr. imagines for poetry-as-woman in *Every Man In His Humour*; see chapter 1, "Burning Verses."

And ye my fellow shepheards which do see
And heare the languours of my too long dying,
Unto the world for ever witnesse bee,
That hers I die, nought to the world denying,
This simple trophe of her great conquest.

(931–51)

Typically, within the context of Petrarchan erotic lyric, "grace" means some-thing rather different, which is to say giving in to the wooer, giving him "relief," "joy," and all the other euphemisms for sexual consummation. Not here. The speech also raises questions about agency in the context of the dis-junction Lucida created between the "faire Maid" who might be allotted the right to choose her own sexual destiny and the divine creature clothed in feminine frailty. Colin asks that Rosalind "vouchsafe to grant" him enough grace to honor her, "and praise her worth," since he "may not" love her. What is meant by loving her here? Not the kind of independent, individual act that, as Lucida had said, cannot be compelled. No: Colin seems to think that if his love is not returned, he cannot love. Or rather that to love Rosalind requires her permission. Since he knows he cannot have that, he seeks an alternative, namely to praise her in song.

He calls this "grace" a "guerdon" and "some relief," but the emphasis in the ensuing lines is his "griefe," "long affliction," and "paine which cannot be recured." It isn't hard to hear all this as passive accusation, leading back, fi-nally to the anger at Rosalind Hobbinol expressed at when the poem turned to this topic. And then the "grace" Colin hopes to receive is finally a sort of hospice care, palliative treatment to the mortal wound he has received—from Rosalind? He does not quite impute agency to her in his destruction, and yet it remains for all to "witness" that if she only had given him the kind of grace he really wanted, life as "too long dying" would be "too soon dy-ing" instead. And the last lines in particular seem to give up excuse-making for Rosalind: he asks "the world"—grandiosely—to "for ever witnesse" that he dies as "hers," a "simple trophe of her great conquest." The adjectives are worth pausing on: he reserves for himself "simple" while to her he grants "great"—why? One almost feels the charge of divinity becoming something more like elitism: the Rosalind thought she was too good for "simple" Colin. And if that is true, it multiplies the resentment that roils through this dia-logue and which Lucida only partly succeeds in mitigating. In *Colin Clout's*

Come Home Againe Colin does indeed come home, but we do not leave him in a good place.

The most striking thing about the Mount Acidale episode of book 6 of *The Faerie Queene*, coming off of *Colin Clout's Come Home Againe*, is "grace." "So much grace," "Such grace," and "Such grace" formed the spine of Colin's final words and here, as Spenser's narrator warms to the task of describing the scene that the Knight of Courtesy finds atop this mountain in canto 10, is grace again, but this time in several senses that are not the erotically tinged one in Colin's plaintive requests. The last two lines of stanza 11 famously set things up:

> An hundred naked maidens lilly white,
> All raunged in a ring, and dauncing in delight.

Calidore's self-envying eyes see farther though, into what the ring contains:

> All they without were raunged in a ring,
>> And daunced round; but in the midst of them
>> Three other Ladies did both daunce and sing,
>> The whilest the rest them round about did hemme,
>> And like a girlond did in compasse stemme:
>> And in the middest of those same three, was placed
>> Another Damzell, as a precious gemme,
>> Amidst a ring most richly well enchaced,
> That with her goodly presence all the rest much graced.
>> (stanza 12)

The other damsel that "with her goodly presence all the rest much graced" I think is Rosalind, a version of Rosalind which in a few stanzas is identified here as not just gracing others, but "another Grace"—another because the three surrounding ladies are the Graces themselves. The focus on the word "grace," however, appears once more in the stanza that is the best evidence that we can read the woman at the center as Rosalind:

> She was to weete that jolly Shepheards lasse,
>> Which piped there unto that merry rout:
>> That jolly shepheard, which there piped, was

> Poore *Colin Clout* (who knowes not *Colin Clout*?)
> He pypt apace, whilest they him daunst about.
> Pype jolly shepheard, pype thou now apace
> Unto thy love, that made thee low to lout;
> Thy love is present there with thee in place,
> Thy love is there aduaunst to be another Grace.

(stanza 16)

The apostrophic language to Colin is particularly striking in its focus on the present, "now," on acceleration, and on lowering, raising, and advancing. He is already piping "apace," but the narrator urges him on, seemingly faster, and "now." He pipes to his love and we are reminded of the collapse she precipitated in "Januarye," the "lout[ing]" that so much has shaped the course of his poetry. The final lines make statements of possible contraries, namely Rosalind's "presence," with the emphatic gesture, "there with thee in place." That, and she is also "advanced" to be another Grace, the kind of advancement that sounds "heavenly" and unworldly indeed—an interpretation supported by her evaporation with all the other dancers when Calidore interrupts the dance. The passive construction is also striking: who has advanced her there? The poem supplies no explanation beyond Colin's urgent piping.

The best reading I know of this scene, that is also thinking about Rosalind, is by Richard Rambuss, who writes that "this figure exists only as an imaginative conjuration in an intensely private, autoerotic fantasy of enfolded desire and poetic production."[43] That is a compelling description, but some of the aspects I have just cited I think resist it. The "conjuration" may have been intended only to please Colin, but it ends up enthralling and pleasing Calidore too. On the other hand, it is hard to argue with Rambuss's nomenclature of "autoerotic fantasy" in that this Rosalind does not speak, but merely stands among a supernatural Busby Berkeley production number. Are we to imagine that this image of Rosalind is connected to the actual woman in any more significant way? Like Laura or Beatrice after their deaths for Petrarch or Dante? Spenser gives us nothing to go on here. But likewise, this is not the Colin of "December" who turns away from his unrequited love to find other satisfying pursuits, the pursuit of knowledge of the natural world, prime among them. Instead he seems to be devoting himself to

---

[43] Richard Rambuss, *Spenser's Secret Career*, Cambridge Studies in Renaissance Literature and Culture (Cambridge: Cambridge University Press, 1993), 122.

the poetic worship of Rosalind as "divine creature," going farther and farther in a direction that presumably would have exacerbated her scorn, if she was remotely involved at this point. So all of that seems less than ideal, and not much worthy of praise. But then again, Colin seems to be scoring some kind of Petrarchan success through the scale and supernatural quality of the spectacle he conjures and, again, its ability to enthrall a stranger. Which is to say, that with the estrangement and alienation that this location on Acidale seems to evoke, Colin also seems to be partaking in a payoff of Petrarchism, of Pan playing the Pan-pipe and hearing the voice of Syrinx, which is to say a sublimating, Platonic aesthetic vision. Not bad.

But I think I have made it clear that in terms of the possible evolutions of Rosalind hinted at by *The Shepheardes Calender*, this does not satisfy. To get our satisfaction we will have to leave Spenser behind and pursue the next stage of Rosalind's history in the work of Thomas Lodge a decade later. Which is what we will now do.

3

Lodge's Rosalind

Virtuous Lightness and Queer Mythography

As You Like It gets off to a running expositional start with a speech from
the male hero Orlando, complaining about his mistreatment by his older
brother since his father's death. Orlando, let's be clear, really is the male hero,
and he really is suffering from mistreatment. Thomas Lodge's *Rosalynde* begins, in contrast, with a something of a fake-out.[1] We are introduced to one
Sir John of Bordeaux, a former "principal" of the Knights of Malta known
for having the wisdom of Nestor and the eloquence of Ulysses, as well as being a hardy fighter against the Turks.[2] All of those references, on reflection,
could be a little ambiguous.[3] The introduction then moves to a deathbed
scene where the aged knight gives a "legacy" of wisdom to his assembled
sons, after altering the strictures of primogeniture enough to cause significant trouble later. Much of the wisdom is innocuous: proverbs, aphorisms,

---

[1] That the opening seems in some ways disconnected from latter parts of the text could be
a function of the circumstances of its writing, while on a sea voyage to the Canaries. Lodge (c.
1558–1625) had a fascinating life. He was educated at Merchant Taylors' School and Oxford,
dabbled in the law, and then began a series of literary efforts including plays, poems (Ovidean
epyllia and verse satire among others), and, as we shall see shortly, pro-literary polemic. He
converted to Catholicism around the end of the century, and medical studies in Avignon were
followed by an MD from Oxford in 1602. His works after that are translations (of Josephus,
Seneca, and Du Bartas) and medical texts.

[2] My text is a modernized edition: *Lodge's "Rosalynde" Being the Original of Shakespeare's "As
You Like It"*, ed. W. W. Greg (New York: Duffield & Co., 1907), 1. I have also kept my eye on a
facsimile of the 1590 printing obtained through EEBO. Parenthetical citations in the text will
henceforth refer to pages of the Greg edition.

[3] The ambivalence in Elizabethan culture about Homeric heroes finds its greatest expression
a decade later in Shakespeare's *Troilus and Cressida*, where Nestor and Ulysses are as much subject to the play's withering satire as anyone else. And of course just adjacent to those characters
are Achilles and Patroclus, who present as powerful an example of the difficulty of translation
of ancient culture into Christianity as Virgil's second eclogue (see chapter 1, "Problems with
Sex and Aesthetics"). By 1590 the Knights of Malta were also just as well known for piracy as
for heroism against the Turks: the latter principally from their victory in the siege of 1565, the
former for their activities in the Mediterranean in the decades following. On charges of piracy,
see Helen Nicholson, *The Knights Hospitaller* (Woodbridge: Boydell Press, 2001), 127.

What Rosalind Likes. Paul J. Hecht, Oxford University Press.
© Paul J. Hecht (2022). DOI: 10.1093/oso/9780192857200.003.0003

and alliterative bromides like "the mean is sweetest melody" (4).[4] But the climax of the speech goes in a startling new direction, which I will quote at some length:

> "But above all," and with that he fetched a deep sigh, "beware of love, for it is far more perilous than pleasant, and yet, I tell you, it allureth as ill as the Sirens. O my sons, fancy is a fickle thing, and beauty's paintings are tricked up with time's colors, which, being set to dry in the sun, perish with the same. Venus is a wanton, and though her laws pretend liberty, yet there is nothing but loss and glistering misery. Cupid's wings are plumed with the feathers of vanity, and his arrows, where they pierce, enforce nothing but deadly desires: a woman's eye, as it is precious to behold, so is it prejudicial to gaze upon; for as it affordeth delight, so it snareth unto death. Trust not their fawning favors, for their loves are like the breath of a man upon steel, which no sooner lighteth on but it leapeth off, and their passions are as momentary as the colors of a polype, which changeth at the sight of every object. My breath waxeth short, and mine eyes dim: the hour is come, and I must away; therefore let this suffice: women are wantons, and yet men cannot want one: and therefore, if you love, choose her that hath eyes of adamant, that will turn only to one point; her heart of a diamond, that will receive but one form; her tongue of a Sethin leaf, that never wags but with a south-east wind: and yet, my sons, if she have all these qualities, to be chaste, obedient, and silent, yet for that she is a woman, shalt thou find in her sufficient vanities to countervail her virtues. Oh now, my sons, even now take these my last words as my latest legacy, for my thread is spun, and my foot is in the grave …" (5–6)

And he says a few more things of that kind before giving up the ghost. So: if Spenser's *Shepheardes Calender* begins with furious hatred from a woman directed against poetry and "shepherds devise," *Rosalynde* begins with what Colin Clout mostly avoids: hatred of women, condemnation of Eros. A series of alliterative and assonantal antitheses (pleasant, perilous; liberty, misery; precious, prejudicial) culminate in gazing on "a woman's eye" that "affordeth

---

[4] Readers of *As You Like It* may note in this section surprising resonances with language in the play, but disordered, like this: "a friend is a precious jewel" (4), says Sir John, as our doubts about his real wisdom continue to grow. That is as clichéd a pairing of adjective and noun as one could find, and yet perhaps the actuator of, or otherwise subconsciously linked to, another patriarch's speech, this time the "senior," exiled duke welcoming everyone to the forest of Arden: "Sweet are the uses of adversity, / Which, like the toad, ugly and venomous, / Wears yet a precious jewel in his head" (2.1.12–14).

delight" and thus "snareth unto death." Despite this mortal danger, however dangerous and "wanton" are women, "men cannot want one," and Sir John gives a list of "qualities" to seek but warns that no matter how chaste, obedient, and silent she may seem, her virtues will be "counterveil[ed]" by "vanities."

What to make of this misogynist screed at the head of the book that inspired one of the most extraordinary and admired female characters in English literature? What to make of the praise for a man whose accumulated wisdom begins with tired saws and degenerates into a gift of paranoid woman-hating and terror of sexuality couched in punning wordplay? Is this meant seriously? Is Lodge satirizing or attacking these views and the way they are expressed? As we will see, ten years earlier, Lodge did attack views arguably allied with Sir John's as he was the first respondent in print to Stephen Gosson's *Schoole of Abuse* (1579). In the first section of this chapter we will return to that polemical scene, both for illumination of Lodge and for the larger context it provides for the tension around aesthetics and sexuality. In the second section of the chapter we will meet Lodge's Rosalind, who despite Sir John's screed, has many of the exuberant and appealing qualities of Shakespeare's Rosalind, along with a few Shakespeare's character lacks—notably scenes in which she both composes poetry and reflects on the experience. All of this is a tenfold advance in the technical history of Rosalind that we are tracing in this book. The final section of the chapter is where we will entertain at greater length the questions provoked by the opening misogynist gambit of Sir John. Absent from Lodge's book is any direct repudiation of these views, but what we do find is a complex, evocative repetition and variation of elements that, when we first see them, look like just more Elizabethan rhetorical cliché, just more expressions of Lodge's deployment of Lyly's overwrought, learned, show-offy style. One of the most important such repeated elements in my reading has indeed already appeared for the first time in Sir John's speech, and that is the Sirens.

The Sirens are familiar, but let's review the details, as they will be important later. The Sirens episode of book 12 of *The Odyssey* begins when Odysseus is warned about them by Circe (36–54); when his ship passes by (153–200), he is prepared to resist the Sirens' supernaturally beautiful songs, which have words, and are expressed as verse paragraphs within the epic, and which lure sailors to approach heedlessly, crash their ships on rocks and be devoured. But despite the warning, he chooses a peculiar form of resistance for himself: his crew stops their ears with wax so they cannot hear and be tempted, while he has himself tied to a mast, ears unstopped. Why? He wants to hear the beautiful song, despite the suicidal desire he knows it will elicit. This is a resonant image with Christianity: to be tied to a mast is to assume a position of martyrdom, aligned with numerous saints, and finally aligned with Christ on the cross—Christ who endures death willingly on behalf of our sins. In Homer's version this is obviously kinky as well, as there is no doubt that the beauty of the Sirens' poetry is an erotic as well as an aesthetic beauty, and carries erotic power. So, Odysseus demonstrates an inclination toward bondage and masochism as he allows himself to be tied up and teased with desire, tortured with longing that will not be fulfilled.

In short, the Sirens turn out to be a promising location in which to explore Elizabethan hang-ups with aesthetics and sexuality, as well as the perils and complications of importing classical aesthetic objects into a Christian context. Sir John's ham-handed reference to "love" that "allureth as ill as the Sirens" (5), does little to exfoliate these layers, but, as we will see, this is just the beginning of the book's engagement with the myth. And one of the most crucial aspects of that engagement is this: in a strange and extended performance of forgetting and whitewashing, later in the book, this scene and Sir John's "precepts" get telescoped and reduced from that problematic and lengthy discourse to a single word—"concord," that finally applies to warring brothers and sectarian combatants equally. But while the dissonance of Sir John's hatred resolves into "concord," the songs of the Sirens continue to echo—indeed they appear an additional eight times, in a series of permutations and variations and inversions, including a full-scale acting-out of temptation and torture and ear-stopping in a bizarre breakfast scene. It is never clear how much of this repetition and variation is conscious or unconscious, and whether the forgetting of Sir John's speech itself is something that happens within the fiction of the book or actually happens to Lodge. But it is not necessary to answer that question for my purposes, for seeing how this book contributes to our biography of poetry at the same time that it hugely advances Rosalind's story. I want to argue that the concept of concord, which as with Spenser is deeply associated with the pastoral mode (of rivals and sects finding a way to look past their differences and live in harmony), is tied to sexual terror *through* the story of the Sirens: the fear that the harmony leading onward to union actually leads to destruction. In our biography of poetry, Lodge's book makes it clear that beauty of all kinds—very much including the beauty of English poetry that had advanced so much since the publication of *The Shepheardes Calender*—could always also be cast under the suspicion of the Sirens' song, extending indeed to the very concept of concord itself. Is concord, the book asks, the rational resolution of difference into harmony? Or is it the forgetting of unresolved discord, resolution by loss, by erasure, a forgotten patrimony that may one day re-emerge or be reborn?

Before *Rosalynde*

Stoppe your eares

If we are interested in the inexpert strong opinions of Elizabethans, Stephen Gosson is an excellent place to start. Gosson fired three salvos in what has generally been taken as a debate about the theater in Elizabethan England, and which extended to the actual closing of the theaters in 1642. Gosson's first publication, *The School of Abuse* (1579) is the one that I will focus on here, since it is what Lodge responded to, in the same year. Gosson's third publication is more steadily aimed at theaters, right down to its structure in "five acts."[5] *The School of Abuse* is much broader in its criticisms, a broadness that may weaken its effectiveness, but for my purposes makes it the more interesting text, since it moves fluidly between plays, poetry, and music, and eventually expands to take in and take on seemingly every form of pastime available to Elizabethans. In his purgative rage, Gosson sees no borders between cultural forms: fencing, bowling, or piping, never mind reading or playgoing, are all "idle[ness]" in his eyes.[6]

Gosson's central move is one that should be familiar from our own culture wars, and that is of the broadly corrupting effect of cultural artifacts that give pleasure and take our time.[7] That pleasure is almost always, for

---

[5] *The School of Abuse* is a much-abbreviated title, which continues, *The schoole of abuse contayning a plesaunt inuective against poets, pipers, players, iesters, and such like caterpillers of a comonwelth* ... and goes on from there. The second publication was *The ephemerides of Phialo* ..., also published in 1579. *Playes confuted in fiue actions* ... appeared in 1582.

[6] E2r. Several versions of the 1579 edition are available through Early English Books Online. This is STC (2nd edn.) / 12097.5, from the Henry E. Huntington Library and Art Gallery and Emmanuel College Library, Cambridge University. Other folio references to this edition will be cited parenthetically in the text. Gosson reminds us that the modern borders between disciplinary areas of expertise—say, Renaissance poetry and drama—were utterly absent in the 1570s and 1580s. Despite Gosson's wrongheadedness, this shedding of the connoisseur's reserve is one of the traits I set out to pursue in this study: Gosson certainly "feels the fury" (see chapter 1, "Feeling the Fury").

[7] For example, rock and roll, hip-hop, video games, and the Internet have all come under criticism of this kind in the latter part of the twentieth century and beginning of the twenty-first.

Gosson, false, a disguise that conceals deadly danger. Thus, when Gosson mentions the Sirens, in the third paragraph of his tract, it is among a list of artful concealments that carry the unsuspecting to their doom:

> I must confesse that Poets are the whetstones of wit, notwithstanding that wit is dearly bought: where hony and gall are mixed, it will be hard to sever the one from the other. The deceitfull Phisition giveth sweete Syrropes to make his poyson goe downe the smoother: The Juggler casteth a myst to worke the closer: The *Syrens* song is the Saylers wrack: The Fowlers whistle, the birdes death: The wholesome bayte, the fishes bane: The Harpies have Virgins faces, and vultures Talentes: *Hyena* speakes like a friend, and de-voures like a Foe: The calmest Seas hide dangerous Rockes: the Woolf jettes in Weathers felles: Many good sentences are spoken by *Danus,* to shadowe his knavery: and written by Poets, as ornaments to beautifye their woorkes, and sette theyr trumperie too sale without suspect. (A2r–v)

What form does the doom take, for Gosson? Sexual corruption is very high on his list, to be sure. Gosson famously sees theaters as rampant markets of sexual vice, and the mere intermingling of men and women in a public place seems as prone to his condemnation as any activity, virtuous or vicious, that could occupy them there. His anxiety about female sexuality leads him to argue that women are best kept at home, best prevented from any encounter whatsoever with anyone not a family member. But it also eventually becomes clear that Gosson sees any and all "pastimes" that are not useful work, or, better, preparations for possible attack from outsiders, as carrying the entire country toward destruction.

But at the same time, Gosson often does not seem aware of how deeply literary are his own apocalyptic views of the dangers of literary culture, and leisure activities of any kind. The citation of the Sirens above demonstrates this: amid a list of possible connivers—evil poisoning physicians and con-men jugglers, as well as hunting techniques, and concealed dangers in animals and the natural world—Gosson mentions the danger of Sirens to sailors, registering not at all that this is a purely poetical danger, supplied by a poet, and functioning as a metaphor. Gosson thus supplies a piece of evidence against his own argument, showing how poetry can function as a cognitive structure to highlight exactly the kinds of concealed dangers he suggests that poets invariably pose. More than that, his reference displays the way specifically classical poetic and mythological reference was inseparable from argument of any kind for Elizabethans. If one will speak, or argue, one will make use of this kind of reference.[8]

Likewise, Gosson's method of seeing the corrupting interconnectedness of art forms also relies on an ability to make metaphorical crossings between like (or not-so-like) things with poetical fury. The Sirens lure their prey by music, and Gosson is ready to condemn all the music of his time as corrupt and corrupting. He doesn't see music as fully separate from other forms though: "For as Poetrie and Piping are Cosen germans: so piping, and playing are of great affinity, and all three chayned in linkes of abuse" (B3r). In particular, he views the use of music *at* theaters as a giveaway that the theaters work to "effeminate the minde, as pricks unto vice" (B3r), rather than any positive purpose. Here is how he summarizes the effect:

> *Ovid* the high martial of *Venus* fielde planteth his maine battell in publique assemblies, sendeth out his scoutes too Theaters to descry the enimie, and in steede of vaunte Curriers, with instruments of musicke, playing, singing, and dauncing, geves the first charge. (B3r)

That is a pretty poetical condemnation of poetic abuse. Ovid here seems to have been metamorphosed, via the *Ars Amatoria*, and *Amores*, presumably, into Cupid himself, as the militant Cupid of the *castra*, for whom the first wave of attack, the "vaunt-currier," is made with musical instruments.[9] The Siren song of poetry, then, can be an actual song, and the corrupting influence of classical culture, the unsupervised reading of the *Amores* or *Ars Amatoria*, for example, can find a parallel in the effeminizing and vice-preparing effects of music.

Gosson's condemnation of Ovid, and his approving citation of Ovid's exile, even as he exuberantly uses Ovidean metaphoric and metamorphosing techniques himself, is one of a number of assaults Gosson makes on the moral influence of the classical culture that has given the Renaissance that name, even as the same culture is the most obvious and sustained influence on his own style. He allows that Elizabethan theater is probably on balance

---

[8] To be fair, although he doesn't show awareness of the way poetry and poetical thinking are integral to his criticisms, he does demonstrate awareness that representing abuses in his text could have the unintended effect of amplifying and replicating them in unsuspecting readers—which is why he doesn't allow himself to get into some of the details of the abuses of current theatrical practice (C3v).

[9] See Ovid, *Amores* 1.9.1: "Militat omnis amans, et habet sua castra Cupido" ("All in love are at war, and Cupid also has a military encampment"). Ovid, *Amores, Medicamina Faciei Feminae, Ars Amatoria, Remedia Amoris* (Oxford: Clarendon Press, 1995), 23 (my translation).

less lewd than, say, the theater of Plautus. But this moral progress has not gone far enough. In other ways, "progress" has clearly been negative. This is at the center of Gosson's wholesale condemnation of the music of his time. It is in every way too complex, and its complexity is an index of its corruption, right down to the excessive number of strings on stringed instruments. Gosson doesn't get into the details of exactly how the corrupting influence of this corrupt, decadent music might work. But it doesn't lift one's thoughts to virtue, nor does it help to win battles—which he says the good kind of ancient music, modeled on the music of the spheres, succeeded in doing. Contrary to what Lodge will say of him, Gosson does seem open to the possibility of a noble, perhaps transcendent music:

> If you will bee good Scholars, and profite well in the Arte of Musicke, shutte your Fidels in their cases, and looke up to heaven: the order of the Spheres, the unfallible motion of the Planets, the juste course of the yeere, and varietie of seasons, the concorde of the Elementes and their qualyties, Fyre, Water, Ayre, Earth, Heate, Colde, Moysture and Drought concurring togeather to the constitution of earthly bodies and sustenance of every creature. (A8r–v)

Above, or all around, is the right "concorde" and "concurring" that should inspire music and scholarship. Contrary to any art that carries Sirenic suspicions, this music is "vnfallible" and "iuste." Gosson does not give any more practical directions for how one could access or deploy this concord, but it is still significant that he both believes in the concept and seems to think that such an art is within the realm of the possible.

It is easy to see why Lodge's *Reply* to Gosson has received so much less attention than Sidney's *Defense*.[10] It is harsher and more personal, and yet at the same time Lodge's disagreement with Gosson can seem one of emphasis rather than substance. In a passage like the one above, Gosson allows the possibility of an uplifting, concord-inducing music; he also allows that poets can provide inspirational role models, and in his very satiric technique allows that poetry and plays can be used in service of exposing abuse. Lodge in general is rather too quick to launch ad hominem attacks on Gosson, suggesting, for example, that he condemns contemporary music because he

---

[10] The most easily accessible version is Saintsbury's lightly modernized edition: Thomas Lodge, "A Reply to Stephen Gosson's Schoole of Abuse in Defence of Poetry, Musick, and Stage Plays," in *Elizabethan and Jacobean Pamphlets*, ed. George Saintsbury (New York: MacMillan, 1892), 1–42. The pamphlet is not included in EEBO. Page references will be made to this edition parenthetically in the text.

doesn't understand it. Elsewhere, though, he scores hits. He is ready to concede that there certainly are "abuses" within various cultural forms, and in Elizabethan society at large. He longs for a voice calling out these abuses parallel to the Old Testament prophets, and for criticism of all that is lacking in plays and poems and music and what have you. But he attacks Gosson for the sweeping, all-encompassing condemnation of his book. "If you had reprehended," he at one point suggests, "ye foolish fantasies of our poets *nomine non re* which they bring forth on stage, my self would have liked of you and allowed your labor" (18). And he would be happy to "find a judge that severely would amende the abuses of Tragedies" (19). That is, he is ready for discerning theatrical criticism that is not categorical. And he likewise would be pleased to see magistrates well advised in such a way as

> to roote out those odd rymes which runnes in every rascales mouth. Savoring of rybaldry, those foolishe ballets, that are admitted make poets good and godly practises to be refused. I like not of a wicked *Nero* that wyll expell *Lucan,* yet admit I of a zealous governour that wil seke to take away the abuse of poetry. I like not of an angrye *Augustus* which wyll banishe *Ovid* for envy. I love a wise Senator, which in wisedome wyll correct him and with advise burne his follyes. (19)

With those provisos, it still sounds as though Lodge is having a version of the fantasy of just judgment and enforcement of good taste that we see enacted at the close of Jonson's *Every Man In His Humour* two decades later, and which I discussed in chapter 1.[11] And we can also note that some of the terms by which Lodge conceives of corrupt and abusive poetry sound remarkably like those Spenser and E.K. use in *The Shepheardes Calender*, in E.K.'s *Epistle*, and in the voice of the shepherd Cuddie in "October"—and as in those cases, we see again "r" alliteration used to conjure bad poetry and its specifically sexual corruption in "rybaldry."[12]

He never quite states it as pointedly as he might, but Lodge gets close to making a baby-bathwater argument that seems one of the smartest ways to meet Gosson's attack, and we might add, attacks that similarly seek to cut out an entire cultural practice on the basis of a corrupting influence that might exist in isolated cases, isolated encounters between the right sort of corruptible person and the wrong sort of art. Gosson opens himself up to charges

---

[11] See "Burning Verses."

[12] As they were published in the same year, it isn't clear whether Lodge could have read a copy of the *Calender* with E.K.'s *Epistle*, or seen some version of it in manuscript. For more on alliteration, see chapter 2, "Chasing the letter."

that his remedies are extreme for a problem of uncertain dimension, and equally extreme is Gosson's vision of perpetual military discipline, which Lodge somewhat unfairly converts, in his rehearsal of Gosson, into a vision of perpetual war (Gosson doesn't advocate perpetual war, but rather perpetual vigilance in a dangerous world). In this line, there is a parallel to the argument in the *Calender* that involves Argus, where the shepherds debate how much vigilance is necessary, how on guard for "wolves" shepherd-priests must be.[13] And that of course parallels the ongoing debate within Elizabeth's administration about religious tolerance and military preparedness, and similar debates that go on in our own time (cf. the debate in the first decade of the twenty-first century on the notion of "the war on terror," and culture wars of various eras).

When it comes to music, Lodge doesn't have much more to say beyond accusing Gosson of ignorance, and that, on the contrary, the sophistication and complexity of contemporary music adds to its virtue. Beyond this, he gives a list of famous biblical and mythological examples of the virtuous power of music—not really on the mark since Gosson here is arguing merely that modern, complex music is corrupt and corrupting, not all music at all times.

With the benefit of hindsight, Lodge's *Reply* seems pretty ineffective, and all too much like modern debates in which the two sides don't really respond to each other's arguments, preach to the choir, and resort to ad hominem attacks. On the other hand, Lodge's level of engagement here makes it possible to consider many things in *Rosalynde* as informed by this debate. The Sirens turn out to be a particularly good classical site at which to extend and deepen the debate with Gosson. This is because Gosson's polemic is engaged, whether or not he acknowledges it, in the question of how corrupt human beings are to begin with, and how much they are at the mercy of impulses and passions, virtuous and vicious. Gosson is quite negative on this, comparing people unfavorably, and at length, with animals, and then reflecting in this way:

> But we which have both sense, reason, wit, and understanding, are ever overlashing, passing our boundes, going beyonde our limites, never keeping our selves within compasse, nor once looking after the place from whence we came, and whither we muste in spighte of our hartes. (D1v–D2r)

---

[13] Lodge also mentions Argus as an exemplar of vigilance, when warning Gosson to watch his back (30). For more on Argus, see chapter 2, "Passive poetics."

Gender and sexuality also have a significant role in Gosson's view of the weakness and danger humans face. Eros is of course a prime impulse that moves us to go viciously "beyonde our limites"; everywhere in *The School of Abuse* Gosson exhibits concern about threats to masculinity, that pleasurable pastimes effeminize and lead to weakness and idleness, as well as more active vices. And as people in general are highly susceptible to temptation, so women are particularly susceptible. So he makes the non-gender-specific call to us all:

> Let us but shut uppe our eares to Poets, Pypers and Players, pull our feete back from resort to Theaters, and turne away our eyes from beholding of vanitie, the greatest storme of abuse will be overblowen, and a fayre path troden to amendment of life. Were not we so foolish to taste every drugge, and buy every trifle, Players would shut in their shoppes, and carry their trashe to some other Countrie. (D3r)

When he specifically singles out women, however, as he does in the appendix to *The School*, addressed "To the Gentlewomen Citizens of London," he advocates complete withdrawal from the cultural scene that is now so replete with vicious temptation. And being shut up behind walls is not enough—walls can be penetrated by alluring sounds:

> And if you perceive your selves in any danger at your owne doores, either allured by curtesie in the day, or assaulted with Musicke in the night; Close up your eyes, stoppe your eares, tye up your tongues; when they speake, aunsweare not; when they hallowe, stoope not; when they sighe, laugh at them; when they sue, scorne them. (F4r–v)

The Sirens are not cited in any of these cases, but the gesture of stopping up one's ears actuates the myth, and fits seamlessly into Gosson's worldview, where temptation assaults us all continually, assaults women especially, and as with Ulysses' crew, our best defense is not to listen, and not to give ourselves the option of listening: we cannot be trusted, so stop up your ears.

Do we hear strains of Gosson in the patriarch on his deathbed at the start of Lodge's *Rosalynde*? Not exactly. Gosson never makes the jump from the version of misogyny that fears everywhere the effeminate and effeminizing, that fears temptations to vice of all kinds, to plain hatred of women. And Lodge's patriarch similarly does not move from his fear and hatred of women and Eros to cultural objects that he can associate with their vicious effects. So at the beginning of *Rosalynde* the hang-up with sex is more closely confined to sex and gender, and not aesthetics. But if "concord" is the real problematic of *Rosalynde*, as I have suggested that it is, we can see the aesthetic territory in which Gosson and Lodge fought still visible here. And this is something that comes into even clearer focus if we move now, following Kimberly Anne Coles's lead, to examine the way Gosson's arguments look in light of earlier ones by Calvin and Augustine.

Calvin, Augustine, and aesthetic suspicion

I have already noted that the Sirens appear in *Rosalynde* nine times, in a dizzying variety of situations and applications, and not all of them by any means negative. But their basic action is to bring into the same gravitational field music, Eros, danger, femininity, and beauty. It seems clear that the Sirens are emblematic of any kind of dangerous temptation, and as such the thinking about temptation is not limited to music, but extends to any other way people might be allured. Sir John lands, more or less, on women as the principal danger to be shunned or if not shunned, then treated with the maximum suspicion. But there is no reason in particular why he might not, with Gosson, have landed on cultural productions as the principal dangers—the Sirens' songs and not the Sirens themselves—and thence into a general aesthetic suspicion or skepticism.

But while the unidimensional women-are-the-root-of-all-evil women-hating enunciated by Sir John is easily undone by the book, this is not the limit of its aesthetic suspicion. We have seen how Gosson was thinking about a constellation of threats that includes both forces that can effeminize and forces that can threaten women—threaten both in the sense of inciting ungovernable lust that targets them and in the sense of corrupting or seducing them. Kimberly Anne Coles has lately argued that we ought to see Gosson and the other notable Elizabethan anti-theatrical, anti-literary polemicists in the context of a significantly larger English Protestant attitude both skeptical and suspicious of all poetry, indeed of any use of the imaginative faculties we might call today "creative." She demonstrates that the views Gosson enunciates were more widespread in English culture than has previously been acknowledged, and that, in particular, one can find similar arguments in such earlier reformers as William Tyndale. Especially relevant for our discussion, however, is the thread of argument she traces through John Calvin back to Augustine on music and musical language, the twin ingredients of the Sirens' song.[14]

Augustine in the *Confessions* addresses music's appeal to hearing as another fleshly weakness that needs to be governed along with the rest of the body's urges. He regards the way he used to listen to music, "hypnotized," as something from which he has been freed, but he remains deeply suspicious, especially of the role of music in the Church. He feels that when "music carries a meaning," as in acting as a delivery device for meaning, it penetrates more deeply into his heart. But he does not know if this is "proper." He expands on the experience he has now:

> A delicious physical sound should not melt our reason, but should attend it as its subordinate partner—but once admitted on these terms, it tends to skip ahead of reason and take the lead from it. When this occurs, I go wrong without realizing it, and only recognize what has happened later on.[15]

That is quite a detailed description of musical and perhaps aesthetic experience, this sense that "a delicious physical sound" might appropriately begin "subordinate" to reason, aiding the primary—semantic meaning, scriptural content—but "once admitted" can "skip ahead." He feels this aesthetic betrayal in such a way that it makes him want to exclude music entirely from society, but he concludes the passage indecisively, since "I increasingly favor the practice of singing in the church, which can strengthen the wavering soul's feeling for religion" (141). This is to say that Augustine recognizes the positive Sirenic qualities of music, the ability to exert influence through its access to feelings, its ability to operate "beneath" thought and indeed to subvert thought, or at least subvert doubt. The latter-day reformers of Lodge's time tend to appear less circumspect than Augustine in balancing the positive and negative qualities of music and musical language.

---

[14] See Kimberly Anne Coles, *Religion, Reform, and Women's Writing in Early Modern England* (Cambridge: Cambridge University Press, 2008), esp. 75–98.
[15] Augustine, *Confessions*, trans. Garry Wills (New York: Penguin, 2008), 141. Subsequent page references to this translation will be made parenthetically in the text. For a translation more contemporary to Rosalind, see William Watts, *Saint Augustines confessions translated: and with some marginall notes illustrated* [...] (London, 1631, STC 912).

For John Calvin, there is much more of a bias toward music's dangers than in favor of its power to do good. The desire to make music a "subordinate partner" is echoed in Calvin's preface to the Geneva Psalter, the Psalter being a place where these concerns tended to congregate, all the more so for the reformers who were so keen to peel away the patina of corrupt interpretation from scripture and restore it to its original sense. As Coles demonstrates, much of that false patina was thought to be aesthetic in nature, sweetening and blurring biblical content. But what then is to be done with biblical lyric? Calvin argues that we should

> make music serve for all honesty, and so that it be not at all an occasion to unleash any dissolution, or to feminise ourselves in disorderly delights … & in fact, we experience its secret, nearly incredible virtue or power to move hearts one way or another. For this reason we must be even more diligent to govern it so that it might be useful to us, and in no way pernicious.[16]

All of this is in the context, not of actual music to be used in church services, as Augustine had been discussing, but of the music of language, that music which in lyrical poetry is highlighted by verse, by metrical structure, and by innumerable other elements that are unnecessary for the conveyance of meaning. One can feel the temptation of the translator with Calvin's concerns to translate the "poetry" right out of scripture altogether, into prose, and avoid having to work with someone like Clément Marot. But if we will have the aesthetic here, those pleasure-giving elements must somehow be kept subordinate. Again, there is the sense of power, and potential usefulness, but also danger and the necessity of careful "governance." Most striking for our discussion is Calvin's use of the feminine to describe the effect of too-loosely governed encounters with music. Women thus are more vulnerable to such dissolution, as men become more like women when they give in to such a Sirens' song. What kinds of "disorderly delights" does he mean? As he feels the need to gender the reader in describing the effect, so the disorder is sexed as well—lock up the dance halls; don't play that rock and roll. And all of that puts us in the territory of the concerns voiced by E.K. in the prefatory material to *The Shepheardes Calender*, where the music of language in alliteration is attached to the same forces that so concern Calvin

---

[16] Quoted in Coles, *Religion, Reform, and Women's Writing*, 95, from *Les Psaumes de David, mis en rime Francoise par Clement Marot, & Theodore de Beze* (Geneva, 1576), fol. iii r–v. The translation, unpublished outside of Coles, is by Anne Coldiron.

and Augustine—and furthermore where "disorder" was associated with the love of Corydon for Alexis in Virgil's second eclogue, from which E.K. went to such lengths to distance Spenser and himself.[17]

It is not a great leap of fearful thinking among Elizabethans from worry of being effeminized by aesthetic forces escaping proper rational governance to worry of being actually seduced by a woman. This kind of thinking seems behind Sir John's advice at the start of the book. But one also need not go far beyond Augustine and Calvin in these passages to arrive at Gosson's argument that the bad aesthetics of Elizabethan culture is nothing less than a national security threat. How does this work? Through many individual acts of effeminizing, seductions from hard work to the opiates of crass entertainments, inducements to fornication and vice, the country gradually loses its ability to defend itself and prepares the way for invading forces.

Gosson gets to this national security level, but where he does not go is into the relative stability of Protestant and Catholic believers, and how music, poetry, or other cultural constructions might contribute to the drama of religious reform playing out in late sixteenth-century Europe. One additional element to explore before we launch into Lodge's contemplative and substantive responses to aesthetic suspicion and fear is to consider the implications of an Englishman setting a fiction in France during the French Wars of Religion. It is a testament to the complexity of those wars, along with the additional complexity of the relationship with those people separated by the English Channel from its activities, that even in the twenty-first century we seem to be rather in the infancy of understanding how someone like Lodge might have perceived the events taking place in France. If we turn to Anne Lake Prescott's landmark study *French Poets and the English Renaissance* (1978), we get a sense that parallels this writer's—at least for most of my career writing about English literature—namely that the French Wars of Religion are so complex and convoluted that anyone could be forgiven for allowing him- or herself to lose track of the details. If poetry is to any extent "its own thing," then might it not be possible for English poets to be interested in French poets for their poetry, and not their religion or their politics?[18] After all, plenty of English Renaissance literature that is set

---

[17] See chapter 1, "Problems with Sex and Aesthetics," and chapter 2, "Static stanzas."

[18] See Anne Lake Prescott, *French Poets and the English Renaissance: Studies in Fame and Transformation* (New Haven: Yale University Press, 1978), and her finding of "a rich and varied confusion" with respect to religious and political and literary affiliation and affection between poets from the two countries, p. xiv.

in Italy makes very little hay of the presiding religious practice on the penin-
sula. Does Catholicism loom large over *Othello*, or is not Venice a place that
could simply be associated with a generalized European, Christian sensibility that England wanted to see itself as part of, despite disagreements on
religious matters?

And yet, there are aspects of Lodge's operations here that call such a view
into question. France is closer to England, its long-running religious tur-
moil harder to lose focus on. And then there is the religious language and
political conflict that frame Lodge's story. In part I am encouraged in being
made more alert to religious and political reference in the book by Shakespeare's version, in which, as I discuss in chapter 4, "conversion" is made into
a prominent motif. But even without that, there is still a thread of religious
language and imagery running through the book that invites interpretation. We never understand what conflict sets in motion the usurpation of
one king by another (and notably the "king" in Lodge is demoted to the
less specific and blurrier "duke" in *As You Like It*), but in the context of
religious war it is hard not to feel this as a religious conflict. In the wors-
ening political and religious atmosphere of the 1580s, the pressures that
led Spenser to give religious conflicts voice in his *Calender* shepherds, and
then imagine paths to "concord," seem all the more pressing for Lodge,
even as it may now be less feasible to voice conflict in such comparatively
overt terms as Spenser uses.[19] And that may be all the more the case for
a writer of great literary ambition who also has Catholic sympathies that
within ten years would be brought into the open. This is, as it were, the
circumstantial evidence. By the end of the chapter I hope to show that not
only does Lodge respond here to aesthetic suspicion in the fuller, religiously
backed sense that can be traced from Gosson through Calvin and Augustine, but he also uses the scene of comparatively open strife in contemporary
France as a way to give the abstraction of aesthetic debate in England a
more profoundly consequential frame. Put simply, setting this aesthetic-
sexual-religious argument in France raises the stakes, because such conflicts
were killing people at a steady rate as they were not, at least not yet, in
England.

---

[19] In "Julye," for example, Spenser uses the thin disguise of "Algrind" to voice support for a
prelate, Edmund Grindal, who had run afoul of the queen for his reforming zeal. Nothing so
topical or forward is to be found in *Rosalynde*.

Lodge's Rosalind

Poetic self-awareness

The Sirens serve as a good vehicle for Sir John's misogyny at the start of *Rosalynde*, encompassing both the allure of specific women and the allure of love itself. But after invoking them he does allow that his sons will need to get married; he just urges them not to fall in love with their wives. He makes this argument by emphasizing that however much some women may display this or that appealing quality, it will always be a ruse: there are no good women. As "Venus is a wanton," so "women are wantons, and yet a man cannot want one." Sir John tells his sons to seek a woman who is "chaste, obedient, and silent," but gives a final warning—"yet for that she is a woman, shalt thou find in her sufficient vanities to countervail her virtues" (5–6). To this purported wisdom, we meet Rosalind as someone who seems in many ways to be a carefully constructed counter to this view.

We first see Rosalind with a group of beautiful courtly ladies looking on at the wrestling match where Rosader (Lodge's name for Shakespeare's Orlando) is so impressive to her. As in Shakespeare, Rosader's exploits as a wrestler cause Rosalind to begin to fall in love with him—but we will return to that very fascinating scene in due time. What is most distinctive about Lodge's approach to introducing Rosalind is that it relies on a monologue, a technique that is typical for Lyly's prose: after the wrestling scene, she goes off by herself and gives us plentiful access to her thoughts.[20] The monologue shows off a level of self-awareness that seems able to meet a number of Sir John's sweeping criticisms of women, and of love. And significantly, the monologue culminates in a "madrigal," an improvised lyric poem that we are told Rosalind sings, and accompanies with her lute. The poem is presented as nothing serious, a "ditty," "warbled" out on the fly. But both in the poem itself and in the attitude by which it is presented, there is a potent answer to the heavy warnings of Sir John: for one thing, Rosalind, despite being open to erotic feelings, is hardly a "wanton"—she is

---

[20] For example, Lucilla's monologue reflecting on her first encounter with Euphues in *The Anatomy of Wit*. See John Lyly, *Euphues: The Anatomy of Wit, Euphues & His England*, ed. Morris Croll and Harry Clemons (London: Routledge, 1916), 39–43. This is in contrast with *As You Like It*, where Rosalind's only real monologue is the half-in-character epilogue after the play is over. Parenthetical citations of page numbers in *Euphues: The Anatomy of Wit* will henceforth refer to this edition.

capable of analyzing those feelings, weighing arguments against encouraging them in herself, analyzing her social surroundings, and resisting being controlled by her passions. And furthermore, the poem-song itself, rather than stoking the fires of uncontrollable passion, concentrates her skeptical thinking in a novel direction, as well as her resolution for how to proceed. And even as her feelings are concentrated in the song, there is also a sense of aesthetic distance that the singing creates, an ability to have the feelings, think about them, and also regard them, now in the form of a song, again in a sense where they do not seem to rule her as Sir John so feared—at the end of the scene she is "smiling to herself to think of her new-entertained passions" (27).

In the introductory paragraph to the monologue, Lodge's narrator suggests both that the "idea" of Rosader is acting physically upon Rosalind and that "the remembrance of her present estate, and the hardness of her fortunes" (24) was capable of counteracting her burgeoning passion. In the monologue itself we see this play out, as she first reflects on that "estate," and then on whether "becometh it women in distress to think of love" (25). This she answers with her assessment of Rosader, "absolute" in both inward and outward qualities, confirmed with "report of his virtue" (26). Then a new consideration comes into focus, that he is an impoverished "younger brother" (26) and therefore materially unable to help her advance her social position. To this she adds quotations of Horace and Ovid advising men not to omit wealth when they are seducing women, which she is then easily able to dismiss as "base thoughts" (26) unworthy of her. Thus, at the end of the monologue, the "Chaos of confused thoughts" (24), imputed to her by the narrator at the start, seems quite dissipated, and her passion for Rosader is authorized by his virtues. This is where the "madrigal" opens up a different meditation on the same topic:

> Love in my bosom like a bee
>> Doth suck his sweet:
> Now with his wings he plays with me,
>> Now with his feet.
> Within mine eyes he makes his nest,
> His bed amidst my tender breast;
> My kisses are his daily feast,
> And yet he robs me of my rest.
>> Ah wanton, will ye?

And if I sleep, then percheth he
    With pretty flight,
And makes his pillow of my knee
    The livelong night.
Strike I my lute, he tunes the string,
He music plays if so I sing;
He lends me every lovely thing,
Yet cruel he my heart doth sting.
    Whist, wanton, still ye!

(27)

From having reflected on love and passion as a set of moral, social, and pe-
cuniary considerations, with pleasure and joy somewhat in the background,
the poem begins from what seems the point of view of one of those women
in whom sonneteers see "Love playing" in various features and attributes.
Instead of that kind of localizing of Eros in one or another "part," this poem
imagines a woman attempting to understand her erotic power over others,
a power not entirely under her control, or perhaps very little under her control. Where Sir John framed the danger of love as being localized in "wanton"
women, Rosalind here performs the kind of internal separation that is a standard move of Petrarchan love lyric, but here between a beautiful women and
the power of her beauty, amplified by Eros, which has effects beyond her
control.

And that relationship, aside from being strange, is quite unproblematic
until we arrive at the "sting" that her heart also receives from Love. This
does not seem like either the inadvertent prick of an arrow that Venus gets
while dandling Cupid that leads to her love of Adonis, or the infusion of
erotic feeling that Dido receives from similarly dandling the god in the form
of her son.[21] Instead, the sting seems the effect of all of the lending of "every
lovely thing," an echo effect of the amplification of her beauty. The poem
depicts her trying to understand her erotic powers as she describes the way
Cupid "nests" in her eyes, and aids (like a Popean sylph) her attractive powers, "tuning" and accompanying her musically. But as all of this aids her in

---

[21] For Venus and Adonis, see Ovid *Metamorphoses* 10:503–59, and for Dido, see Virgil *Aeneid*
1:717–19.

attracting lovers and admiration, also it "robs me of my rest" and "my heart doth sting." In the second half of the poem, she considers resistance:

> Else I with roses every day
>   Will whip you hence,
> And bind you, when you long to play,
>   For your offence;
> I'll shut mine eyes to keep you in,
> I'll make you fast it for your sin,
> I'll count your power not worth a pin.
>   (27–8)

But the notion does not last long:

> Alas, what hereby shall I win,
>   If he gainsay me?
>
> What if I beat the wanton boy
>   With many a rod?
> He will repay me with annoy.
>   Because a God.
> Then sit thou safely on my knee,
> And let thy bower my bosom be;
> Lurk in mine eyes, I like of thee.
> O Cupid, so thou pity me,
>   Spare not but play thee.
>   (28)

Part of the poem envisions scourging and binding Cupid, part imagines curtailing his power by shutting her eyes "to keep you in." But this course of beating and confinement is finally rejected because, though a little boy, he is still divine and will "repay me with annoy." And so finally she embraces his presence in her eyes and bosom, and ends by asking his pity.

All of this is quite resonant both with the bald misogyny of Sir John and the more complex fears and suspicions of Gosson, Calvin, and Augustine. Before the poem begins Rosalind has already demonstrated a far-reaching ability to see her own feelings from a variety of points of view (including those of men), and to tame them. In this little mythology of the relationship between beauty and Eros, she further considers applying the kinds of repressive strategies advocated by reformers like Gosson (and encouraged in various ways by Christian tradition) before rejecting them. One might argue that the poem ends by advocating a passive relationship of a woman with her own erotic powers, and thus a passive relationship with their effects—as in accepting any sexual advance that they produce. I am more inclined, however, to see this as a serious rejoinder to Sir John, Gosson, and Calvin and Augustine as well: the poem's mythology "naturalizes" erotic power, and argues that repressive measures can only lead to more suffering, not less. In the unshackling and urging of "play" at the end we might also read advocacy against repressive measures especially for the dress of women—at least against such measures as the requirement of wearing masks. True, such an argument must be gathered from Rosalind's actions here—it is not yet an explicit feminist position or argument countering specifically the anti-feminist positions taken by Gosson and the rest, though it does seem explicitly to counter the narrower misogyny of Sir John.

Furthermore, the poem enacts some of the effects it describes, not only in the fact that we are to imagine it sung, and accompanied by Rosalind's lute playing, but also because it might be seen as an example of the love-amplified beauty that it also describes. As such it gains the expressive and consolatory effect that has been imputed to poetry since Pan grabbed up the reeds that were Syrinx and breathed music into them: the poem describes the conclusion that there can only be limited control of the force of Eros, and that at some level we must all hope for pity. That is to say, Rosalind displays both wide-ranging rational control of her situation, in prose, and the ability to concentrate what she cannot control, the potentially tragic undersong of all love stories, in an expressive aesthetic object, a song, or what for us is a lyric poem. In the technical history of Rosalind, all of this makes for an extraordinary leap forward.[22]

---

[22] Clare Kinney, in contrast, notes the madrigal episode, but views it as subsumed by Rosalind's embrace of pastoral and Petrarchan conventions later in the book. See Clare R. Kinney, "Feigning Female Faining: Spenser, Lodge, Shakespeare, and Rosalind," *Modern Philology* 95 (February 1998): 291–315, at 298. What has changed since 1998? There seems an increased interest in developing perceptions of female agency within male-authored fictions, or within dynamics of power and sexuality that had seemed unidimensionally patriarchal or misogynist. In a near space to this, I might suggest Kathryn Schwarz's readings of Lear's daughters, or Phyllis Rackin's reading of Cleopatra, or, more distantly, Amber Jamilla Musser's reading of "O" in *The Story of O*, who argues that through a dual subject position, through her very complicity in her role, she develops a Foucaultian "technology of the self" that creates a space for agency in the context of extreme non-agency. See Schwarz, *What You Will*, ch. 7; Rackin, *Shakespeare and Women*, ch. 6; and Musser, *Sensational Flesh*, 63.

How far this is from the fearful music imputed to the Sirens, and the aesthetic suspicion of Gosson, Calvin, and Augustine. Instead, this is "harmony" that extends the joint work of reason and affection, that raises mind and spirit without condemning the body. Surely this is virtuous music, but it is not a knee-jerk virtue that condemns—all women, or all sex, or all aesthetic claims on the mind and senses. It is also worth noting how much Rosalind by this point has already advanced beyond the Rosalind of the *Calender* or, for that matter, any other female literary character that I know of in Elizabethan literature prior to this time.[23] Far from being a force for anti-literary, anti-aesthetic suspicion and condemnation, this Rosalind is a practitioner and a connoisseuse, who after this scene will arrive in Arden fully authorized in having a penetrating understanding of virtue and passion, and also having displayed the ability to "warble" off a serious lyric on the fly. It is this sensibility that she carries into her first critical encounters with the lovers of forest, with one additional critical angle to play—that of having assumed the identity of Jove's page, and begun to play a man.

The characters of men

Readers coming to Lodge after Shakespeare, as most do, are likely to find the prose to be off-puttingly "straight," missing the dirty humor of Jaques and Touchstone, and comparatively tightly laced. This is a mistake. In fact Rosalind and Alinda use the occasion of Rosalind's cross-dressing to make penis jokes, which are indeed a bit of a running theme in the book, and beyond that to joke about the male desire to "write once" on the heart of a woman, and leave an indelible impression, or if they can't do that, then engrave their verses on trees.[24] It's all the same instrument. That joke on pens, weapons, and phalluses circulates under a satirical treatment of anti-feminist

---

[23] Examples from literature in general are hard to come by. Sappho was the famous exemplar of a woman poet, and her poems certainly display her managing or attempting to manage passions. And in ancient literature there are many women who express themselves in verse about their passions, but I have not been able to locate an example of a woman who self-consciously expresses herself in a poem or song separate from her ordinary discourse, with the exception of Ovid's *Heroides* where a number of the women include inset epitaphs in their complaints (e.g., Dido at the end of part 7). The effect is very different from this.

[24] Sir John, in his deathbed speech discussed at the beginning of the chapter, is the first in the book to reference this fantasy, as he lists the qualities that he ultimately admits that no woman possesses: his ideal would have "her heart of a diamond, that will receive but one form" (5).

discourse, a satirical treatment which is in Shakespeare, but the other difference is that the poetry that provokes all this is of a very different quality from what is in the play: as with Rosalind's madrigal, and pretty much everywhere in Lodge, the verse is serious. This is in marked contrast with the pastoral verse that Shakespeare's city characters find when they enter the forest, much of which is deliberately "rustic" in its extreme simplicity, if it is not simply bad, and subject to immediate lampooning or mocking derision. In Lodge, we do some satiric rehearsal of various ways of interpreting poetry, but then leave the poetry itself in a different, uncritical zone: the sense here is that all the lyric that Lodge includes is meant to be appreciated consistently, like musical numbers in a Broadway show. Nonetheless, despite this critical separation between the "talk" and the poetry of these scenes, Lodge still sets up structures that gesture in the direction of more complex dynamics to come in later writers. The way that Rosalind and Alinda mock the "decorous" responses of men and women to erotic poetry seems like it could be a way to manage aesthetic response—to clear the way for response and interpretation free of the confines of decorum. And, even more incipiently, Rosalind's adoption of Ganymede as her masculine disguise also contributes to what I will describe here as virtuous lightness, that might be a feminist alternative to the patriarchal disjunction of cold feminine hardness and promiscuous lightness. The queerness of Ganymede, and the text's diffidence on the topic, makes the alternative that much more complex to isolate and define, but it will be something to which we return as we continue to trace the book's deployment of myths and its search for concord.

To the penis. The setup is done with a sword: "I will buy me a suit," says Rosalind, when she resolves that traveling male is the way to go in Arden, "and have my rapier very handsomely at my side, and if any knave offer wrong, your page will show him the point of his weapon" (34). Then, shortly after arriving in Arden, they find a poem written on a tree, complaining of the stony hardness of a woman, giving no "relief" to the male writer, which provokes Rosalind-Ganymede to complain "what mad cattle you women be, whose hearts sometimes are made of adamant that will touch with no impression, and sometime of wax that is fit for every form" (36). It is clear what most directly makes such impressions, and so while Ganymede articulates the patriarchal disjunction, it is subverted by a stronger satire of phallic egomania, along with the fact that a woman is saying this to "keep decorum." The egomania is in the desire, if they cannot "write" themselves permanently on women, to seek consolatory permanence through writing, substituting the pen for the phallus, and in this case engraving their "characters" on hapless trees. The substitution of the sword remains in the background here, except that of course writing on trees requires a sharp pen indeed. The connection is cinched by Lodge's emphasis on recognizability, that the tree-writing is instantly identifiable as male, as "the figures of men":

> At last Ganymede casting up his eye espied where on a tree was engraven certain verses; which as soon as he espied, he cried out:
> "Be of good cheer, mistress, I spy the figures of men; for here in these trees be engraven certain verses of shepherds, or some other swains that inhabit here about." (35)

And that is certain even though the poem itself has no definitive identification of gender. Indeed, the only specifically gendered identification is of the speaker with Mirrha. Yet the character of men is sufficiently self-evident that there is no room for doubt.

Ganymede and Aliena (Alinda's assumed name in the forest) then proceed to play their own obvious parts, and thus do the relatively easy work of skewering the standard lines of argument, as well as mythic and literary reference and imagery, for this particular conundrum. Alinda expresses sympathy for the "perplexed shepherd" as against "the cruelty of his mistress" (36). Ganymede then condemns women full stop, with the "mad cattle" line quoted above. Women, she continues, "delight to be courted, and then they glory to seem coy, and when they are most desired then they freeze in disdain: and this fault is so common to the sex, that you see it painted out in the shepherd's passions, who found his mistress as froward as he was enamoured" (36). To that Aliena protests:

> "And I pray you," quoth Aliena, "if your robes were off, what mettle are you made of that you are so satirical against women? Is it not a foul bird defiles the [sic] own nest?²⁵ Beware, Ganymede, that Rosader hear you not, if he do, perchance you will make him leap so far from love, that he will anger every vein in your heart."
> "Thus," quoth Ganymede, "I keep decorum: I speak now as I am Aliena's page, not as I am Gerismond's daughter; for put me but into a petticoat, and I will stand in defiance to the uttermost, that women are courteous, constant, virtuous, and what not." (37)

---

²⁵ The "the" is in the original published text, 15.

Despite Rosalind's offhand "what not," we can recognize the potential of the performance of this kind of decorum-keeping. For of course Rosader *has* heard an assault on women in very similar terms to the ones Ganymede employs, in the deathbed "precepts" received from his father Sir John. And to frame that as merely the usual positions in anti-feminist and feminist debate between the sexes does much to undermine Sir John's wisdom as just gendered "what not."

This is not the only place that this scene comes into alignment with Sir John's advice to his sons—it also invokes the Sirens myth for a second time. But this time we hear women charging that male poetry is a lure to vice, and so not a Siren song of female beauty or heteroeroticism in general, but the seductive songs of men, poetry doing phallic seductive work after all, and the Sirens now gendered male. It is Aliena who, after taking in another tree-poem, gives us this:

> but see, I pray, when poor women seek to keep themselves chaste, how men woo them with many feigned promises; alluring with sweet words as the Sirens, and after proving as trothless as Aeneas. Thus promised Demophoon to his Phyllis, but who at last grew more false? (38)[26]

So: the Sirens here are only their "sweet words" and not their monstrous forms and piles of carcasses—we need Aeneas to get to the betrayal Aliena seeks, which makes for two slightly tendentious myth-readings in one sentence. Ganymede has the appropriate comeback, namely that both men were "women's sons"—women are the root of all evil, that is to say, including the evil of men. The argument that all such "sweet words" betray the same seductive "character" of men is thus subjected to as much irony as the assault

---

[26] In citing Demophoon and Phyllis, a woman canonized for constancy in the face of male betrayal in Ovid's *Heroides* as well as Chaucer's *Legend of Good Women*, Lodge also draws very near the font of Euphuism in Lyly's *Anatomy of Wit*, here as the object of Euphues' desires, Lucilla, questions the earnestness and durability of Euphues' overtures, especially given that he is a stranger to Naples:

> But alas, Euphues, what truth can there be found in a traveller, what stay in a stranger; whose words and bodies both watch but for a wind, whose feet are ever fleeting, whose faith plighted on the shore is turned to perjury when they hoist sail? Who more traitorous to Phyllis than Demophon? Yet he a traveller. Who more perjured to Dido than Aeneas? And he a stranger. Both these queens, both they caitiffs.

(61–2)

on women that Ganymede launches because, well, she needs to speak the part.

The implication of Rosalind-Ganymede's role-playing is the weakness of both arguments, or that the accusation leads to a situation where neither side is listening, each entrenched in comfortable positions—indeed, we might say, "stopping their ears" to the arguments of those they condemn. If this broader critique of "decorum" is satiric, to use Aliena's term, then that might lead us to conclude that everyone here is ridiculous. But if the book as a whole is really interested in "concord," then our next question is—how do we proceed forward from this location where we have successfully perceived the ridiculousness of all sides of the argument at hand? I see two possible answers to that question in this scene. The first is to consider more carefully the poetry that contrasts so sharply with the doggerel that Shakespeare exhibits for ridicule in parallel scenes in *As You Like It*. And the second is to consider the queerness of Rosalind's assumption of "Ganymede" for playing the part of a man. First to the poems.

For one thing, in Shakespeare's Arden the city folk do not immediately find anything written; instead they overhear the same unhappy shepherd speaking:

> If thou remember'st not the slightest folly
> That ever love did make thee run into,
> Thou hast not loved.
> Or if thou hast not sat as I do now,
> Wearying thy hearer in thy mistress' praise,
> Thou hast not loved.
> Or if thou hast not broke from company
> Abruptly, as my passion now makes me,
> Thou hast not loved.
> O Phoebe, Phoebe, Phoebe!
>
> (2.4.31–40)

Compare this with the first tree-poem around which Ganymede and Aliena have their satiric dialogue:

> Hadst thou been born whereas perpetual cold
> Makes Tanais hard, and mountains silver old;
> Had I complained unto a marble stone,

Or to the floods bewrayed my bitter moan,
   I then could bear the burthen of my grief:
But even the pride of countries at thy birth,
Whilst heavens did smile, did new array the earth
   With flowers chief;
Yet thou, the flower of beauty blessèd born,
Hast pretty looks, but all attired in scorn.

Had I the power to weep sweet Mirrha's tears,
Or by my plaints to pierce repining ears;
Hadst thou the heart to smile at my complaint,
To scorn the woes that doth my heart attaint,
   I then could bear the burthen of my grief:
But not my tears, but truth with thee prevails,
And seeming sour my sorrows thee assails:
   Yet small relief:
For if thou wilt thou art of marble hard,
And if thou please my suit shall soon be heard.

(35–36)

To Shakespeare's simple, stylized verses we have a ten-line stanza, including a shortened line 8, more akin to the intricacy of the "April" eclogue in *The Shepheardes Calender*. Indeed, if there is a complaint about this poem it might be that the complex structure is almost too handily resolved. "I then could bear the burthen of my grief" is a strong line to repeat, and it impressively balances the stanzas in which it is placed, coming out of the twin contrary-to-fact clauses that fill the previous four lines. In the vein of poets like Daniel and Drayton, if the poem is Spenserian, it seems a Spenser smoothed by the prevailing sense of poetry that was taking hold in 1590. Its chief pleasure is in its smooth unfurling through a complex and demanding form. And it is not bad at accomplishing this.

If the general observation holds, if Shakespeare presents deliberate doggerel as the natural poetry of forest rustics, then we may understand this as making fun of one of the central conventions of pastoral, that Tityrus and Melibœus are ordinary people who can sing effortlessly, like Sirens. We will return to this: in chapter 4 I will be especially interested in examining the way Shakespeare manages expectations about the poetic content of his play—the complex methods he uses to condition and prepare moments of earnestness, where the satiric point of view can fall away. In our biography of poetry we can see in Lodge the elements that will be incorporated into that management. But Lodge seems much less concerned here with managing or countering a truly skeptical reader: while there is plenty of knowing discussion of the ways that, for men, poetry can be a substitute for or expression of phallic egomania, when the poetry arrives, there seems an uncritical confidence that it needs no defense with readers. And that might have actually been the case in 1590, if the popularity of Lodge's book is any guide.[27] But by 1600, or facing the broader or more mixed audience of the Globe, it seems very much not to have been true for Shakespeare.

But if an examination of the poetry seems to see it as an unsatisfyingly disconnected advance from the scorched ground left by the satiric play of the two women, another way of understanding how we might find a way forward from a satiric display of ridiculousness all around is by concentrating on what it means for Rosalind to choose "Ganymede" as her page-name. Ganymede is the supposed etymology for "catamite," and invokes the most famous affair between Jove and a male mortal.[28] From this it is clear that Ganymede could be shorthand for pederasty, a myth about how powerful men—who might have wives and mistresses as well—like to have sex with boys. This significance is greatly amplified on the Elizabethan stage, of course, where Rosalind will be played by a boy involved in romantic scenes with adult male actors. But to read Leonard Barkan on Ganymede in *Transuming Passion* is to be made aware of a much larger range of resonance in Western culture surrounding this particular myth.[29] What is frustrating

[27] It was reprinted nine times after 1590, the latest edition appearing in 1640. See Greg's introduction to this edition, p. xxii.

[28] One good indicator of an Elizabethan understanding of Ganymede along these lines can be found in Marlowe's portrayal of him in *Dido, Queen of Carthage*, a play that might have preceded *Rosalynde* by a few years. It was published in 1594 but there is much uncertainty about its first performance date. See E. K. Chambers's note on the text in *The Elizabethan Stage* (Oxford: Clarendon Press, 1923), 3: 426–7. I am of course hardly the first critic to have noticed the name Ganymede and contemplated its significance for destabilizing gender and sexuality here, though most of this kind of attention has gone toward Shakespeare and not Lodge. However, after initial readings and statements by, for example, Mario DiGangi (on *As You Like It*) and Stephen Orgel (one of the chapters of whose standard-setting book *Impersonations* is named "Call Me Ganymede"), attention to the significance of the name seems largely to have dissipated, along with the subsidence of the ferocious interest in cross-dressing and gender destabilization in 1980s and 1990s. See DiGangi, *The Homoerotics of Early Modern Drama*, Cambridge Studies in Renaissance Literature and Culture (Cambridge: Cambridge University Press, 1997), 50–63; and Orgel, *Impersonations: The Performance of Gender in Shakespeare's England* (Cambridge: Cambridge University Press, 1996).

[29] See Leonard Barkan, *Transuming Passion: Ganymede and the Erotics of Humanism* (Stanford, CA: Stanford University Press, 1991). Teasing out the resonance and function of the myth is the book's whole project, but see "The History of a Myth" for an overview, 27–40.

about both Shakespeare's and Lodge's invocation of Ganymede is how little else we are given to navigate the versions of Ganymede being invoked here, but I will for the moment hazard a try, based on what we have seen so far of Lodge's satiric treatment of gender "decorum" in this forest. Even just bringing to bear the most basic set of associations with Ganymede, we might be ready to read that particular name selection as a serious encouragement to see it as the basis for what Judith Butler famously called a subversive gender performance.[30] Rosalind shifts effortlessly between male and female arguments about sexual integrity, lightness versus hardness, but "Ganymede" occupies a position that is in neither pole, or is a position that stands somehow and unstably outside of both. Other than being entertained and (perhaps) fascinated by this performance, what do we get? That is not yet clear. But we will presently explore an allied possibility, namely that Lodge begins to map out a concept of virtuous lightness, as an answer to the knee-jerk misogyny of Sir John, or the commensurate moral condemnation of masculinity by women.

To be sure, the figure of the cross-dressed woman is so common in Elizabethan literature as to lose some of its force as a conduit for critical energy. But in the light of Sir John's misogyny, to see a woman dressed as a man, satirically rehearsing male arguments against love, against women, is as far as imaginable from the silent, chaste, only once "impressed" woman that Sir John suggests for a wife if his sons cannot be persuaded to forswear women altogether. And where John's fears and the fears of the reformers and church fathers come together is over the impressionability of women and people in general: that impressions of virtue made upon people by faith and reason might be undone by the aesthetic, by the aesthetic that makes more feminine, which is to say more easily and multifariously impressionable. So far in the book, then, we have satiric energy directed at the notion that this obsession with permanence and permanent impressions might be a specifically phallic egotism and neurosis, which women, lacking phalluses, are in an advantageous position to highlight and lampoon—especially by dressing up as men.

---

[30] See Judith Butler, *Gender Trouble: Feminism and the Subversion of Identity* (2nd edn., New York: Routledge, 1999), *passim*, e.g. 44–5. Within queer studies and feminism, the phenomenon remains of central interest, even as its meaning and limits are much debated. Lynne Huffer, for example, discusses the ways that queer of color critique "begins with a recognition of historical marginalization as a desubjectivating experience to be remediated by critical resubjectivation." Thus, if one reads Butlerian identity disruption as going "all the way down," such that "there are neither selves nor intersections," then "queer theory's relation to intersectional feminism becomes more fraught." See Huffer, *Lips*, 16.

Virtuous lightness, feminine poetic virtue

Let us continue to follow the argument emerging against the "single impression" desideratum for women. This is not to say that Rosalind and Alinda are polyamorous or that they sleep around. But they are variously impressionable in that they have feelings about various things, various people, and they are variously moved by song and poetry. So that is virtuous lightness at one level: here we are, young women of intelligence and sympathy who can love, and also be moved by art including erotic art: their hearts and minds are capable of contemplating this, responding, participating, and not being corrupted. That is a general sense of things that answers Sir John, and answers those behind him to an extent as well, and though a simple argument, it is a powerful one: people, men and women, can take pleasure from art and not be corrupted or drawn into vice by it: they demonstrate this through their virtuous lives. I refute it thus.

But can anything more specific be drawn from extensive talk and poems exchanged in the forest? I think so, but it is harder to demonstrate in Rosalind or Alinda, than it is to demonstrate, as in the *Calender*, as an effect of the women's discourse, their critical pressure on the main poet-figure of the book, which is to say Rosader. The scene that concentrates this best is in Rosader's second encounter with the women in the forest. The theme of the exchange seems to be temperance, which could also be a more positive way of putting "lightness." That is to say that being variously impressionable, which looks like looseness and lightness from one point of view, might from another look like the ability to temper passion and not be consumed by it.

This particular scene begins with Rosalind-Ganymede advising Rosader that "'Tis good … to love, but not to overlove" (77). Rosader responds that, while love robs him of rest, he finds comfort walking in the forest:

> here, although everywhere passionate, yet I brook love with more patience, in that every object feeds mine eye with variety of fancies. When I look on Flora's beauteous tapestry, checked with the pride of all her treasure, I call to mind the fair face of Rosalynde, whose heavenly hue exceeds the rose and the lily in their highest excellence: the brightness of Phoebus' shine puts me in mind to think of the sparkling flames that flew from her eyes, and set my heart first on fire: the sweet harmony of the birds, puts me in remembrance of the rare melody of her voice, which like the Siren enchanteth the ears of the hearer. Thus in contemplation I salve my sorrows, with applying the perfection of every object to the excellence of her qualities. (77–8)

It is frustrating that neither Aliena nor Ganymede respond to this directly: has Rosader "answered" the warning about "overlove" through this description? We might suggest that instead Rosader sounds like the speaker of Shakespeare's Sonnet 147, "feeding on that which doth preserve the ill" (3), and that such a cycle of association and amplification is just what Ganymede warns against. Or not. The position of the Sirens here is especially striking. In its original negative configuration, the poem-song is luring to destruction, beauty that tempts the otherwise virtuous off the true path to perdition. The sense is linear and singular: one true path, one temptation, one event of destruction. But this positive configuration for the Sirens is instead cyclical. The Sirens appear as an association with a memory: I hear the "sweet harmony" of birdsong, which reminds me of her voice, which like the Sirens enchants all who hear it, and we might go on to say that the birds then likewise enchant all who hear. I say that this is a positive configuration of the Sirens because it surely does not appear negative: none of this cycle of association and enhanced feeling seems bad to him: he is wandering in a natural echo chamber of his desire, and such "contemplation" seems to keep sorrow at bay.

But in other respects we might consider the Sirens here to be somewhat more neutral, or at least not a positive inversion of the Homeric story: they are not accomplishing the reverse operation of tempting the person on the path of vice onto a path of virtue—and that is the way the myth will be retold, finally, with respect to Saladyne, Rosader's fratricidal brother, and Rosader's own impulses to hold a grudge against Saladyne and leave him to the mercy of a hungry lion. And furthermore, it is not at all clear that Rosader would agree that anyone who hears the birds singing would be sirenically enchanted in the same way that he is via the link to Rosalind's voice. It is his love that powers this association, powers the enchantment.

The narrative addresses none of this directly. But there is at least circumstantial evidence that this state of cyclic association and amplification is linked to poetry writing. How? Because when Ganymede decides to change subjects, and ask Rosader to read them some of "those sonnets, which you said were at home in your lodge" (79), he assents, and, far from any modest preface, tells them to prepare themselves to take in "what a poetical fury love will infuse into a man" (79). The implication is that the poem, which explores the same paradoxical state of pain and pleasure that he has just described in prose, is the product of that state. It is a dream vision where the lover's tears and sighs merge with the natural world in a manner reminiscent of the associations of his walk in the forest, but which ends by imagining his own destruction and renewal like the phoenix:

> Meanwhile my sighs yield truce unto my tears,
>   By them the winds increased and fiercely blow:
> Yet when I sigh the flame more plain appears,
>   And by their force with greater power doth glow:
>   Amid these pains, all phoenix-like I thrive
>   Since love, that yields me death, may life revive.
>
>   (80)

I suggested that when we first see Rosalind by herself, the poetry she spontaneously sings serves to counter Gosson by showing off poetry as a technique for passion management that can be wielded by women. We will recall that in her poem, she decides not to attempt to suppress the erotic power of her own beauty, not to take on Cupid directly, but rather to allow him some rein, and pray for mercy. But there is indeed a lightness to the entire scene that contrasts with Rosader's description of his wanderings in the woods, and with the *Liebestod* evoked by this poem.

Indeed, once she hears this poem, Rosalind-Ganymede finds the moment ripe to respond with a most Gosson-like tirade, that is worth quoting at some length:

"I can smile," quoth Ganymede, "at the sonettos, canzones, madrigals, rounds and roundelays, that these pensive patients pour out when their eyes are more full of wantonness, than their hearts of passions. Then, as the fishers put the sweetest bait to the fairest fish, so these Ovidians, holding *amo* in their tongues, when their thoughts come at haphazard, write that they be rapt in an endless labyrinth of sorrow, when walking in the large lease of liberty, they only have their humours in their inkpot. If they find women so fond, that they will with such painted lures come to their lust, then they triumph till they be full-gorged with pleasures; and then fly they away, like ramage kites, to their own content, leaving the tame fool, their mistress, full of fancy, yet without even a feather. If they miss, as dealing with some wary wanton, that wants not such a one as themselves, but spies their subtlety, they end their amours with a few feigned sighs; and so their excuse is, their mistress is cruel, and they smother passion with patience. Such, gentle forester, we may deem you to be, that rather pass away the time here in these woods with writing amorets, than to be deeply enamoured, as you say, of your Rosalynde." (80–1)

The most Gosson-like part of this is the charge that poetry is used for vicious temptation, not called Sirens' songs here, but used by men to lure women like fish to their destruction. But the response to Rosader is also more specific, in that she suggests that the state he has described in himself is really one that churns out a "haphazard" stream of low-grade Ovidean erotic blather. And so the "fury" that Rosader claims for himself is self-induced froth that powers the conquests of would-be womanizers, or attempts to power them: when the poems don't work, the "poets" just target another mistress in hope that she will be a "tame fool" unable to see through the ruse. Most damningly, she suggests, all of this is superficial: "writing amorets" has no correspondence with being "deeply enamoured."

Rosader's response is straightforward: you are wrong, or at least you are wrong about me. Beneath his writing are "deep impressions" (82). But can we claim any remainder here for the notion of virtuous lightness? There are a couple of paths: first, there is the very conversation, the discursive zone in which, if Rosader's feelings and expressions are not light, then at least we are able to make light of them. Second, we can ask whether Rosader's love-suffering is indeed lightened by his poetry writing, whether the cycle of association and amplification he describes, his "contemplation" really does "salve" his sorrows and not simply make further and deeper impressions. Rosalind in the scene does not really bring out the double nature of the danger she perceives. There really must be some concept of "overlove" operating here: there must be a version of this "contemplation" that is, if not negatively effeminizing, then at least enervating, and thus a "depth" that is too deep. And so even though the dialogue ends with seemingly conventional assurances that Rosader isn't like those bad poets or bad men, and that he is "true and trusty" (81) and appropriately deep, I argue that we retain some interest in the lightness Rosalind displayed when on her own.

The question that remains open is the nature of lyric poetry within this dynamic. When Rosalind is alone, it certainly seems as though the act of singing does make her feel better, that the "making" of the poem-song both concentrates the difficulty of her position, and lightens the load. Is this just some version of the speaking cure? The confessional poem doing confessional work? Does poetry then act as both an enabler of deeper contemplation and as it were a float to grab onto to save one from sinking too far into the depths? Does such poetry model a virtuous lightness that can be imitated by either sex? Does poetry model a mean of thinking and feeling, a philosophical harmony that gives pleasure as it salves sorrows and authenticates depth? We will leave these questions open as we move now from this extension of the technical history of Rosalind, focused on her character, her actions, and immediate surroundings, to the biography of poetry in the text at large, and work our way back around to the notion of "concord" falsely imputed to Sir John, and refracted through the various citations of the Sirens.

Queer mythography: the Sirens

It does not take long for Sir John's Sirens to begin to migrate from their starting signification of female danger to other meanings. But another myth tends to remain more stable, and that is the story of Ixion. Ixion is a kind of negative Pygmalion in that he falls for a false image of a goddess, and the moment of embrace is the one that Lodge's narrative keeps coming back to. Ixion has the temerity to try to seduce Jove's wife Juno, and Jove sets him up by substituting a Juno-like "cloud" for the real thing. At the end of the scene we were just examining, Rosalind invokes the myth as a warning to Rosader, what she indeed prays will happen if he proves to be superficial: "I pray God, when you think your fortunes at the highest, and your desires to be most excellent, then that you may with Ixion embrace Juno in a cloud, and have nothing but a marble mistress to release your martyrdom" (81). She prays, that is, that Rosader meet the fate of a martyr of a false religion, who when he thinks to embrace (or be embraced by) the deity he has worshipped, he finds everything dissolve in a mist.[31] We shift here from surface-depth to substance versus the insubstantial, embodied and disembodied as the appropriate test. And in such a moment, suddenly all the talk of affections and passions is obviously portable to the field of religious faith in a time of hotly competing versions of the truth, in a time of "real" martyrdom, martyrs dying by the sword and on the scaffold and at the stake.

As Ixion gives us an inversion of Pygmalion, where life is revealed as illusory at the point of bodily contact, he also gives an inversion of sorts of the Sirens, or at least of the moral nature of Sirens story. That is to say, the listener is presumed to be virtuous with respect to the corrupting influence of the Sirens. In the Ixion story, by contrast, his desire is thoroughly vicious, but what he pursues is not, and the metamorphosis at the end seems more to reflect his false desire: that false, selfish, vicious desire is ultimately rewarded

---

[31] Although, interestingly, the "marble" (which could mean simply "white," as in the whiteness of a cloud) gets us still closer to Pygmalion, coming home after praying to Venus and hoping that the marble of his mistress has become flesh, only to find that it remains stone. For Pygmalion's classic Ovidean telling, see *Metamorphoses* 10:243–97.

with empty, false beauty. The other significant difference between the Ixion situation and that of Odysseus and the Sirens is that Ixion's story is about the relations of mortals and deities, and it explores the dynamics and ends of false desire for true deity—it is primarily about religion and secondarily about Eros.[32] As the myth inverts aspects of both the Sirens and Pygmalion, it allows Lodge to move from queer mythography into the territory of queer theology.[33] Rosalind embodies a response to Sir John's misogyny, and her criticism of poetry along with her original verse respond to the larger atmosphere of misogynist anti-aestheticism in Gosson, Calvin, and Augustine. In the scenes I explore below, the tables are turned on Christianity, as some of its central narrative components, images, and moral gambits are subjected to the same various, improvisational, and critical handling as the myths. Specifically, this will take us to three locations: the wrestling scene close to the start of the book; the persecution of Rosader by Saladyne and Saladyne's redemptive trajectory following this; and the mock wedding that happens when Rosader declares that he is tired of all this talk in the forest and longs for action.

First, to the wrestling: Shakespeare's wrestling scene in *As You Like It* turns on the identification of Orlando with the dissenting party to the Duke; in Lodge that does not happen, but the scene is more deeply imbued with religious associations. The introduction for the main combat between the king's champion (here identified as "the Norman") and Rosader is, as in Shakespeare, the champion's brutal defeat of some other challengers. In Shakespeare, we don't know if the challengers survive. In Lodge there is no doubt. A "lusty franklin" presents his sons, "two tall men," to take him on. The eldest goes first—"and presented himself to the Norman, who straight coped with him, and as a man that would triumph in the glory of his strength, roused himself with such fury, that not only he gave him the fall, but killed him with the weight of his corpulent personage" (17–18). The death is clear, but the religious resonance becomes more apparent in the

---

[32] I am not sure where Lodge would have read about Ixion: he is only alluded to in Ovid and Virgil; Pindar, *Pythian Odes* 2.21–48 seems the fullest classical source, but Lodge might have gotten it from somewhere else—perhaps a French source. Given the influence of Desportes in this book that is my first suspicion. It might be further noted that Apollo isn't much better in the Daphne story—but Apollo has a lot of other redeeming qualities.

[33] I alluded to queer theology in chapter 1, "Problems with Sex and Aesthetics," with respect to recent readings of Virgil's Eclogue 2, and such seminal work as that of Jonathan Goldberg, *Sodometries: Renaissance Texts, Modern Sexualities* (Stanford, CA: Stanford University Press, 1992), and Richard Rambuss, "The Straightest Story Ever Told," *GLQ: A Journal of Gay and Lesbian Studies* 17, no. 4 (2011): 542–73.

follow-up to the Norman's second combat, where he kills an additional tall franklin's son by throwing him against the ground and breaking his neck:

> At this unlooked for massacre the people murmured, and were all in a deep passion of pity; but the franklin, father unto these, never changed his countenance, but as a man of a courageous resolution took up the bodies of his sons without show of outward discontent. (18)

The franklin's "courageous resolution" puts him into the position of a martyr, nobly accepting his suffering; the use of "massacre" also arguably signals Lodge's interest in actuating the dynamics of so many scenes of suffering in France that were making their way to the attention of the English, and behind them the looming image of St Bartholomew's Day.[34] If the political struggle in the play can be read against the religious struggle in France, and if we see this tournament as an attempt to distract people from that struggle, this seems like a place where the underlying tension might be coming through—because rather than "sport," the scene has become yet another "massacre." The differences with Shakespeare are telling, even as it is initially tempting to see them simply as a product of genre conventions: that Elizabethan comedy in 1600 couldn't brook onstage death, even of minor characters, though it could brook critical injury and the threat of death just fine. But for Lodge it seems important that the crowd in this scene is experiencing something like a shared sense of religious and political oppression: their sympathy for the franklin is as for a representative of a persecuted politics or religion, made to suffer—in this case to watch the violent death of his children—for his beliefs.

Lodge now turns our attention to the sequence of events that leads Rosader into the combat, and what allows him to win; this overlaps with the process of seeing Rosalind for the first time and falling in love with her. This is also one of a number of places in the book where Lodge shows something of a rage for process, or obsession with tracing the causal path that leads from an event to a responsive action (one might call the impulse scientific—perhaps part of the same impulse that would eventually lead him to study medicine in France). The obsession is especially striking because it

---

[34] In a forthcoming book, Brian Sandberg will argue that "massacre" comes into English in the sixteenth century with St Bartholomew's Day, and carries that association everywhere. A version of this argument was presented to the Chicago Area Renaissance Seminar in October 2016 under the title "The Massacre of the Innocents: Gender and Martyrdom in the French Wars of Religion."

is so absent in Shakespeare's play. The beginning of the process Lodge traces is Rosader's agreement with "the people," as he beholds this "tragedy," and is impressed by "the undoubted virtue of the franklin's mind" (18). That is, Rosader begins by aligning himself with the aggrieved (but patient) franklin, as though he might be fighting for the honor of the Reformed Church and its martyrs as much as for this man. We never find out if this would be enough motivation to bring him victory. Rosader leaps into the "lists" and this affords him a view of the "troop of ladies that glistered there like the stars of heaven" (19). Enter "Love": "Love, willing to make him as amorous as he was valiant, presented him with the sight of Rosalind, whose admirable beauty so inveigled the eye of Rosader, that forgetting himself, he stood and fed his looks on the favour of Rosalind's face" (19). This makes her blush, which "doubles" her "beauteous excellence," and presumably its effect on Rosader. The experience seems entirely to displace the sympathy for the martyred franklin that was his first motivation, along with its civic nature—participating in the sympathy of the crowd. As the scene progresses, Lodge attempts to integrate the two, but as he does so, we continue to mix religious and erotic and civic impulses: in language familiar from Lyly's narratives, we hear that Rosader is ready to worship "his saint."[35] On one level, that is a straightforward Petrarchan claim, which might also participate in the more problematic and aggressive valences of Petrarchism.[36] But on another level, in this context, the phrase raises the question of what comes next: should Rosader passively worship Rosalind from afar, and never act on his desires? Should Rosader martyr himself with the Norman, turn the other cheek before his violence, and allow the moral case against him to grow concomitantly?

Lodge invests a great deal of description and psychological analysis into the scene, but it ends indeterminately. At the start, seeing Rosalind in fact does not lead directly either to action or submission but rather appears as gross distraction. The Norman is forced to shake Rosader by the shoulder in order to break what Lodge describes as Rosader's "*memento*," a sort of state of thunderstruckness that in Shakespeare happens after the combat is over and Orlando is unable to give a reply to Rosalind's compliments.[37] It is being

---

[35] See e.g. Euphues in conversation with Lucilla: "Euphues (being rapt with the sight of his saint) answered ..." (56).

[36] See chapter 1, "Active and Passive Art."

[37] This is a very odd term, used only otherwise by Greene and Nashe, according to the *OED*, and as the *OED* alerts us appears at the start of several passages in the Latin Bible as well as other "liturgical passages."

disturbed from this state that launches Rosader into the fight. All consideration of the franklin and his dead sons disappears; rather it is Rosader's anger
that his reverie in contemplating Rosalind has been broken. Lodge adds several more layers of motivation to the scene, including doubt attributed to
"the people" about whether Rosader, a man of self-evidently "high thoughts"
should be involved in the wrestling's "base action," as well as some thoughts
in Rosader also of his father's reputation and the honor of his "house," before the scene comes to its violent resolution: Rosader "roused himself and
threw the Norman against the ground, falling upon his chest with so willing
a weight, that the Norman yielded nature her due, and Rosader the victory"
(20).

In Shakespeare's version of the scene, Orlando's success signals that the
usurping duke's reign is vulnerable—the fall of the state's champion is a
proxy for the weakness of the state, and the duke sees it as such, at least
when he knows that the winner is from a dissenting family. Here, on the
contrary, Rosader's victory seems to ease us from the "murmur" precipitated by the death of the franklin's sons—it seems a political boon for the
regime. And what of Rosader's motivation, the power on which he draws
for his victory? Lodge calls it "love": what it looks like is a contemplation of
a "heavenly" beauty that is literally on high. That contemplation is capable of
mesmerizing Rosader into unworldliness, and indeed seems to have nothing
to do with bodies "coping," "clapping," crushing, or "rousing" themselves in
any way other than longing upward toward the heavenly. And yet all that
"base action" is somehow connected to the "high thoughts." How? It seems
that bodies clasped together, straining to wrest the life from one another,
is being submitted to us as a substantiation of the heavenly desire, a way of
satisfying the longing it produces—through some combination of frustrated
physicality or the "glory" of one body mastering another.

With all the layers of psychology and motivation that Lodge adds—
slathers perhaps—on the scene, it is notably free of mythological reference.
But we will note that the dynamic of attraction and embrace, of thought
and action, is another way of reading the two myths to which Lodge is re-
peatedly drawn: Ixion desires (basely) an actual goddess, and embraces a
false substantiation of her; Odysseus is drawn toward the divine song of the
Sirens, which if he were able to follow, would result in a violent embrace
indeed. And we might as well keep Pygmalion in the mix too, transgres-
sively drawn toward his own inanimate creation, only to embrace it as it is
endued with life. To this set of possible relations, the wrestling scene invests
Christian resonance, and resonance with contemporary religious struggle.

We see violence classified as a potential "massacre" of the faithful; we are brought into the moral zone of the martyr, of wondering if the best Christian response to violence and threat and force is with passive acceptance; and we wonder whether "high thoughts"—of a religious champion who receives support and motivation from a "saint"—receive almost supernatural force in crushing an opponent who is motivated by greed. And if that is what has happened, if Rosalind has been the conduit for divine support, then that would of course be a significant counter to Sir John's misogyny, that women are only to be feared and loathed. All of these components will remain in play as we turn to the bizarre breakfast that Rosader's brother hosts for his friends.

The wrestling scene involves Rosalind in a complex process of motivation and substantiation of possibly divine energies. It also invokes the language of martyrdom even as it sets aside a martyr's passivity in favor of the violent overthrowing of the persecutor. In this process, Rosalind seems to play a Siren-like role, but emanating virtue or inspiration to high or heroic deeds. But Lodge does not make that connection explicitly—either to the Sirens or to Sir John's misogynist precepts. The plot line in which this does happen is the one that follows Rosader's evil brother Saladyne on his path to redemption. As we will see, Saladyne is not the only character redeemed here: so too is Sir John himself, whose message of fear and hatred is posthumously converted into one of "golden principles of brotherly concord," and explicitly a Sirens' song of "philosophical harmony" that Sir John urges his sons to hearken to. In that case there is another name we can give for the redemption: nostalgic lying.

As with Shakespeare, following the failed plot to kill his troublesome younger brother in the wrestling match, the aggrieved older brother is driven to more extreme means to try to dispense with Rosader. When Saladyne comes to the conclusion that he must act directly against his brother, he rises one morning, "very early," gets some servants, and grabs Rosader out of his bed. Then, "in the midst of his hall" Rosader is "chained ... to a post" (52). In response to questioning about the cause of this treatment, Saladyne answers only "with a look of disdain," and gives orders that Rosader is to receive neither food nor drink. This goes on for "two or three days." We might also note that there seems to be no provision for Rosader to accomplish the natural offices of excretion, though Lodge's narrator doesn't mention it. Still, there has to be a reasonable sense of the cruelty of such a punishment, especially if, as seems the intention, it ends in Rosader's death. Then, as if this isn't enough, Saladyne seeks a wider audience, a group which Adam Spencer—who is the original for the faithful servant of the same name in Shakespeare's play, and who supplies Rosader with secret provisions during this period— describes as "all your kindred and allies" (53). Saladyne invites these to "a solemn breakfast" in the same hall in which Rosader is tied, and he tells everyone who comes that his brother is mad, "and fain to be tied to a post" (53). It is at that point that we can recognize that we have entered a version of the Sirens story, with Rosader playing the role of Ulysses.

And this is true in more ways than are apparent to the breakfast guests: one aspect of Rosader's link with Ulysses is that by this point he is actually restrained willingly. When Adam comes one night and gives Rosader refreshment he also frees him from his chains, and after considering immediate revenge, Adam convinces him to follow a different, much stranger course. Adam tells him about Saladyne's plans for the breakfast, and suggests that he should "complain to them of the abuse proffered to you by Saladyne. If they redress you, why so: but if they pass over your plaints *sicco pede*, and hold with the violence of your brother before your innocence, then thus" (53), the "thus" being that he will leave him unlocked, leave some poleaxes conveniently placed in the hall, and when Adam gives "a wink" the two will grab the weapons and, in a striking invocation of Butlerian gender performance, "play the men, and make havoc amongst them" (53). Before that, he will be playing Ulysses—voluntarily restraining himself—and also playing the Sirens, singing a reasonable song begging for mercy which if the hearers ignore, will result in their violent death. Why would Rosader's kindred and allies not listen to him? Lodge provides just two explanations: Saladyne's generosity with this sumptuous breakfast, and his brazen cover story. Saladyne ingratiates himself with the guests "with courteous and curious entertainment, as they all perceived their welcome to be great" (54). As for Rosader, he is introduced "as a man lunatic." Hospitality coupled with that charge of lunacy seems enough. When Rosader attempts to win this group over to his plight, he finds his efforts "in vain," for "they had stopped their ears with Ulysses, that were his words never so forceable, he breathed only his passions into the wind" (54). Lodge's mistake here seems genuine, and a mark of the hasty production of the book—because of course Ulysses is the only human being in this story who does *not* stop his ears. But it is also a welcome development in the spirit of queer mythography, a pleasing reshuffling of the elements of the myth, which, as we will see, Lodge continues to make use of as we follow Saladyne's redemptive path.

The reshuffle also places Rosader for the second time close to the role of Christian martyr—the role he decides to play prior to "playing the man." In the wrestling scene his first impulse was recognizing the patient fortitude of the franklin watching the deaths of his sons, which them moves him to risk his life against steep odds. At this breakfast, for a time, he resembles Christ on the cross, heckled by unsympathetic onlookers. Except of course that he then frees himself and slaughters a good portion of those onlookers, and then sits down with Adam to partake of some of the remaining breakfast courses. When Saladyne returns with a posse, the two make a violent escape and end up in the forest to meet Rosalind and commence the book's pastoral phase. We will return to that phase shortly. For now, let us stick with Saladyne.

Saladyne's redemption follows the general path of what we find in Shakespeare's play, but where in the play that redemption is accomplished by report of events that have already taken place, narrated by Oliver, the Saladyne character, to Rosalind and Celia (a scene at the center of my analysis of *As You Like It* in chapter 4), here it is simply narrated. Saladyne has been banished and is wandering through the forest. Rosader comes upon him asleep and threatened by a lion (Shakespeare adds a serpent). Rosader is at first tempted to kill Saladyne or leave him to the lion, but upon misremembering his father's advice, he changes course. He addresses himself: "Did not thy father at his last gasp breathe out this golden principle: Brothers' amity is like the drop of balsamum, that salveth the most dangerous sores? Did he make a large exhort unto concord, and wilt thou show thyself careless?" (96). No, he did not. Then again, after being rescued, but before he recognizes his brother in his rustic garb, Saladyne reports the same "principle," this time as nothing less than an unheeded Sirens' song: he should have been kinder to his brother, he admits,

> having two brethren committed by my father at his death to my charge, with such golden principles of brotherly concord, as might have pierced like the Sirens' melody into any human ear. But I, with Ulysses, became deaf against his philosophical harmony, and made more value of profit than of virtue, esteeming gold sufficient honor, and wealth the fittest title for a gentleman's dignity. (98–9)

The first mistake of arrangement of plot elements of the Sirens story seemed a genuine mistake, but here that mistake is linked with a radical rewriting of the framing scene of the book. Saladyne claims he became deaf with Ulysses, but Ulysses was never deaf; the Sirens' song was poetic, but it was never "philosophical harmony," and Sir John's advice on his deathbed sowed fraternal discord, fear of sexuality, and hatred of women—women cast as sirenic monsters whose beauty lures men to disaster like the Sirens' songs. One searches that scene in vain for any sign of "golden principles of brotherly concord." As we follow the Saladyne plot to its conclusion, we will see one more turn of these elements as Saladyne completes his redemption and enters into marriage.

The chief contrast in the courtship of Saladyne and Alinda (masquerading as the shepherdess Aliena) with that of Rosader and Ganymede, is that, first, it is relatively brief, and second that it is much more action-oriented than the long-unfolding discourse between the other characters. With that said, it is still lengthy compared to the lightning flash of Shakespeare's play. There is a solo meditation by Aliena, and then when they meet, Aliena gets Saladyne to read the love poem he has tucked in his shirt. There is some semi-interpretive discussion ("descant" [127]) of the poem, but beyond that the resemblance ends: when Aliena trots out some arguments skeptical of male erotic-aesthetic eloquence, Saladyne responds by saying that he wants her to marry him, "to consummate my faithful desires in the honourable end of marriage" (131), and the end of the scene is in fact their physical union of a sort, "as they strained one another's hand" (132), which broadcasts to the nearby Ganymede that the dialogue has ended in "a match" (132).

The ending comes after a return to some of the criticisms of poetic eloquence that had earlier been deployed by Aliena and Ganymede, this time charging that poetry is more about displaying "quickness of the wit" (129), as Saladyne puts it, or that courtiers' discursive wooing was more "to discover their eloquence" (126) as Aliena puts it. To this is initially opposed, more authentic, "naked" speech. Saladyne describes it this way:

> since I became a forester, Love hath taught me such a lesson that I must confess his deity and dignity, and say as there is nothing so precious as beauty, so there is nothing more piercing than fancy. For since first I arrived at this place, and mine eye took a curious survey of your excellence, I have been so fettered with your beauty and virtue, as, sweet Aliena, Saladyne without further circumstance loves Aliena. I could paint out my desires with long ambages; but seeing in many words lies mistrust, and that truth is ever naked, let this suffice for a country wooing, Saladyne loves Aliena, and none but Aliena. (129)

Despite the nakedness of this declaration, we are told that "these words were the most heavenly harmony in the ears of the shepherdess" (129). Is Sir John rolling over in his grave? It seems so, but it is left to Aliena to invoke the Sirens to her aid: "If such Sirens sing, we poor women had need stop our ears, lest in hearing we prove so foolish hardy as to believe them, and so perish in trusting much and suspecting little" (130). So had Gosson urged the women of England, to preserve their virtue, and preserve the state against the vicious onslaught of effeminizing discourses, pastimes, and melodies. But at the end of *Rosalynde*, these honest erotic notes might as well be "philosophical harmonies": Saladyne giving himself over to his love of Aliena, and the two of them confessing their passion in an erotic "shrift" is nothing less than the final phase of the brother's redemption and return into a community that has escaped the most dangerous and lethal of fraternal strife.

"Shrift" in this context again appears as daringly religious language, but it is not the most daring moment of Lodge's engagement with religious imagery and iconography, as we merge the language of myth and the language of religion, and replace Sir John's Christian terror at sexuality with a liturgy that includes a woman priest and is overseen by Rosalind, cross-dressed as Ganymede, and transubstantiated into Rosalind once more.

Queer theology: a wedding feast

If the fraternal strife between Saladyne and Rosader is a proxy for the political and religious strife convulsing France in this period, and smoldering in England, what is it exactly that Lodge is offering his readers as a cure? And if *Rosalynde* is a step in a biography of poetry that is also a step in the reception of Virgilian pastoral into English, where is it that the book ultimately arrives? My sense is that the answer to both questions may be the same. As I discussed in chapter 1, the twin challenges of Virgilian pastoral to Western poets are, first, Virgil's technical sophistication, in the context of a language that works very differently from European vernaculars, and second, the poetry's frank homoeroticism. *Rosalynde* is a book that begins by telescoping to relatively simple misogyny a much broader set of fears about sexuality, effeminacy, and aesthetics in the English cultural scene and in Christian culture at large. But eventually most of the complexity is restored: in the final scene I wish to examine, we see Lodge pushing to the limit the elements he is more or less coherently marshalling.

The myth of Ixion once again seems in the background when we arrive at the first place where we get into serious play with Ganymede's disguise. Ganymede asks Rosader for a description of this Rosalind "at the full, as one that hast surveyed all her parts with a curious eye" (70). He obliges her with a conventional but not terrible poem that devotes stanzas to hair, eyes, cheeks, lips, neck, breasts, and then how all these fit nicely together. This makes Ganymede blush, which he explains this way: "it makes me blush to hear how women should be so excellent, and pages so unperfect" (72); to which Rosader replies, "Truly, gentle page, thou hast cause to complain thee wert thou the substance, but resembling the shadow content thyself; for it is excellence enough to be like the excellence of nature" (72). This confusing statement might mean "If you were a woman and looked the way you do, you would have cause for complaint, but you're just a copy of a copy," that boys "resemble the shadows" of women through their lack of masculine features like beards and Adam's apples and lowered voices, all of which is fine. But if you are a woman who looks like a boy then, yes, that is something to complain about.

That Rosader is able to assert all this while staring at the cross-dressed object of all his desire creates irony—he mistakes the "substance" for a copy of a copy—that is enhanced by the argument Ganymede makes in response, which imputes political force to the "substance" to which Rosader refers. "You say that boys can content themselves by being second-order copies of sovereign female beauty," the argument goes, "I say that it's all in the clothing: if boys dressed up as women, they would have all of their beauty and power." And this argument gains strength, sort of, by coming from a woman who has usurped male authority by dressing up as a boy. It is a pretty packed bit of reference and irony, not much given room to breathe or be understood. And where does it lead? What can Rosader see by staring into the eyes of Ganymede, he who resembles a shadow of the ineffable, unembraceable substance of his mistress? It leads, much more clearly and logically than in Shakespeare's play, to a wedding.

In the interim, Rosader is induced to play along with Ganymede and Aliena, and to accept that Ganymede can "play" Rosalind, going a step beyond Shakespeare in that the two join together in a "wooing eclogue" accompanied by Aliena, on recorder. This pastoral-poetic version of Rosalind gives in to Rosader's advances, but the experience leaves the extra-poetic, prose Rosader unsatisfied. "Rosader hath his Rosalynde," he says, but only "as Ixion had Juno" (90). All this stuff is just the "imaginary fruitions of fancy." He feels like the birds that went for "Zuexis' painted grapes," or "Aesop's cock." But yet he still has "hope" that "these feigned affections do divine some unfeigned end" (90). Unfeigned end? Aliena has just the thing: "I'll play the priest: from this day forth Ganymede shall call thee husband, and

thou shall call Ganymede wife, and so we'll have a marriage" (90). "Content,"
quoth both the other two.

Lodge withdraws a bit from the action here and has his narrator comment
on it: "let the forester awhile shape himself to his shadow, and tarry fortune's leisure, till she may make a metamorphosis fit for his purpose" (91).
His shadow? As in the mirror image of his own gender? As in the masculine, secondary-version of Ganymede-to-Rosalind? As in Pygmalion's
plastic shadow awaiting metamorphosis? Not clear. But as we avert our eyes
and ears from the ritual words of marriage, from the "playing" of the priest
that Aliena promises, we look instead at the spectacle of the postnuptial
feasting. Aliena says the wedding "was not worth a pin" unless accompanied by "cheer" and "a cup of wine": "and therefore she willed Ganymede
to set out such cates as they had, and to draw out her bottle, charging
the forester, as he had imagined his loves, so to *conceit these cates* to be a
most sumptuous banquet, and to take a mazer of wine and to drink to his
Rosalynde" (91, my emphasis). This I would argue is the more noteworthy
priest-playing of the scene, and moves us from considerations of "substance"
to the trans-substantial. There is an implied answer for Rosader: if you can
"conceit" this food into sumptuous fare, then you can conceive Ganymede
as/into your wife. Aliena's suggestion of a wedding also presents the ceremony as a conduit for sexual desire—just as, I suggested, Lodge seemed to
indicate the violence of the wrestling could be. Here, however, the symbolic
and euphemistic qualities of the marriage ceremony are made that much
more emphatic, even as it is drawn closer, in the accompanying feast, to
the last supper and the conceit of cates and wine. In any case, Lodge seems
acutely interested in where desire leads and how it works: whether to a crush
of bodies, or a doubling-down of imagination, fancy, conceit, or into an
aporetic house of mirrors where substance is shadow and shadow substance.
Is violence between men a symptom of unrequited desire for women? Are
weddings as much playful "conceits" of real relations of amity as pretend-
ing that simple rustic fare is a sumptuous feast? When people embrace each
other erotically, are they drawn to difference or similarity? When men embrace each other, is this the more "substantial" form of amity, or does it
"shadow" the love of men and women? And how substantial is the love of the
divine that also underwrites the Ixion myth, and underwrites the conceptual
feasting that follows the mock wedding?

It is a striking proliferation of questions. Compared with the cognitive disruption caused by this mock wedding, the sort of lightness contemplated in

earlier discussion and surrounding lyric poetry seems quite tame. We have seen women in the throes of erotic desire managing that desire through discursive means, and poetry-songs an important component of this. In a discussion with an amorous and poetically inclined young man, a further lightness was pursued, finding balance between depth of feeling and rational control. All of that seems like quite a serious response to Calvin and Augustine, and the more hysterical Gosson, and the misogynistically telescoped anxiety of the paterfamilias Sir John. So this attempts to meet objections to the non-rational aesthetic, to music and beauty that can stir passions and beliefs in men and women, at least on the level of their erotic attraction. But what beyond? What about the association of aesthetic-erotic engagements and virtuous action? The story here is more mixed. Saladyne's virtuous transformation is very much about becoming open to beauty, to the natural world, to art, and to love. It is not clear precisely where this "golden harmony" of brotherly concord and its aesthetic-erotic accompaniments figure in his transformation, though it seems like being stripped of his worldly pretensions, his hope of taking his father's place and dominating his brothers, and becoming a penniless exile, is a necessary preparation for the rest of the change. And so the father's precious advice remains precious, but is utterly transformed. With Rosader, who begins as a virtuous young man with a penchant for martyrdom, it is less clear what transformation occurs, or what transformation for the good.

The first substantiation of his desire for Rosalind is crushing the body of the Duke's champion wrestler. Deep into a seductive discourse with his cross-dressed beloved we seem to go further into moral complexities without easy resolutions. How much is love a self-reflective exercise? How much can he hope that his desire, once fulfilled, will continue? The writing pushes us closer to the contradiction of physical desire behind all this: what is the relationship between the "height" of love, of fancy, of natural beauty, all that is and could be the Sirens' song, to the crush of bodies toward which it tends? What is that relationship when we see gender as performance, as a role a man or woman or boy or girl might play? And finally, how does all this reflect back upon the sacrament of marriage, the union of spirit and body grudgingly sanctioned by what casts itself as the ultimate moral authority? What if this is revealed to be just another kind of "play" around what this culture is too uncomfortable to face as it is? And what of the extraordinary resonances between this sacred joining of bodies and the even more central actions and rituals of Christianity?—the embodiment of deity, the union of

believers with the blood and body of the Christ. It is a physical union that relies on "fancy" for its accomplishment, on the tools of poets and artists (and
false seducers and false prophets): conceit. It is an action all right, an action
of the mind, an action of desire and against all reasonable reservations or
doubts.

It remains uncertain at the end of *Rosalynde* how much of this Lodge himself had clearly in view, and how much is the accidental, felicitous product
of the elements that he stirred together in hot pursuit of a literary success
riding on the coattails of Lyly's *Euphues*. But nonetheless what the book
offers us for the overall project of this study is considerable. To return to
language of technical history and biography, we get a multidimensional Rosalind as a counter to Elizabethan misogyny tied to cultural and religious
suspicion of art. This Rosalind is able to appreciate poetry and music, to
compose her own, and quite specifically to engage poetry as a way of managing passions—the opposite of being a helpless victim before their corrupting
power. Instead, she performs a version of that "lightness" so often used to
accuse women of weakness and vulnerability, but lightness that appears as
flexibility and insouciance and self-awareness, an aid to virtue in an unpredictable world. With Rosalind cross-dressed as Ganymede, Lodge goes
further, highlighting the performative quality of gender full stop. Where
in Spenser, we saw E.K. terrified by the "disorderly love" of Virgil's second eclogue, in *Rosalynde*, pagan myths provide structures specifically to
interrogate Christian morality, especially about sex. What I have called
Lodge's queer mythography—his repeated, varied citation of the Sirens, of
Ixion—ends up casting the central figures of Christian iconography in their
problematic and interchangeable roles.

And finally, Lodge's book is surprisingly forward in its engagement with
the France of its time, of the search for "concord" amid the endless slow
grind of sectarian conflict. To this Rosalind herself may offer something as
well, as a kind of myth to place beside those ancient ones that Lodge and
his Elizabethan contemporaries were so fond of repeating. In the book's historical engagement is perhaps an answer at the national security level to the
argument made by Gosson about art and women as risking the fate of the
nation. Far from the leading edge of moral collapse, could the virtuous lightness of a woman like Rosalind actually be the key to escape from the endless
conflict submerging France? That would mean that an irreverent display of
the queerness of the fundamental structure of religion and national belief
might actually be the key to escaping sectarian conflict while also doing

nothing to lower the nation's preparedness to resist invasion—a virtuous lightness that saves a nation from itself.

Coda: Making Fun of Phoebe

If Gosson followed Lodge this far, one presumes, he would not feel comforted—nor would Calvin or Augustine. But if there is a limit to Lodge's radical thinking, it is around the love between women. In Lodge's Arden, the only person who really suffers for love is Phoebe, and by suffering I don't mean falling into the sort of melancholy that allows one to get a lot of poetry writing done—lots of people in *Rosalynde* experience that. What Phoebe experiences is an entirely different degree of love-suffering: she is made physically ill to the point of death. But in the face of this extreme of suffering, the text is remarkably unsympathetic. Rosalind and Alinda, in fact, find the whole thing to be quite a joke, to the point of making more overt anatomical jokes than they did about forest poets' pens. Hearing about her mortal illness and receiving her love poetry, the two fall "into a great laughter" and Aliena whispers to Ganymede, "Knew Phoebe what want there were in thee to perform her will, and how unfit thy kind is to be kind to her, she would be more wise, and less enamoured" (138). The more generous interpretation of this is that it is a concession to the moralists, or a demonstration of the limits of what Lodge thought he could get away with in an age of censorship and potential danger for writers. The less generous interpretation is that Lodge sees something fundamentally distinct and inferior in the potential of love relationship between women and other women. This will be an important point to revisit once we come to Shakespeare's Arden. But for now all one can say is that Aliena in that moment seems to have missed all of the lessons of the preceding book, with respect to wisdom and love, with respect to "fitness" in the less obscene sense. And indeed, though Rosalind and Aliena do not acknowledge it and seem to enjoy Phoebe's pain, Phoebe herself is given a poem that might answer them if they could listen.

Phoebe's "scornful warble" references one of the key examples of women betrayed by the false promises of men—in this case Phyllis, who is all the more appropriate for a shepherdess since the name is also a standard one in classical pastoral.

Down a down,
    Thus Phyllis sung,
        By fancy once distressed;
Whoso by foolish love are stung
    Are worthily oppressed.
        And so sing I. With a down, down, &c.

When Love was first begot,
    And by the mover's will
Did fall to human lot
    His solace to fulfil,
Devoid of all deceit,
    A chaste and holy fire
Did quicken man's conceit,
    And women's breast inspire.
The gods that saw the good
    That mortals did approve,
With kind and holy mood
    Began to talk of Love.

Down a down
    Thus Phyllis sung
        By fancy once distressed, &c.
    But during this accord,
        A wonder strange to hear,
    Whilst Love in deed and word
        Most faithful did appear,
    False-semblance came in place,
        By Jealousy attended,
    And with a double face
        Both love and fancy blended;
    Which made the gods forsake,
        And men from fancy fly,
    And maidens scorn a make,
        Forsooth, and so will I.

> Down a down,
>> Thus Phyllis sung,
>>> By fancy once distressed;
> Who so by foolish love are stung
>> Are worthily oppressed.
>>> And so sing I.
> With down a down, a down down, a down a.
>>>>> (118–19)

It is not completely clear that this is the Phyllis associated with Demophoon referenced earlier in the book, that one who appears in the *Heroides* and *Legend of Good Women*. The reasoning here is etiological and metaphysical, and perhaps Christian, in the sense that Phoebe references a sort of prelapsarian love devoid of falseness. The introduction of "fancy" as a term to describe what is mixed with the original pure love to make it "double" and "false" and associated with jealousy is interesting and confusing.

It is hard not at least to consider "false-semblance" in light of what is about to occur: namely that Phoebe will be answered, momentarily, by the eavesdropping Ganymede, or, as Lodge's narrator will soon dub him, "the amorous girl-boy" (123). But what would be the implication of linking this general "falseness" and unpredictability of love, its inherent risk, with the Rosalind-Ganymede figure? That would be problematic especially since for Lodge, the "falseness" of Ganymede's ambiguous gender seems a tool by which to discredit conventional misogyny, and promote "concord" with respect to Eros as well as relations between "brothers"—both within the family and within the body politic. It is hard not to wonder as well whether the falseness and jealousy that has infected Eros may have rendered heterosexual relationships unsalvageable, and whether this poem might in fact be opening up the way for same-sex relationships to substitute for heterosexual relationships because, roughly, of their lack of worldly baggage. Note how, in the first stanza, the "chaste and holy fire" of passion is entertained for both men and women, without saying that it links them. As well, the stanza gestures toward Eros resulting not in sex, but in virtuous action, or rather, virtuous thought: it "quicken[s] man's conceit" and "women's breast inspire[s]." The poem does not get into details, but it surely isn't difficult to see same-sex relationships as potentially free of the corruptions that plague heterosexual lovers, marriage negotiations, and the like, never mind the even more disturbing questions at the heart of the marriage ceremony and the church itself.

In Shakespeare's version, to which we are about to turn, the mock wedding goes by with much less emphasis, while Phoebe is a more significant character, and a poem she writes is the vehicle that brings to a breaking point Rosalind's impulse to gather tyrannical power to herself. Phoebe is also a figure in a play that develops the relationship between its two principal female characters in a very different way, and in the context of other Shakespeare representations of female friendship like that of Hermia and Helena in *A Midsummer Night's Dream*.[38] A moment of special intensity in that relationship, between Rosalind and Celia, comes after the Duke banishes Rosalind:

> Shall we be sundered? Shall we part, sweet girl?
> No, let my father seek another heir!
> Therefore devise with me how we may fly,
> Whither to go and what to bear with us,
> And do not seek to take your change upon you
> To bear your griefs yourself and leave me out.
> For by this heaven, now at our sorrows pale,
> Say what thou canst, I'll go along with thee.
>
> (1.3.95–102)

And perhaps most resonantly with the scene of *Rosalynde*, Ruth's speech to Naomi, here in the Geneva version:

> Entreat me not to leave thee, nor to depart from thee: for whither thou goest, I will go: and where thou dwellest, I will dwell: thy people shall be my people, and thy God my God.
> Where thou diest, will I die, and there will I be buried. The Lord do so to me and more also, if ought but death depart thee and me. (Ruth 1:16–17)

If Lodge uses Rosalind to develop a notion of fraternal concord that might save a country from sinking into internecine conflict, Shakespeare in *As You Like It* seems to have in his ears this vow of a woman to a woman at the start of his play.

---

[38] Valerie Traub emphasizes these relationships as having more to say about lesbian desire than the situations produced by cross-dressing, in *The Renaissance of Lesbianism in Early Modern England* (Cambridge: Cambridge University Press, 2002), 171.

4

Shakespeare's Rosalind

Homoeroticism, Tyranny, and Pastoral Concord

The time has come to return to 1600, to the moment when Jaques—one of
the new characters Shakespeare brings to Lodge's Arden—can hear someone speak in blank verse and lose his temper, to the moment when our
technical history of Rosalind and our biography of poetry arrive at their Elizabethan conclusion. And at last, having spent time with Spenser's passive
poetics, shadow-Rosalind, and technical struggles, as well as with Lodge's
greatly expanded Rosalind and queer mythography, we get to return to this
much more familiar territory and see where we are. I also promised a few
things when we started out in chapter 1. I promised that we would see something of a restaging or rematch of Rosalind's takedown of Colin Clout in the
"Januarye" eclogue of *The Shepheardes Calender*. I promised that the project
of the translation of Virgilian pastoral into Elizabethan poetry would be
brought to another level in Shakespeare, that we would arrive at some version of the telos of Virgilian poetic sophistication longed for in 1579—even
if we do not get clear of the sexual hang-ups that Virgil provokes upon translation. I promised that we would see the arrival of the Rosalind with which
the world has fallen in love—at least some version of that Rosalind, keeping
in mind that we would have to wait until the eighteenth century for her to
begin her career as a star vehicle for actors. But I promised that we would see
her freedom and agency reach new heights, as well as her power as a critical
thinker and incisive satirist.

And so that is what we now set about doing. The structure of this chapter
is similar to previous ones in that its two major sections correspond to the
two major projects of this book. The first section, the technical history of
Rosalind, focuses on innovations that Shakespeare's Rosalind brings to the
table. The second section, the biography of poetry, traces the threads that
converge in the play's performance of Virgilian pastoral dialogue. Together,
the two sections illuminate the scene that is the culminating moment in the

What Rosalind Likes. Paul J. Hecht, Oxford University Press.
© Paul J. Hecht (2022). DOI: 10.1093/oso/9780192857200.003.0004

history I have been tracing, which takes place in act 4, scene 3. I read this scene as staging a confrontation between a version of feminist agency and critical insight that Rosalind has lately been embodying, but which also has associations with tyranny, and the comparatively quiet Virgilian pastoral, characterized by sympathy and selfless singing. But to get to that moment and perceive the dynamics that I am arguing for will require some work.[1]

Ferocious Rosalind

Devising sports

In Lodge, we are introduced to Rosalind at the wrestling match, seen on high by Rosader, and when we first hear from her, she is already managing her passion for him. In *As You Like It*, we are first introduced to Rosalind and Celia by themselves, before they have met Orlando. And whereas in Lodge, the first relationship we see of Rosalind to poetry is that she improvises a

---

[1] In chapter 3, "The characters of men," I noted the subsidence of interest in cross-dressing and gender destabilization in Shakespearean comedy since the 1990s; this has included arguably a turn away from *As You Like It*. The relative paucity of discussion has been consistent enough to be noted by two critics in recent years. First, quite tartly, by Bruce R. Smith, that, "curiously," for many critics since the 1970, "they *don't* like it," and more then more broadly by William N. West that "the play was largely bypassed by New Historicists" in favor of "darker, more obviously fraught comedies" like *Twelfth Night* and *A Midsummer Night's Dream*. This in Smith, *Phenomenal Shakespeare* (Chichester: Wiley-Blackwell, 2010), 5 and West, *As If: Essays in "As You Like It"* (Earth: Dead Letter Office, BABEL Working Group, 2016), 16. In the 1990s and to an extent afterward, criticism had also been highly concerned with how to address the play's ending. The ending is crucial to Louis Montrose's memorable statement that, as much as the play is "a vehicle for Rosalind's exuberance, it is also a structure for her containment," in Montrose, " 'The Place of a Brother' in *As You Like It*: Social Process and Comic Form," *Shakespeare Quarterly* 32 (1981): 52. Readings focused on homosexuality have tended to push back on that statement, including Bruce R. Smith and Mario DiGangi, and more recently Jeffrey Masten has contributed a reading focusing on textual cruxes and (in a moment resonant with my reading of Spenser's "September") gendered pronouns, wondering if they call more attention to what remains queerly uncontained at the play's marriage-bonanza close. See Smith, *Homosexual Desire in Shakespeare's England: A Cultural Poetics* (Chicago: University of Chicago Press, 1991), 154; DiGangi, *The Homoerotics of Early Modern Drama*, Cambridge Studies in Renaissance Literature and Culture. (Cambridge: Cambridge University Press, 1997), 50–63; and Masten, *Queer Philologies: Sex, Language, and Affect in Shakespeare's Time* (Philadelphia: University of Pennsylvania Press, 2016), 60–5. When Paul Alpers summed up his views and the critical traditions around the play in 1996, he saw critics like Montrose as continuous with skeptical views of the play stretching much farther back, in Alpers, *What Is Pastoral?* (Chicago: University of Chicago Press, 1996), 134. I certainly see my own work as on the side of the play's power and achievement, and I am unimpressed by the forces of containment marshaled by the ending. But my view is that there are aspects of exuberant power and scathing critical vision that have not been fully realized, and thus our understanding of a climactic moment within the play is more important than the constraining power or impotence of the ending.

"madrigal" that aids in passion management and self-understanding, in *As You Like It*, it is much less clear that Rosalind has any special interest in or appreciation of poetry, much less that she would ever write or sing as a response to emotions or "passion." Indeed, her initial view seems much closer to Stephen Gosson's—not, to be sure, Gosson's crusading zeal against Elizabethan culture, but rather his view of the cultural scene, in that she sees poetry as just one of many kinds of diversions, or what she calls "sports."[2] I want to take seriously this low-stakes strain of thought in the play because it helps us to understand key differences between the way Lodge's and Shakespeare's characters encounter poetry in the forest of Arden. It is also an important view of poetry for understanding the other ways that Shakespeare's Rosalind engages with poetry, and the way the expectations of audiences and readers are managed as we make our way to the moments when poetry becomes much more than a diversion. To see how Rosalind and her friends can adopt this view of poetry as a diversion, a low-stakes "sport," we need to link her introductory scene to her first encounters with poetry in the forest of Arden after she has been banished. In terms of her character and technical history, we are developing multiple facets of someone who is also quite capable of thinking with piercing seriousness and political insight. But at this initial stage, Rosalind and her friends look to be embracing a version of virtuous lightness where we might just go ahead and drop the "virtuous"—which is to say that where in Lodge, emotional vulnerability and delight in pleasure in the female characters seemed to be a pointed response to the misogynist terror of Sir John, here similar qualities, appearing outside of any particular misogynist charge, seem more like superficiality full stop.[3]

As Orlando opens the play by bemoaning his insufferable position as oppressed younger brother, Rosalind lets us know immediately that she has reason for unhappiness, in that her father has been banished. Celia reminds her cousin of their love, and, in anticipation of where we will soon find her loyalties lie, urges Rosalind to look to a future in which the usurping duke her father will die, Celia will inherit his position, and will restore Rosalind's. Be happy, she argues, for the blessings that you have (in my love) and those that you will have in the future, and, "therefore," she concludes, "my sweet Rose, my dear Rose, be merry" (1.2.22–23). Rosalind agrees: "From henceforth I will, coz, and devise sports" (24–5). Celia's emotional logic is good but not good enough, Rosalind implies: diversions, "sports," are also required to

---

[2] See chapter 3, "Stoppe your eares."
[3] For virtuous lightness, see chapter 3, "Virtuous lightness, feminine poetic virtue."

keep away the sadness of thinking of her absent father.[4] So the purpose of such sports is diversion and distraction from a reality that if contemplated soberly is not merry at all. Though poetry isn't mentioned here, we can see that from this point of view, poetry would be valuable to the extent that it can succeed in diverting. Whereas in Lodge, Rosalind first seeks to compose poetry as a way of expressing and managing her passions, the desire for sports here implies poetry of the kind described and condemned by Cuddie in "October," "faining" men's follies and rolling in more or less ribald rhymes to Tom Piper's tunes.[5] That is, a means not to extend thought or understanding, but to avoid thinking—cheap escapism. And as well we can say that if poetry is diverting "sport," it is much less likely people are engaged in attempting to improve it, to match or surpass the achievements of ancient poets, and one person's view is as good as another: good poetry is poetry that works for you, for helping you ignore your particular problems, nothing more.

That is a view of poetry that we might posit from the concept of "sport" as diversion or escapism, but when Rosalind follows her promise to "devise sports" with an opening suggestion, "what think you of falling in love?" (25), it is clear that we are not going to stay in the realm of card games and street spectacles. Celia responds to Rosalind that this is a fine idea, but only "to make sport withal," as in, to demote to the level of sport, and avoid any but superficial relations that "with the safety of a pure blush thou mayst in honour come off again" (26, 28–9). So no love that might penetrate to the level of the relationships that matter—Celia, Rosalind's father—and, we hardly need add, sex would be out of the question. The "pure blush" here is sexual, but sexual in its denotation of sexual innocence.[6] The other phrase Celia uses to describe this love is more straightforward: love away, as long as you "love no man in good earnest" (26–7). Before the end of the scene, though, Rosalind will have observed Orlando, that "excellent young man" (204), and been captivated enough to tell him "Sir, you have wrestled well and overthrown / More than your enemies" (243–4). The result of this is that we do not know how serious Rosalind is here, how much her love is "in good earnest." And one of the places where this instability plays out is in the first encounters of

---

[4] For "sport" in its Elizabethan sense as "diversion, see *OED*, s.v. "sport," I.i.a., "diversion, entertainment, fun."

[5] See chapter 2, "Passive poetics."

[6] The blush is a physical marker of a state very difficult to determine otherwise; but Celia's confidence that a "pure blush" can be distinguished from an impure is undermined by the ambivalent reception of Hero's blush in *Much Ado About Nothing*, 4.1.

our trio of banished courtly ladies and clown with the pastoral poetry and "pageant" of Arden.

When Rosalind first encounters a literary spectacle, she likes it, and indeed professes to like it because she sees in it a reflection of her own love-sorrow, the depth of her love. So at first it seems as though "the literary" as encountered in Arden might not qualify as "sport," might focus attention on painful realities rather than acting as a pleasant diversion. But this isn't the case—rather, Rosalind displays easy approbation of the "relatable" here—the poetic display of lovers' passion she encounters is generally reminiscent of her own feelings, but that is as far as it goes. In act 2, scene 4, Rosalind, Celia, and Touchstone have arrived in the forest of Arden; in Lodge, they first encounter some written lyric poetry by Montanus before coming upon shepherds in verse dialogue. In *As You Like It*, the dialogue is what happens first, with Silvius (Montanus's replacement) protesting his desperate love, Corin counseling patience, and Silvius insisting that he can't possibly understand the depth of his passion, since Corin is old. After Silvius rushes offstage crying "O Phoebe, Phoebe, Phoebe," Rosalind responds, continuing in verse: "Alas, poor shepherd, searching of thy wound, / I have by hard adventure found mine own" (41–2). That might sound like the beginning of a Lodgean period of straight, admiring response, if what we knew of Rosalind did not already teach us to be suspicious of such apparent plainness. But this is immediately followed by a contrasting response from Touchstone:

> And I mine. I remember, when I was in love I broke my sword upon a stone and bid him take that for coming a-night to Jane Smile; and I remember the kissing of her batlet and the cow's dugs that her pretty chopped hands had milked; and I remember the wooing of a peascod instead of her, from whom I took two cods, and, giving her them again, said with weeping tears "Wear these for my sake." We that are true lovers run into strange capers. But as all is mortal in nature, so is all nature in love mortal in folly. (43–52)

This is a riddling speech, teasingly pornographic, presenting an unsorted catalog of swords, batlets, dugs, cods, and "mortal folly." If the sexual content remains elusive, its effect on the scene is easier to register: Touchstone undermines the apparent seriousness of Rosalind's ability to "relate" to the shepherd's passion. But there is no evidence Rosalind takes much offence at this—on the contrary, her response to Touchstone is "Thou speak'st wiser than thou art ware of" (53), before repeating that she relates to the shepherd's passion. Celia notes that she is still hungry, and the entire episode feels finally like just more diversion, more sport, here observing literary shepherds doing what we expect of pastoral, and having unproblematically diverse reactions or non-reactions to what they see and hear.

Rosalind is certainly far away from Spenser's Rosalind here, and her sweeping rejection of all "shepherds devise"—on the contrary, she likes shepherds' diverting devices, but only as amusements, appropriate instantiations of her desire to "devise sports." This is a marked contrast as well with the initial stance of Lodge's women: indeed, the satire of phallic egomania that characterizes their first reception of pastoral poetry seems to have its only remnant in Touchstone's bawdry—much lower-stakes, and very difficult to see as in any way feminist. That contrast continues as the group encounters actual poems in Arden.

This happens in act 3, scene 2, where Rosalind, Celia, and Touchstone handle, read aloud, and criticize two poems by Orlando that they have found attached to trees. There is no sense that the poems are bad because they fail in their deeper objectives, in this case to praise Rosalind, but rather because they are boring and metrically uninventive, and perhaps rough and unrefined. I already tipped my hand on this matter in chapter 3: where in Spenser, Rosalind condemned pastoral poetry categorically, and in Lodge, all the inset poetry in the book is presented as equally fine, here Shakespeare presents deliberate doggerel, as he is quite capable of doing elsewhere both in comedy and tragedy.[7] And where in their responses to Silvius and Corin, the group displayed easy aesthetic diversity, letting everyone's taste be expressed without judgment, here the group displays the arrival of settled poetic sophistication in Elizabethan culture. While we may disagree on the technical meaning of their criticisms, the upshot is clear: all three of them find Orlando's poems to be obviously technically flawed.

This is how their sensibility is displayed: after hearing the first poem that Rosalind reads as she walks on stage, Touchstone makes a remark that has had metrical analysts scratching their heads through the ages, that "it is the right butter-women's rank to market" (94–5).[8] That has been thought to refer to the poem's "gait," in part because his next remark is more obviously

[7] See chapter 3, "The characters of men." For other examples, see Benedick's self-consciously inept versifying in *Much Ado About Nothing*, 5.2 and Hamlet's execrable verses to Ophelia in *Hamlet*, 2.2.

[8] See the selection of comments provided by Richard Knowles in his New Variorum Edition of *As You Like It* (New York: Modern Language Association of America, 1977), 155–6, e.g. Walter Whiter in a commentary from 1794 explaining it as "vulgar uniformity of rhythm" (quoted on 156). Many emendations and explanations have been suggested without, thus far, resolving the issue. Dusinberre's edition notes the additional light cast on butterwomen and their favored

rhythmic: "This is the very false gallop of verses. Why do you infect yourself with them?" (110–11). A gratingly repetitive rhythm, then, to which we can add the monophonic rhyme scheme on "Rosalind." Touchstone provides his own parodic extension to the poem, demonstrating both features, and taking the content in a direction that, as with his reaction to Corin and Silvius, presses the modest, "pure" quality of the original in a bawdy and pornographic direction:

> Winter garments must be lined,
> So must slender Rosalind.
> They that reap must sheaf and bind,
> Then to cart with Rosalind.
> Sweetest nut hath sourest rind,
> Such a nut is Rosalind.
> He that sweetest rose will find
> Must find love's prick—and Rosalind.
>
> (102–9)

Rosalind's own criticisms of the poetry are not so technical: when Celia comes onstage reading a longer poem, Rosalind merely finds it overly pious and boring. "What tedious homily of love," she asks, has the "pulpiter" wearied his audience with (152–3)? Rosalind seemed like she might have found the poem Touchstone roasted to be, at least, mildly pleasing, but she has no patience for the second.

In both cases, we see low-stakes sophistication in the way these people encounter and read poetry, in line with a sense that poetry, including the poetry of characteristically literary pastoral scenes, can be a pleasant diversion even as it is received diversely. An eclogue-pageant by some literary shepherds might be diverting, or it might be fuel for bawdy parody; love poems encountered on trees might be cute, and they might be ridiculous or wearying. But they are not going to be profound. As this is a point of view not formed with analytic rigor, nor with much moral force, but is simply an attitude, it may not seem serious enough to merit response. But of course it is, as anyone who has ever faced an undergraduate classroom will attest: the limit of readers' expectations can be exceedingly difficult to shift. And though the play makes little of it, we can see in Jaques's offhand dismissal

forms of expression supplied by Sara Mendelson and Patricia Crawford, *Women in Early Modern England 1550–1720* (Oxford: Oxford University Press, 1998), 210, 212; and Gary Taylor, "Touchstone's Butterwoman," *RES*, NS 32 (1981), 187–93.

of Orlando in act 4, scene 1, when he responds to Orlando's friendly, but metrical, greeting with "Nay then, God b'wi' you an you talk in blank verse" (28–9), it is a short step from Touchstone's brand of literary criticism to one that would condemn the verse form upon which Shakespeare's entire poetic output is built.[9] And a short step from there to "oh it's in poetry: I don't like poetry, so it's not for me"—a loose, low-stakes commitment can lead to a broad, categorical condemnation.

Jaques's dismissal was of course what I used to start off this entire enterprise, connecting it with Spenser's Rosalind and her categorical dismissal of pastoral "devise." I am arguing then that seeing poetry as sport and diversion is what is behind the particular flavor of "fury" Jaques displays there: it is fury at boredom, at not being properly diverted. It is nothing like the fury that might underwrite the feminist zeal of Lodge's characters, pressing back on misogyny and hypocrisy—at least, not in these scenes, not in these encounters with poetry and literary spectacle. But it is nonetheless one component of Rosalind's technical history that in *As You Like It*, Rosalind can at times inhabit this attitude of sophistication verging on snobbery, breezy skepticism next to self-indulgence that also borders on ennui and bawdry and fury displayed in the attitudes of her companions—a "lightness" where presence or lack of "virtuous" is at the least not an object of concern. That is one important component of what *As You Like It* brings us.

But from almost the same moment—the "urban" scene that introduces us to Rosalind and Celia and Touchstone, we also find a strand of satiric and critical thought which, although the stakes certainly seem lower at first, is finally as ferocious as anything we have seen in Spenser and Lodge, and that is what we will examine next.

Pancakes and mustard

The same scene that introduces us to Rosalind and to the light, sporting, and sophisticated attitude in her and her friends, and which later gets shown off in her encounters with literary shepherds and forest-poems, also has a different phase that jokes its way into a serious incursion into the relative stability of the truth, thence into the instability of who gets to decide what is true,

---

[9] G. B. Shaw seems to agree with Jaques as he largely condemns the blank verse in this play relative to its prose and, for example, suggests that much of Rosalind's popularity comes from the fact that she speaks relatively little verse. See "Toujours Shakespeare," in Harold Bloom, ed., *Bloom's Shakespeare Through the Ages: "As You Like It"* (New York: Infobase, 2008), 93.

and along with that, the instability of social position and identity itself, and finally the politics of all this. This produces something that I would like to call knowledge, and include in the sense I am building of "what Rosalind knows," crucial in this phase of her technical history. But to do this, I have to make a side-argument for what kinds of knowledge Shakespeare's characters display passively, particularly his female characters. For Shakespeare's women, knowledge can be displayed through small signs and short speeches in scenes and plays where men speak at much greater length. This is not a surprising phenomenon in a patriarchal culture that often explicitly values silence in women.[10] The example I use to support this idea of knowledge is of Gertrude, a woman of few words but great understanding.

Of course, Rosalind is no Gertrude—on the contrary, Rosalind speaks more than almost any other female character in Shakespeare's plays, and enough to put her line-count actually in the running with the largest male roles. But in my view, the early ensemble scene that I want to examine next, led by the clown Touchstone, displays an aspect of what Rosalind knows that is both crucial to understanding her development in the rest of the play, and is also expressed in this indirect manner characteristic of women in the usual patriarchal backdrop to Shakespeare.

The part of the scene I want to examine contains a series of binary evaluations, where judgments of taste—literally evaluating food—shift in a flash to judgments of people. When Touchstone approaches Rosalind and Celia in act 1, scene 2, he interrupts their talk about gifts of fortune and nature, and says that Celia must come to her father (odd, since her father is actually on his way to her). Celia asks whether Touchstone was "made the messenger" by the duke, and he replies "No, by mine honor, but I was bid to come for you" (58, 59–60). (The messenger is Monsieur Le Beau, who will arrive presently.) Here it feels as though we are entering the territory of cheeky replies by clever servants, punning, or otherwise exploiting the potential for confusion in sensible questions by their masters (e.g., the Dromios, Grumio, Dogberry). Rosalind protests, however, not the contradictory information Touchstone conveys, but instead the accompanying "by my honor" with which he packages it: "Where learned you that oath, fool?" she asks (61). There is an implied criticism in that question, and it aligns with other, more literarily focused protests elsewhere in the play.[11] Outside of Shakespeare,

---

[10] For a proximate example, see Sir John at the start of Lodge's *Rosalynde*: "chaste, obedient, and silent" (6). See the opening of chapter 3 for the full quotation.

[11] Jaques's protest about blank verse (4.1.28–9) is of course one of these; one might also cite his critique of Orlando's pretty sentimental speech: when Jaques asks Orlando the "stature"

the implied criticism lines up with an entire critical-comic theme in *Every Man In His Humour*, where a braggart soldier, Bobadilla, impresses gulls and appalls the educated with his outlandish oaths, and starts an outbreak of pretentious and affected swearing accompanying every claim from the most inconsequential to the most momentous.[12]

The source of Touchstone's oath, this unnamed knight, sounds a lot like Jonson's Bobadilla. But in any case, it is Touchstone's response to Rosalind's question that leads into a parody of absolutist thinking, and dizzying consideration of parallel binary judgments. Touchstone says he learned the oath

> Of a certain knight that swore by his honor they were good pancakes, and swore by his honor the mustard was naught. Now I'll stand to it: the pancakes were naught and the mustard was good, and yet was not the knight forsworn. (62–6)

Touchstone doesn't dispute that the value of mustard and pancakes can be seen in absolute terms, that the mustard is "good" and the pancakes "naught." But he also gamely acknowledges that he lives in a world where another person could come to exactly the opposite conclusion about that truth, get it exactly wrong. And so at first, despite the absoluteness of the evaluations here, we might conclude that we are still in the territory of low-stakes individual judgments that no one will get very exercised about: diversions, sport.

But Rosalind and Celia both find their interest piqued by the riddle that ends the speech: "How prove you that in the great heap of your knowledge?" asks Celia; "Ay, marry, now unmuzzle your wisdom," says Rosalind (67–9).

of Rosalind, he replies, "Just as high as my heart," which provokes this: "You are full of pretty answers. Have you not been acquainted with goldsmiths' wives, and conned them out of rings?" (3.2.261–5). Jonson also focuses satiric energy on the poor quality of the "posy" inscribed in cheap rings in both editions of *Every Man In His Humour*. See Bevington's Quarto, 2.1.24–36.

[12] The theme is intact in both printed versions of the play, including the earlier one thought to have been performed in 1598. For additional discussion of *Every Man In His Humour* and differences between the 1601 Quarto and 1616 Folio, see chapter 1, "Burning Verses." Stephano, 2.3.95, is fascinated with and does his best to imitate the oaths; Lorenzo Sr., the sober-minded father-figure, "like[s] not these affected oaths" when he hears them from the lips of the disguised Musco (2.2.88). Oaths are so general in the play that *not* swearing can become grounds for fervid suspicion, as when Thorello notes in an aside of his servant, "He will not swear. He has some meaning, sure, / Else, being urged so much, how should he choose / But lend an oath to all this protestation?" (3.1.70–2). Bevington discusses the evidence for the earliest performances in his introduction to *The Cambridge Edition of the Works of Ben Jonson*, ed. Bevington (Cambridge: Cambridge University Press, 2012), 1:113.

Touchstone obliges, and his solution is to apply similar absolute evaluation to the knight's honor, to move from judgments of pancakes to people. Touchstone's riddle is answered through an analysis of the oath, funny because the knight certainly didn't intend for the oath to be analyzed—the oath functions as an intensifier, not a serious application of his honor to the matter of the pancakes and mustard. But for Touchstone, the problem of the knight coming to the opposite conclusion to the truth is resolved by the oath: the knight has no honor; therefore swearing by it negates or possibly inverts his judgment: "if you swear by that that is not, you are not forsworn" (74–5). But behind this clever syllogism is something else, namely that whether statements are true or not depends on who is making them. What has been simultaneously introduced is the topic of who has access to the truth, what constitutes, for Elizabethans, a person appropriately authorized to speak and be listened to, to speak and be believed. And what emerges next is increasing attention called to the fact that none of these three speakers have that status.

That attention comes in the form of the "example" that Touchstone uses to demonstrate his logical analysis of the knight's statement:

TOUCHSTONE Stand you both forth now. Stroke your chins, and swear by
    your beards that I am a knave.
CELIA By our beards—if we had them—thou art.
TOUCHSTONE By my knavery—if I had it—then I were. But if you swear by
    that that is not, you are not forsworn. (70–5)

Part of the joke, and the way this "argument" slips beyond its supposed bounds is that we are treated, if the characters follow Touchstone's direction, to the spectacle of these two boy-actors playing women stroking their chins. If we follow the sense of who was authorized to speak truth in Elizabethan society that has been established by scholars like Steven Shapin, then we are led to think that Elizabethan audiences would have understood that we are calling attention to the fact that only gentlemen have full access to the truth, are authorized to speak and not be "forsworn"—that is, one must have a beard, a real one, and be an adult male, and also have status.[13] This

---

[13] See Steven Shapin, *A Social History of Truth: Civility and Science in Seventeenth-Century England* (Chicago: University of Chicago Press, 1994), esp. ch. 3, "A Social History of Truth-Telling: Knowledge, Social Practice, and the Credibility of Gentlemen." For more on beards and masculinity, and their prosthetic nature on the early modern English stage, see Will Fisher,

sense is actuated by Touchstone, but it is also being subjected to satirical and critical pressure. Touchstone shifts us from honor conceived as an absolutely present or absent quality to something, a beard, that seems much more clearly to submit to binary analysis of being or not-being. The only trouble is that what is signified by its presence or absence is not absolute. It might signify the absence of manhood, as in the onset of puberty—absent for the boy actors playing Rosalind and Celia, incipient for the character Orlando, who both refers several times to his burgeoning manhood (in the opening scene) and is the object of comment on his youthful delicacy ("Nay, he hath but a little beard," says Celia at 3.2.201). Or it might signify the absence of maleness altogether, woman- or girlhood, within the fiction of the play. Before Rosalind has cross-dressed as Ganymede, that is, the play already calls attention to the ambivalent illusion of gender that is part of the theatrical foundation of Shakespeare's drama, and simultaneously calls attention to the link between women and boys through their absent beards.

The beard binary is the odd one out among a series that are all overtly concerned with overall worth: good or naught, honorable or dishonorable, wise man or knave. It is easy to see having a beard as a marker of worth, and not having one, a marker of worthlessness, and indeed, in broad terms in the social marketplace, this is the case: women and boys are linked by their inferior status and lack of power. The language of the pancakes and mustard, "good" or "naught," also takes on an erotic cast here. Rosalind and Celia had just been speaking of the presence or absence of "honesty" in women, the razor's edge of sexual propriety that Elizabethan women had to walk, the least slip-up raising the prospect of the utter destruction of their marriageability, converting them to "naught"—a word with common sexual significance.[14] The scene also contains offhand references to an erotic marketplace for both women and men. Celia jokes that Le Beau will cram the ladies with news as a pigeon feeds her young, which she jokes will make them "more marketable," presumably like fatter pigeons brought to market (95). But the implication is that there is a market for young ladies, and a variety of factors that might influence their value and salability.[15] And of course, the actual wrestling

---

Materializing Gender in Early Modern English Literature and Culture (Cambridge: Cambridge University Press, 2006), 83–128.

[14] See *OED*, s.v. "naught" C.adj.2.b. "promiscuous, licentious."

[15] Economic language and the notion of an erotic "marketplace" is most pronounced in act 3, scene 5 when Rosalind tells Phoebe that she is "not for all markets" (61). Though he does not

scene will be one in which Rosalind and Celia engage in much evaluation of Orlando, and he returns the favor—where men and women are "checking each other out." Finally, of course, for many Elizabethans, to be a woman at all is to be "naught," the absence of a beard alluding to their genital absence and lack of phallic virtue, that is, the genital binary that supposedly constitutes the gender binary: I/O. There is a hint in this language of absolute condemnation of what is otherwise entirely absent from *As You Like It*: the bald, categorical misogyny of Sir John's condemnation of women at the start of Lodge's *Rosalynde*.

All of this serves to place an exceedingly inconsequential judgment about food, which could just as easily be a judgment reflecting taste in poems, in a line of judgments about human worth, and that could be, depending on who makes them, extremely consequential. The dialogue displays a genuinely disturbing "slippery slope," where absolute evaluations slide all too easily from minor to major and back again, wreaking potential havoc on the evaluated. The contrast with the breezy evaluative sophistication discussed above in "Devising sports" could hardly be stronger: to the extent that reading or evaluating literary spectacles or poetry works in the same absolute terms as erotic or other evaluation of people, it evokes not a pleasingly low-stakes world of individual taste, but a terrifying, unreliable, and volatile marketplace where one's social standing can plummet or soar with little warning or provocation.

If we follow the dialogue a little farther, however, we find another crucial layer applied. Celia next asks Touchstone "who is't that thou mean'st?" (79)—a question at least a little surprising, since it seems quite possible that a jokester like Touchstone could have made up the whole story. He replies not with a name, but a category: the knight is "one that old Frederick, your father, loves" (80–1). Celia's back immediately comes up: "My father's love," she says, "is enough to honor him" (82).[16] That construction neatly undermines Touchstone's series of present/absent evaluations.

comment on this play, my understanding of Shakespeare's thinking about "markets" is strongly influenced by Lars Engle, *Shakespearean Pragmatism: Market of His Time* (Chicago: University of Chicago Press, 1993), esp. his reading of *Hamlet*, at 54–73.

[16] This is the site of a notable crux: the speaker of the "my father's love" line is identified in F1 and F2 as Rosalind. But her father can't be named Frederick, so either the speech belongs to Celia and "Rosalind" is a compositor's error, or "Frederick" is a compositor's substitution for the name of the otherwise unnamed exiled duke. Dusinberre has gone with "Ferdinand" and the F identification of speaker, based on the Douai manuscript. These identifications do not affect my reading significantly, however, since I see little differentiation between Celia and Rosalind's arguing positions in this scene.

"Honor" shifts from a noun and an attribute that one may have or not have, like a beard, to a verb, whereby Celia's father's love "honors" the knight, bestows honor on him. The construction equally means "is enough for me and you to honor him"—if my father loves him then we should honor him. This can be taken as simply pointing out Celia's duty to her father. But we can also read it as a reminder that Touchstone is living in a state with an absolute ruler whose judgments trump anyone else's. To dishonor those that the state loves risks incurring the wrath of the state. Thus she continues, "Enough! Speak no more of him. You'll be whipped for taxation one of these days" (83–4). Whipping is not something we see the duke deploy in this play; this duke is more in the habit of banishing those who represent the least hint of political liability or risk to him.

So evaluations of people take place within structures of social and political obligation that can render moot individual evaluations. This may to an extent lend stability, may give a sense of a less volatile marketplace open to influence from every quarter. But it does so at the expense of individual freedom and control. Celia recognizes, as surely Rosalind does too, that their evaluations have only limited efficacy. Celia can be forced to marry a man she hates; Rosalind can be banished on a whim.

What I would like to do is claim all of this as "knowledge" for Shakespeare's Rosalind, and a waypoint in her technical history. Talking about what Lodge's Rosalind knows, by comparison, is much easier—there we have a character who presents her knowledge and her technical poetic abilities in a nicely secluded scene, complete with monologues and improvised madrigal. Here the claim is for a knowledge that is social and communal: it is authorized by the fact that all of these three get each other's jokes, that no one is thrown by the lightning moves that Touchstone makes—that there is no telling who is the most witty of these three. But for support, let us look outside *As You Like It* to see if I can show something similar elsewhere. To me it seems that for every direct performance of virtuous understanding— Adriana condemning the double standard of sexual propriety, Hermione condemning the injustice of her treatment—there are as many scenes where knowledge is implied by action or by silence.

Much of the power of Cordelia's character in *Lear* comes from this kind of tacit understanding, but let us consider for a moment Gertrude in her closet, and the famous confrontation with her son—a scene that Shakespeare likely wrote within a year or two of writing *As You Like It*. The point I would make about this scene is simply that even as Gertrude speaks very little compared with Hamlet, the scene conveys the sense that she understands every word he says, that she understands and accepts the critical view of herself, of the "black and grained spots" in her soul, and yet she also can understand his "madness," both in the hallucinatory sense of someone who sees invisible spirits and converses with them, and in the sense of the social madness of such a view as underlies Hamlet's criticism. It is tragic to forget the memory of old Hamlet, and to note the deficiencies of Claudius when put side by side with him. But this too is the way of the world. Thus Gertrude is able to follow Hamlet's critical line of thought, to feel its purchase on herself, to sympathize with his agony as he perceives and thinks this, to continue to love him, and to continue to operate as Claudius's queen, and to lament both the death of Polonius, and soon, the death of Ophelia. Gertrude, without ever making a disquisition on how all of this can coexist in her, nonetheless performs this capacious sympathy and knowledge through her unwavering and assured engagement in every scene in which she appears. And it is this kind of indirect knowledge that I want to say Rosalind displays in the scene of the pancakes and mustard.[17]

Mark how the tyrant writes

I noted in chapter 3 that Lodge's book has more topical resonance with the contemporary political situation in France than does Shakespeare's play. One of the ways that is visible is through the change of "kings" in *Rosalynde* to ambiguously situated "dukes" in *As You Like It*.[18] The political struggle in *As You Like It* also never results in warfare or significant deaths, as it does

---

[17] The topic "what women know in Shakespeare" seems too general for recent Shakespeare studies to have treated as such. But claims of this kind are not out of the ordinary in various contexts of analysis. For example, Janet Adelman's landmark study, *Suffocating Mothers*, begins with a reading of Gertrude that agrees with mine in many specific moments of her understanding, but is finally inclined to emphasize "how little we know" about her and how much "her character remains relatively closed to us." See Adelman, *Suffocating Mothers: Fantasies of Maternal Origin in Shakespeare's Plays, "Hamlet" to "The Tempest"* (New York: Routledge, 1992), 15, 16. More recently, Kathryn Schwarz, in analyzing the gendered power dynamics of *King Lear*, is quite confident in elucidating what the relatively close-lipped Cordelia knows, and also bringing out the "sharp knowledge" of her sisters Goneril and Regan. See Schwarz, *What You Will: Gender, Contract, and Shakespearean Social Space* (Philadelphia: University of Pennsylvania Press, 2011), 190. Still, the importance I am claiming for moments of tacit understanding, or implied communal knowledge, in the context of Shakespeare's most voluble female character, makes me wonder whether there is room for further exploration of this particular thread across more women in more plays.

[18] See chapter 3, "Calvin, Augustine, and aesthetic suspicion."

in Lodge. But being less topically resonant does not mean the play is un-interested in politics—on the contrary, as we will explore in this section, the play has a running interest in tyranny in particular, a word that keeps appearing in widely different contexts. The tyranny that will most interest us, however, is that which involves and in some ways entangles Rosalind. So far I have been working to establish how Shakespeare's Rosalind advances the technical history of Rosalind overall: that she is an advance on the virtuous lightness of Lodge's Rosalind to a new level of sophistication and easy ca-maraderie among a diverse group of consumers of diversions, someone able to grasp and laugh at technical flaws of verse, and also uncritically to appre-ciate displays of passion that she is in the mood for, unthrown by bawdry and semi-pornographic critique; and that she is also able effortlessly to see the connections between low-stakes judgments of taste, and judgments of character; to see how a patriarchal society with a bright line around the gen-try attempts to preserve what counts as knowledge, and how accoutrements like dress and beards and gender performance can subvert those structures; and finally how, under a "humorous" tyrant, all judgments can be rendered moot by the judgment of the prince.

That is a very modern package of qualities, which I hope gets us closer to seeing why someone like Martha Nussbaum might say that Rosalind is someone whom she would like to be.[19] But the final advance that I want to chronicle is more complex and more problematic, and this is the nature of the power that Rosalind assumes in the play and the way she attempts to use it. Thus the politics I am most interested in here is the manner in which Rosalind assumes some of the qualities of tyranny, and some of the spe-cific qualities of the tyrant Duke Frederick who banishes her father and her to the forest. To an extent this assumption of power raises difficulties and questions that are general to feminism, and to what happens when any op-pressed group gains agency and autonomy and the opportunity of wielding power over others. But there are also aspects to this phase of Rosalind that are highly specific to her technical history in Elizabethan culture. In the rela-tionship where "tyranny" becomes an accusation against her, she has moved closer to the Rosalind of twenty years earlier, Spenser's Rosalind, she who condemned "shepherds devise." This is because, while Rosalind begins her sojourn in Arden declaring her predilection for pastoral literary spectacle,

---

[19] This was a comment made during a roundtable discussion at "Shakespeare and the Law," a conference at the University of Chicago Law School, May 15, 2009.

she soon enough becomes a fearsome critic of pastoral tropes and the literary in general. This is true of her famous, Plato-inspired assault on the "lies" of famous poems in which men are reputed to have died for love (4.1.86–99), and it is true most of all for her intervention in the Petrarchan impasse of Silvius and Phoebe in act 3, scene 5.

But an additional complication for our technical history is that the style that Rosalind appropriates to exert power over those two pastoral lovers is nothing but the blank verse that remains the most celebrated technical achievement of the Elizabethan stage. To be sure, it is not blank verse in general—we will see that what counters Rosalind in this tyrannical phase is also blank verse, which is also the best vehicle for Virgilian pastoral—but blank verse as wielded by someone in power, someone imposing that power on others, by, indeed, the tyrant Duke Frederick. This poetry gains this association in the play through two dramatic and unforgettable deployments—at least, they are unforgettable once one is looking out for them.

In chapter 1, I brought in components of Leo Bersani's important work in queer theory from the 1980s (and more recent feminist reflections on that work).[20] In tracing Rosalind's tyrannical turn, I will also argue that we make our way to Rosalind at her queerest. This is because I argue that her tyranny is caught up in the erotic charge of her relationship with Phoebe. Roughly, my reading of that relationship is this: Rosalind, annoyed at the power that Phoebe is exerting over Silvius, attempts to puncture the erotic situation of imperious female beauty holding a desperate suitor at bay by calling the whole thing ridiculous, but particularly by calling beauty into question as a delay or motivator: just get on with it. At this first moment, her intervention might be understood as feminist to the extent that it attacks gender roles in which women try to maximize their ability to induce desire and prolong the suffering of men. But the intervention goes awry and, just as is the case in Lodge, Phoebe falls for Rosalind cross-dressed as Ganymede. Here, however, the play diverges in remarkable ways from its predecessor. Whereas in Lodge, Phoebe's passion is simply the butt of jokes, including fairly homophobic jokes, in Shakespeare, something far more complex takes place. The understanding I would like to advance here is that the dynamic between Rosalind and Phoebe finally takes into account the same metatheatrical dynamics that surfaced in the pancakes and mustard dialogue: that is, the erotic charge and tension between Phoebe and Rosalind resonates with their joint identity as "Ganymede," in that both roles would have been played at the Globe by young men. This interpretation I offer as a way of solving a notable crux in the play, namely whether and why Rosalind so mercilessly attacks Phoebe's "beauty," even as in Lodge there is never any question that she is the most beautiful shepherdess in Arden. Our analysis here will take us to the moment of maximum tension in this relationship, which is also the exact moment of the arrival of Virgilian pastoral, and the culmination of the biography of poetry that is the subject of the second half of this chapter.

But what, for the play, is a tyrant? By simply tracing the use of the word, *As You Like It* provides four distinct answers, and implies a fifth.[21] The political tyrant is of course Duke Frederick. His tyranny includes several common components, but also omits others. He seems to have taken power illegitimately—we only hear of him as a usurper, but hear nothing else about the circumstances under which he assumed the title of duke and banished his older brother along with some of his close followers (unlike, say, Prospero's narration to Miranda in *The Tempest*). Within the action of the play we see no evidence of corruption, hear nothing of him abusing his power at the expense of the state, but we do see evidence of excessive sensitivity about his legitimacy and his public standing, which leads him to his single most tyrannical act, the banishment of Rosalind in act 1, scene 3. This seems based only on his personal suspicions, and unsupported analysis of public opinion. His subjects describe him as "humorous," but he is not humorous in the sense of Angelo of *Measure for Measure*, using his power to satisfy his lust. He is also not, so far as we know, a killer. Banishment is backed up by "pain of death," but we hear of no resolution of his to kill until, at the end of the play, we learn that just before his religious conversion, he had resolved to take soldiers to the forest of Arden and put his brother, and perhaps others, "to the sword" (5.4.156). That would be an entrance into "bloody tyranny" of the sort that is commonplace among other infamous Shakespearean tyrants— Richard III, Macbeth. Frederick avoids this, and though there is no question about his tyranny in the play, the lack of blood on his hands make his actions revocable, himself redeemable, as he is, finally, and in stark contrast to his counterpart, killed on the battlefield in Lodge's *Rosalynde*, redeemed.

But even before we hear of this version of political tyranny in the play, we hear of a domestic tyrant, Oliver, the eldest brother of Orlando de Boys. Orlando begins the play by decrying his treatment under this tyrant

[21] This is in marked contrast with Lodge's *Rosalynde*, where the word is applied only in one instance to anyone other than the tyrant king Torismond, and this is to Cupid, in French, in a poem by Desportes quoted by Montanus on p. 117. The opening up of multiple applications and significances of the word is Shakespeare's invention.

brother. The charges are similar to political tyranny but more specific: Orlando feels he is being denied "the place of a brother" (1.1.18) within the mini-state of the de Boys household, and instead has been reduced to the status of servant or even domestic animal ("His horses are bred better" [10]). There is no broader claim that Oliver is mismanaging the estate, running it into the ground, or abusing its members other than Orlando. But from Orlando's point of view, Oliver's persecution, and especially his fratricidal machinations—again, the threat of death, without its actual appearance—are enough to justify the name "tyrant brother" that Oliver bestows upon him at the end of act 1, scene 2. And like Frederick, failing to achieve his fratricidal ambitions keeps the way clear for conversion and redemption.

The next version of tyranny the play supplies, at the start of act 2, involves the relationship of humans and the natural world, and it does involve actual deaths, in this case of deer: Jaques, we hear through the report of a Lord who heard him say it, is distressed at the tyranny of humans over animals. The terms of his criticism play directly on those of the exiled duke in whose company Jaques has been staying. The duke (he is never named in the play—a seeming oversight, and is identified in most editions as "Duke Senior") might have been unjustly deprived of power and exiled, but his moral position is undermined by hunting deer, the "native burghers of this desert city" as the duke himself puts it (2.1.23). The duke's ability to suggest this point of view himself, and to take pleasure in the line of thought that leads Jaques to call him and his human company "usurpers, tyrants" (2.1.61), makes this read more as endearing self-awareness, rather than, as in the case of Oliver and Frederick, grounds for rebellion or insurgency. But the point is nevertheless made: a version of tyranny could be the relationship of human beings in general with the natural world, over which they could both unjustly invade and abuse their power over weaker creatures. In this respect, we might all be tyrants.[22]

There is one more version of tyranny that I want to mention here, even though it does not as explicitly appear in the play as the four I list above, and this is the potential tyranny of a god or gods over human beings. Although

[22] For a recent discussion that highlights this moment in *As You Like It*, and sets it in the context of Renaissance thinking about the relations of humans and non-humans, see Laurie Shannon, *The Accommodated Animal: Cosmopolity in Shakespearean Locales* (Chicago: Chicago University Press, 2013), 80–1. It is worth noting, however, that for Jaques and the duke, this line of thought seems to provide primarily aesthetic pleasure more than anything else—the duke seeks out Jaques for the pleasure of hearing such arguments, while Jaques uses the idea to "suck" out more of the melancholy to which he is addicted (2.5.10).

it is in a very lighthearted dialogue, this potential is audible in the discussion of Fortune and Nature in act 1, scene 2, as Rosalind and Celia note how irrational seem to be the "gifts" of both. This is a long way from the indictments of deity made in Shakespearean tragedy, but it is still noteworthy. And also noteworthy is the invocation of Ganymede in the play, which alludes in some way to Jove's penchant for rape—that for this pagan deity, the most violent form of erotic tyranny is one of his most defining characteristics.[23]

All of these instances add to the resonances available for the word in the play, and all are available as we examine the charges of tyranny around the erotic relationships of Silvius, Phoebe, and Rosalind. But before turning to those scenes, I want to trace the resonances around the deployment of blank verse in the play that also have an important role to play in these scenes, and supply a version of tyrannical style for the play to draw upon. This resonance arises from two prominent early moments when the play shifts from prose into poetry. Duke Frederick doesn't begin the play speaking in verse (and neither does anyone else)—he only shifts into verse when he realizes that Orlando is part of a family that is politically threatening to him, after Orlando defeats Charles the wrestler and, upon request, identifies himself. So, with the line "I would thou hadst been son to some man else" (1.2.213), after 374 lines of prose, the duke shifts into *As You Like It*'s first blank verse. As if doing so makes some socially recognizable move that requires compliance from all, the other characters follow his lead, and even after he leaves, speak in verse until the end of the scene.[24] In the next scene, the duke does it again, and interrupts the intimate and confidential prose dialogue of Celia and Rosalind to announce that he is banishing Rosalind. This time he doesn't just

---

[23] For more on Ganymede, see chapter 3, "The characters of men."

[24] It is momentarily tempting here to associate blank verse itself, as Pierre Bourdieu might encourage, with tyranny. But the effect of the association of the tyrant duke acting tyrannically with shifts into verse cuts more than one way: on the one hand, it seems ironic that the arrival of verse, instead of breaking out like sunshine, casts a shadow over the play and is aligned with hard political realities that had up to this point been set to one side in the excitement surrounding the wrestling match and the erotic energies that accompany it. But on the other hand, those political realities raise the stakes of everything that is happening in the play, and the duke's ferocity is dramatic, motivating dramatic actions in other characters as well as impassioned speech, also in blank verse, to protest and resist the duke's pronouncements. All of which is to say that while the duke's tyrannical blank-verse style is bad for those he fears or dislikes, it is good for the play. For more on the dynamics of shifts between prose and verse in Shakespearean drama, see the excellent articles by Jonas Barish: "Mixed Verse and Prose in Shakespearean Comedy," in *English Comedy*, ed. Michael Cordner, Peter Holland, and John Kerrigan (Cambridge: Cambridge University Press, 1994), 55–67; and "Mixed Prose-Verse Scenes in Shakespearean Tragedy," in *Shakespeare and Dramatic Tradition: Essays in Honor of S. F. Johnson*, ed. W. R. Elton and William B. Long (Newark: University of Delaware Press, 1989), 32–46.

exercise his authority to change the level of formality of speech; his formal speech actually imposes his will, "pronounces" his sentence upon Rosalind:

DUKE Mistress, dispatch you with your safest haste
   And get you from our court.
ROSALIND   Me, uncle?
DUKE   You, cousin.
   Within these ten days if that thou be'st found
   So near our public court as twenty miles,
   Thou diest for it.
             (1.3.38–42)

This combination of exerting authority over the mode of speech of others, and actual orders, imperatives, that inform the hearer of the summary judgment of the state, establishes the tyrannical style in this play that is later audible in Rosalind. When in act 3, scene 5, Rosalind intervenes in the dialogue and relationship of Phoebe and Silvius, and imperiously addresses Phoebe—"But mistress, know yourself; down on your knees / And thank heaven fasting for a good man's love" (58–9)—she is echoing that style. The intensity of Rosalind's feelings in act 4, scene 3 seems to me inspired by both of these things: her frustration (coupled with some perhaps grudging pleasure) that her attempt to join Silvius and Phoebe has gone so far awry, and her sense that the role of erotic "tyrant" fits her, that by inserting herself into the affairs of these people, with some arrogance, and some contempt of unintended consequences, she is acting and sounding like her tyrant uncle.

The association of blank verse in these situations with political tyranny is an impression strengthened by comparison of these scenes with their origins in Lodge. There is nothing comparable in Lodge to the dramatic entrance of blank verse in the wrestling scene: it is conducted in prose, and furthermore the usurping king does not have a negative reaction when he finds out about Rosader's heritage—there is no change in tone, never mind a change from prose to verse. In general, characters do not unselfconsciously express themselves in verse in Lodge's book—this is a feature of Elizabethan theatre, but one that is highlighted by the long absence of verse at the start of this particular play. Similarly, the king's concern about Rosalind's effect on public support for him is something we read about through third-person narration as hatched sui generis, and when he walks into her quarters to banish her, he does so in prose, and we are not given access through dialogue to Rosalind's protestations—only Alinda replies, again in prose. Finally, the scene in which Rosalind intervenes with Phoebe is conducted entirely in prose.

When Duke Frederick deploys blank verse and imposes it upon his interlocutors, first with Orlando after he reveals his parentage, and then with
Rosalind, banishing her from his realm, he is also imposing his interpretation of the political situation on people who vigorously dispute that
interpretation. Orlando does not claim, in his father, a critical view of Duke
Frederick; and Rosalind, despite being the daughter of the usurped former
duke, has no ambitions to oppose or undermine the usurper. But in both
cases, while he succeeds in forcing those he is addressing to respond in blank
verse, it is much less clear that he succeeds in imposing his interpretation,
or that the intervention has any success in consolidating or boosting his
power. In the same way, Rosalind's intervention to insert economic ratio-
nalism and pragmatism into sexual relations goes wildly awry, and ignites
a passion in Phoebe for herself. But much less understood is the extent to
which the intervention depends on an "interpretation" as well, specifically
Rosalind's attack on Phoebe's beauty. The relevant lines, over which extraordinary amounts of editorial ink have been spilt, are the following. After, from
her position as eavesdropper, hearing Phoebe declare that she will not under
any circumstances "pity" Silvius, she reveals herself thus:

> And why, I pray you? Who might be your mother,
> That you insult, exult, and all at once,
> Over the wretched? What though you have no beauty—
> As, by my faith, I see no more in you
> Than without candle may go dark to bed—
> Must you be therefore proud and pitiless?
>
> (3.5.36–41)

Commentators have suggested that maybe that "no" is really "mo," as they
have tried to argue that Rosalind cannot really be calling Phoebe ugly.[25] The
details that Rosalind adds later in the speech do not help much, as she disputes what she claims mid-speech is an ongoing effort to "tangle" Rosalind's
eyes too:

> No, faith, proud mistress, hope not after it.
> 'Tis not your inky brows, your black silk hair,
> Your bugle eyeballs, nor your cheek of cream,
> That can entame my spirits to your worship.
>
> (46–9)

[25] "Mo" is Malone's suggestion, in his edition of 1790, as Dusinberre notes; for the full range
of options, see Knowles's *Variorum Edition*.

These are ambiguous adjectives that seem more prosodically ugly than se-matically so: it is as if Rosalind is trying to denigrate her beauty through bad poetry but cannot allow herself actually to say falsehoods. There is nothing wrong with silken hair, and "bugle eyeballs" is certainly unflattering as lan-guage, but might describe simply striking eyes. By the end of the speech, she seems simply to be saying that Phoebe's attitude of "scoffer" toward Silvius is the only thing that is making her unattractive. As Phoebe starts speaking in adoring tones, and Rosalind, breaking into prose, sees that she appears to be falling in love "with my anger" she strikes a more concilia-tory note: "I pray you do not fall in love with me, / For I am falser than vows made in wine. / Besides, I like you not" (73–5). But this sudden self-denigration is followed by what I think it is quite reasonable to read as the Elizabethan pastoral equivalent of a meaningful handover of contact infor-mation: "If you will know my house, / 'Tis at the tuft of olives here hard by" (75–6).

All of this leads me to think that, in a way that really never seems on display with her relationship with Orlando, Rosalind is thoroughly dis-composed by this encounter with Phoebe. The ostensible result of her intervention is, to be sure, a failure: there is no evidence that she has ad-vanced Silvius's love-cause or made their relations any more rational. But the above shows considerable evidence that, at the very least, she is interested in the erotic effect of her "anger," is interested in this unexpected result of the appropriation of the language of power added to the performance of male-ness under the name of "Ganymede." What also keeps this dynamic much more deeply ambiguous than its corresponding scene in Lodge is the utter lack of homophobic joking that characterizes the book: there is no reference here to how Rosalind cannot "satisfy" Phoebe's needs because of what she "lacks."[26]

This brings us to the even more confusing start of act 4, scene 3, where Silvius comes upon Rosalind and Celia and delivers to the former a verse epistle. Rosalind gives an opening response to it before reading it aloud and providing commentary, the main claim of which is to accuse Phoebe of tyranny—"Mark how the tyrant writes," she says, before beginning her reading. But of course it is Phoebe who is begging for mercy from the per-son who now tyrannizes her: Phoebe finds herself tyrannized by love and by Ganymede, and Rosalind finds herself unable to shake the role of tyrant that

---

[26] See chapter 3, "Coda: Making Fun of Phoebe."

she adopted while attempting to remedy a tyrannical relationship. When Rosalind says "mark how the tyrant writes" (4.3.39), she is partly being unreasonable, speaking from the frustrated position I have outlined above, but she is also getting at something true, namely that Phoebe's exaggerated praise *makes* Rosalind into a tyrant, and in so doing is itself tyrannical, and sustaining of tyrannical relationships. At this moment, we also connect to two other discourses of tyranny in the play, namely the tyranny of human beings over animals, and the terrifying proposition of a tyrannous deity, that god is a tyrant and the political constitution of the universe, tyranny. "Art thou god to shepherd turned?" (40), asks Phoebe, and as the poem continues on this line, Rosalind finds a way to invert Phoebe's claim that she is superhuman to an insult that she is subhuman: "Whiles the eye of man did woo me, / That could do no vengeance to me" (47–8) says the poem; "Meaning me a beast" (49) interprets Rosalind. But the poem and the erotic relations it participates in do both: Eros makes the lover worship her beloved as a god, but a cruel and tyrannous one, a god that acts with the moral compass of an animal, or a god that treats human beings not as exceptional creatures made in his image, but as any other beast.

This scene of reading and interpreting is challenging enough, but the dialogue through which Rosalind introduces the letter is even more forbidding, as it both provides interpretations that are the opposite of what the letter actually says, and vigorously disputes the notion that Phoebe, or any lowborn woman, or any woman, or any Christian woman, or any white woman, could write such a letter. These are the relevant passages:

> I saw her hand—she has a leathern hand,
> A freestone-colored hand—I verily did think
> That her old gloves were on, but 'twas her hands.
> She has a housewife's hand—but that's no matter.
> I say she never did invent this letter;
> This is a man's invention and his hand.
>
> (24–9)

And then further:

> Why, 'tis a boisterous and a cruel style,
> A style for challengers. Why, she defies me,
> Like Turk to Christian. Women's gentle brain

> Could not drop forth such giant-rude invention,
> Such Ethiop words, blacker in their effect
> Than in their countenance.
>
> (31–6)

The actuation of all of those dimensions of identity—gender, class, religion, race—signals to me that Rosalind sees the dynamics of erotic tyranny to have much wider implications than are otherwise readily apparent. But what precisely is at stake here? If we have on one side, say, the thinking that leads Hamlet to tell Ophelia to go to a nunnery, then we might think that it is sexuality itself, or the Christian demand of "honesty" and chastity from women, that is responsible for Rosalind's accusations. That is, there is no room in Christian, Western culture for women to express desire and to pursue love.[27]

But to my mind, bringing all these dimensions of identity to bear here bespeaks a still deeper challenge to Western order, and that is the prospect of homosexual desire. The play has earlier called attention (in the pancakes and mustard scene) to the fact that the women in this play are boys, and Rosalind will famously do so once more in the play's beard-focused epilogue. Here it seems quite relevant that within the fiction of the play, there is demonstrable erotic tension between two women, tension that is never discredited on the grounds of anatomy the way it is in Lodge. But of course Lodge's jokes about missing penises could never work here anyway—because, extra-diagetically, they aren't missing. And so "this is a man's invention and his hand" is both a baldly contrafactual statement and a statement of truth. And as from the start of this study we have focused attention on how the project of translating Virgil into European vernaculars also elicits the conflicts and difficulties of

---

[27] For a recent discussion thinking these together in the context of Spenser, see Melissa E. Sanchez, "'To Giue Faire Colour': Sexuality, Courtesy, and Whiteness in *The Faerie Queene*," *Spenser Studies* 35 (2021): 245–84. For example: "Spenser's consistent reliance on 'black' and 'savage' bodies to allegorize the perverse and lustful parts of the soul must be understood as contributing to the establishment of racial hierarchies that in his own day justified both the restraint of White female sexual agency and nascent slavery and colonialism" (246). Rosalind's "Ethiop words" also seems to play out the distinction between "dogma line" and "color line" racism, inner and outer "blackness," the inner kind being a greater source of fear because of its difficulty to detect. And at the same time this is applied to the blackness of inked words, which, through slander, can be used successfully to "blacken" their targets. To assert that "woman's gentle brain" could not "drop" such words ironically enunciates precisely the fear of inner "blackening" that Sanchez writes leads to arguments and policies of female "restraint." For "dogma line" and "color line" racism, see Leerom Medovoi, "Dogma-Line Racism: Islamaphobia and the Second Axis of Race," *Social Text* 30, no. 2 (2012): 43–74.

dealing with classical sexuality, where gender is openly and unproblematically substitutable, in an early modern context, so it seems that the intensive othering of desire in this passage—attributing Phoebe's desire, and its answering response from Rosalind, to peasants, to Muslims, and to Africans, but never to a Christian woman—seems to acknowledge the truth before our eyes, the truth trumpeted by "Ganymede," that beautiful shepherd boy raped by the king of the gods for his eternal pleasure. The tyranny of love is everywhere, and you love seeing its dominion, very much including the homosexual spectacle of the Elizabethan theater.

The Throwdown: Translation, Conversion, and Virgilian Pastoral

So far then we have followed the technical history of Rosalind out to this furious and thrilling breaking point, and this turns out to be exactly the point at which Virgilian pastoral dialogue arrives in the play, and likewise arrives in English literary history, the culminating moment in the biography of poetry that I chronicle here. In keeping with Virgil, there are not a lot of fireworks in the writing, which is why, as far as I know, no one has made such an argument before me. I will get to the poetic details in a little while. Before that, I want to trace the other threads that inform and power the moment—both the moment of dialogue and the rest of the scene that ends in Rosalind's swoon. Those threads concern two words that the play puts into productive conversation, namely translation and conversion. As we will see, the power of the Virgilian dialogue that emerges at this moment has everything to do with its initiator, Oliver, one of the "convertites" (as Jaques refers to them at 5.4.182) that show up in the play. It is Oliver's narrative of conversion that leads directly to Rosalind's overthrow, but that dynamic has been prepared by an earlier moment with conversion dynamics, namely the wrestling scene—with its literal throwdown of bodies—in which Rosalind and Orlando are introduced to one another. The play also ends with further consideration of the dynamics of conversion.

But before examining that thread, I want to examine how the play thinks about "translation." The most important point to get before us with respect to translation is that it can describe a very powerful effect of literary language indeed, namely the ability of poetry to transform and redefine its own surroundings. In this active, reframing version of translation, the play also draws attention to the limits and instability of such power—that like a delicate spell, it might be punctured with the right kind of skeptical or irreverent response. We also see translation in its more common modern sense of providing two versions of the same discourse, but with a difference—in the example I want to look at, translation is also persuasion and reassurance: I can speak your language, and make it my own, and thus I display the grounds of our fellowship. In this form, translation also approaches a key effect that I identified in chapter 1 about Virgilian pastoral, in the sympathetic interplay of Melibœus and Tityrus. Here "concord" is introduced through the ability of a listener to sympathize with a stranger's suffering, and through song to transform it—translate it—into something beautiful.

Even from these brief descriptions we can begin to see how there are areas of overlap between conversion and translation, and the place where that overlap is most acute is act 4, scene 3. Onward, then, to pick up the first of these threads, translation.

Sweet translation

Act 2 carries us from the city and court to Arden, and introduces us to the exiled duke and his followers. Given the sparseness of scenery in the Globe, a substantial burden of the duke's first speech is setting this scene, translating, that is, the bare thrust stage into a forest—not quite as magical and mysterious a forest as that of *A Midsummer Night's Dream*, perhaps, but still a forest that is capable of working itself upon the imagination. But this speech does quite a bit more than that, and to see its complexities, I will quote it in full, along with the initial response from Amiens:

DUKE SENIOR   Now, my co-mates and brothers in exile,
    Hath not old custom made this life more sweet
    Than that of painted pomp? Are not these woods
    More free from peril than the envious court?
    Here feel we but the penalty of Adam,
    The seasons' difference—as the icy fang
    And churlish chiding of the winter's wind,
    Which when it bites and blows upon my body
    Even till I shrink with cold, I smile and say:
    "This is no flattery. These are counsellors

That feelingly persuade me what I am."
Sweet are the uses of adversity,
Which, like the toad, ugly and venomous,
Wears yet a precious jewel in his head;
And this our life, exempt from public haunt
Finds tongues in trees, books in the running brooks,
Sermons in stones, and good in every thing.
AMIENS   I would not change it. Happy is your grace,
That can translate the stubbornness of fortune
Into so quiet and so sweet a style.

(2.1.1–20)

Amiens's comment is obviously crucial for the particular interpretive line I will follow here, and by referring to "stubbornness of fortune" he also associates this moment with the work of "devising sports" that Celia and Rosalind were engaged in when we first met them in act 1, scene 2. But his comment also cuts more than one way, since it implies that not everyone is so capable of such a successful translation, that not everyone, perhaps not even Amiens, is so capable of finding the "good" in everything that surrounds them. In that case, they are left with "the stubbornness of fortune," and the "quiet" and "sweet ... style" the duke deploys is just a momentary diversion from that harsh reality.

But by invoking translation and style, Amiens also calls attention to the literary situation of this moment in the play, and this moment in the biography of poetry we have been tracing. While this is not yet the moment of Virgilian translation in the play that I will argue meets the poetic standard Virgil set, it is nonetheless a moment evocative of Virgilian pastoral. The key aspect of Virgil's first eclogue to bring to bear here is that the land that Tityrus uses for his sheep and goat-herding, and upon which the encounter with Melibœus and the eclogue's verse dialogue takes place, is in fact quite undesirable—swampy and full of rocks. The poem's famous opening lines then, where Melibœus describes Tityrus's idyllic pose, singing of Amaryllis beneath a wide-spreading birch, and accompanying himself on an oaten flute—that is already an act of translation, imposing a poetic pastoral imagination on the rough ground of reality, just as it also translates the vocabulary and conventions of Theocritus from Greek into Latin. So Amiens calls attention to this dimension of the pastoral tradition, which has also always already been translating—more or less questionably—the "stubbornness of fortune."

But the reference to translation and style also calls attention to the details of the poetic style the duke deploys here. "Quiet" and "sweet" are not particularly illuminating adjectives, even as "sweet" is a word with deep pastoral significance—the first and repeated word of Theocritus's *Idylls*. I would add another adjective: Spenserian. Take the alliteration in these three lines:

> And churlish chiding of the winter's wind,
> Which when it bites and blows upon my body
> Even till I shrink with cold, I smile and say

In the density of alliteration, and the interest in balanced pairs of alliteration across a line, these lines evoke the style of *The Shepheardes Calender*. If that is true, it argues that the act of "translation" Amiens imputes to the duke is also an act of literary nostalgia, translating us to situation of adversity experienced by Colin Clout.[28] And if that is true it also places the play in literary history in a way that nothing we have seen so far does: Spenser evoked Chaucer and folk poetry, but without nostalgia; Lodge writes as though all poetry is in the literary present. This is the first moment where the biography of poetry is evoked and where affection for it is mixed with skepticism of its efficacy.

The other moment of translation I want to examine also involves the banished duke, and also evokes Virgilian circumstances, this time as a desperate Orlando, seeking food for himself and for his dying servant Adam, comes upon the duke and asks for help—thus aligning with the primal scene of hospitality of Eclogue 1. After first thinking that he will need to acquire nourishment by force, Orlando quickly realizes this won't be necessary. We need to see his full speech, along with the duke's response, in order to focus on the version of translation of interest here:

ORLANDO   Speak you so gently? Pardon me, I pray you.
I thought that all things had been savage here
And therefore put I on the countenance
Of stern commandment. But whate'er you are,
That in this desert inaccessible,

---

[28] The speech's references to winter also connect it with Spenser's *Calender* since, as has often been remarked, there are few corroborating references to place the play in winter anywhere else. The forest's principal adversity for other characters is lack of food.

Under the shade of melancholy boughs,
Lose and neglect the creeping hours of time—
If ever you have looked on better days,
If ever been where bells have knolled to church,
If ever sat at any good man's feast,
If ever from your eyelids wiped a tear,
And know what 'tis to pity and be pitied—
Let gentleness my strong enforcement be,
In the which hope, I blush and hide my sword.
DUKE SENIOR   True is it that we have seen better days,
And have with holy bell been knolled to church,
And sat at good men's feasts, and wiped our eyes
Of drops that sacred pity hath engendered;
And therefore sit you down in gentleness
And take upon command what help we have
That to your wanting may be ministered.

(2.7.107–27)

There is an effect comparable to this, and perhaps inspired by it, at the end of book 10 of *Paradise Lost*, where the narrator approvingly echoes Adam's plan for contrition and prayer as the couple's best path forward. But that straight echo, with change of pronouns, is simpler than what is happening here, the full complexity of which becomes clear when the two echoing passages are set side by side:

If ever you have looked on better days,	True is it that we have seen better days,
If ever been where bells have knolled to church,	And have with holy bell been knolled to church,
If ever sat at any good man's feast,	And sat at good men's feasts, and wiped our eyes
If ever from your eyelids wiped a tear,	Of drops that sacred pity hath engendered;
And know what 'tis to pity and be pitied—	And therefore sit you down in gentleness
Let gentleness my strong enforcement be,	And take upon command what help we have
In the which hope, I blush and hide my sword.	That to your wanting may be ministered.

The two speeches take up the same amount of room, but after closely following Orlando's structure for two lines, the duke departs in the third, compressing adeptly Orlando's next three lines into two, in the process connecting the pity as the cause of tears. The compression allows the duke to use the "And" of the fifth line to begin his exhortation to sit, brilliantly transforming "gentleness" to the quality of the entire meeting. In other ways, the duke's verse displays greater sophistication and finesse than Orlando's: in compressing his response to lines 3–5, the duke also introduces enjambment, "eyes / Of drops," which is entirely absent in Orlando. So too, the duke's speech is metrically more subtle and varied than Orlando's—his speech might not earn the opprobrium of "butter-women's rank to the market," but it verges on singsonginess, on the jagged line with which Ezra Pound criticized Eliot's blank verse in *The Waste Land*.[29] So too, there is at least one syntactic inversion—"let gentleness my strong enforcement be"—that smacks of metrical enforcement of the kind that is invisible in the duke's speech.

If the duke himself was at the start of act 2 indulging in nostalgia for an earlier Elizabethan alliterative style, then we would not want to say that his "translation" of Orlando here is pure improvement: I don't think we should read the scene as implicitly condemning Orlando for being a poetic rube. But what it does seem to do is give us a sense of what it might have been like if Shakespeare or one of his contemporaries of the 1590s had decided to translate *The Shepheardes Calender* to reflect more of the poetic sophistication that had become the norm. We might look at a stanza like this from "Januarye," that shows off a straight, uncomplicated approach to anaphora that resembles Orlando's:

> Such rage as winters, reigneth in my heart,
> My life bloud friesing with unkindly cold:
> Such stormy stoures do breede my balefull smart,
> As if my yeare were wast, and woxen old.
> And yet alas, but now my spring begonne,
> And yet alas, yt is already donne.
>
> (25–30)

Perhaps then, rather than strictly improvement, we might understand the duke's translation as a friendly improvisation on the materials supplied by the first speech which, because it is natural to the duke's sophisticated expression, naturally exhibits that sophistication, which also recapitulates some key features of the biography of poetry from 1579 to this moment somewhere close to the end of the century. To be sure, the exchange solidifies Orlando's transformation of stance and attitude away from the violence he thought he would have at least to threaten to get food for himself and his servant. So while Orlando is certainly not a "bad" character in need of redemption and transformation—like the "convertites" Oliver and Frederick that we will discuss presently—he nonetheless participates in this moment when words are used to diffuse violence and generate harmony—concord—among potential combatants. That is a "translation" at least as useful as

---

[29] The markings are visible on several pages, and in one instance, Pound also writes, "too penty." See T. S. Eliot, *The Waste Land: A Facsimile and Transcript of the Original Drafts*, ed. Valerie Eliot (New York: Harcourt, Brace & Co., 1971), 11.

the duke's first imaginative transformation of their surroundings and the adverse circumstances delivered to them by fortune.

How much is the sophistication and finesse supplied by the duke to Orlando's rougher materials a part of the de-escalation of tensions in the scene? Is it enough that the two speakers find that they can speak the same language? Surely, if the "translation" were made in haughtier fashion, it might have the opposite effect, and sound like mockery. But the duke clearly avoids that here: the improvements are "gentle," and the touch light. Indeed, that is one of the things about the biography of poetry that he is showing off. Poets in 1600—some poets anyway—are capable of deploying subtle effects with seeming effortlessness, meeting the requirements of form while also sounding like natural speech. And at least in this scene, that is all a force for good.

Thou art overthrown

Translation as we have observed it in these two scenes is a powerful but delicate force, capable of transforming adverse surroundings, or generating goodwill between mistrusting strangers. In the hands of the banished duke it is also active, a gentle but firm imposition on landscapes and people, and an imposition done with, as we have seen, a sense of literary history, and with technical precision. As we move into the allied phenomenon of conversion in the play, we move likewise into an area that is more passive, more something that happens to people, often without warning, and not necessarily by choice or with consent. As I stated earlier, translation and conversion eventually come together in act 4, scene 3. I will now trace the prominent versions of conversion that inform that scene. In order to do this with maximum clarity, it makes sense to begin at the end, with the play's last and most literal conversion, the conversion of the tyrant Duke Frederick.

The first thing to say about the duke's conversion is what it is not. While it is clearly religious, it does not reference the most charged senses of conversion for Elizabethans. Those are, first, conversion from Protestantism to Catholicism or vice versa, and second a conversion to Christianity from non-Christianity, as in the famous forced conversion at the end of *The Merchant of Venice*.[30] The play does seem interested in the two phenomena at the historical origins of Christian conversion—and here I am relying on

---

[30] Dennis Austin Britton's important work on conversion and race is largely focused on the conversion of non-Christians. See Dennis Austin Britton, *Becoming Christian: Race, Reformation, and Early Modern English Romance* (New York: Fordham University Press, 2014).

Molly Murray's excellent study of 2009—namely the ritual of baptism and *metanoia*, the Greek word for change in spirit or mind "often translated into English as 'repentance' or 'penitence.'"[31] The nature of conversion is paradoxical from the start, as Murray elaborates:

> Conversion can be a deliberate, voluntary action, and the passive receipt of the grace of God. It can be incremental and painfully protracted, and it can be instantaneous and cataclysmic. It can be a matter of refusal and rejection, and a matter of intensifying commitments that already exist. It can bolster individual and communal identities, and it can destroy and refashion them. (7)

The two most famous early Christian conversions, of Saul and Augustine, demonstrate some of this variety: Augustine's is textual, brought on by reading the Word; Saul's just comes out of the sky. The medieval *conversio* was short for *conversio morum*, or "a Christian's turn to the deeper piety of monasticism" (11), which is to say a conversion of living, rather than a conversion from non-Christianity to the faith.[32] But while neither Lodge nor Shakespeare explicitly address the topic of conversion from one version of Christianity to another, one could hardly depict instances of *conversio morum* without feeling the tensions this could create: if one is converted in the wrong way, one could end up suddenly at odds with one's government or culture: conversion could equally entail alienation. As Murray sums it up, "conversion was an experience that most Christians desired and dreaded in equal measure, depending on how it was defined" (22).

Though it comes a little later than the period of *As You Like It*, and from a person who could hardly be called an average Englishman, I want to give Murray's demonstration of that dread, in a diary entry she supplies from from William Laud:

> I came to London. The night following I dreamt that I was reconciled to the Church of Rome. This troubled me much; and I wondered exceedingly, how it should happen. Nor was I aggrieved with myself only by reason of the errors of that church, but also upon account of the scandal, which from that my fall would be cast upon many eminent and learned men of the

---

[31] Molly Murray, *The Poetics of Conversion in Early Modern English Literature: Verse and Change from Donne to Dryden* (Cambridge: Cambridge University Press, 2009), 7. Subsequent page references will be made parenthetically in the text.

[32] Murray uses the example of the twelfth-century Bernard of Clairvaux: "For Bernard, as for Paul and Augustine, conversion involves self-scrutiny, atonement for past sins, and preparation for a culminative union with God" (11).

church of England. So being troubled at my dream, I said with myself, that I would go immediately, and, confessing my fault, would beg pardon of the Church of England. Going with this resolution, a certain priest met me, and would have stopped me. But moved with indignation, I went on my way. And while I wearied myself with these troublesome thoughts, I awoke. (22–3)

He dreams, that is, that he has been converted—that he, as it were, wakes up in the dream to find this to be the state of affairs, and then feels intense guilt, which leads him to desire to confess and, presumably, convert back again. But the dream ends before that can happen. Would it have worked? Hard to say. Surely a large measure of the terror derives from the possibility that conversion operates at a level beyond or below agency or consciousness or reason, that, positively, people might be spontaneously or miraculously converted to the faith, but that as well, they might find themselves converted in such a way that they are alienated and at odds with their colleagues, friends, family, country—a terrifying prospect.

Agency or lack thereof remains a fascinating topic as we move through the play's conversions. In Lodge, the tyrant king is defeated in battle and killed. In *As You Like It*, Duke Frederick is on his way to massacre the exiles in Arden, but is converted before he can do so. Here is the narrative of that conversion, as told in the final moments of the play and sworn to be true by Orlando's other brother, confusingly also named Jaques:

> Duke Frederick, hearing how that every day
> Men of great worth resorted to this forest,
> Addressed a mighty power, which were on foot,
> In his own conduct, purposely to take
> His brother here and put him to the sword;
> And to the skirts of this wild wood he came,
> Where meeting with an old religious man,
> After some question with him, was converted
> Both from his enterprise and from the world,
> His crown bequeathing to his banished brother,
> And all their lands restored to them again
> That were with him exiled.
>
> (5.4.152–63)

We have just a little more to go on about this, as the other Jaques, the one who has been a significant character in the play up till this point, asks "If I heard you rightly, / The duke hath put on a religious life / And thrown into neglect the pompous court." Jaques De Boys confirms, "He hath" (178–81).

This is a clear *conversio morum*, and a finding of grace. Frederick's conversion has almost the abruptness of Paul's, but it also involves dialogue, "some question," the content of which is not disclosed. In any case, the "turning" is described as more negative than positive. Jaques describes it positively as to "put on a religious life," but the first telling gives only what he puts off: he is "converted / Both from his enterprise and from the world," that is indeed more encompassing than "the pompous court" that Jaques supplies, as if he would see Frederick as just another newly appreciative denizen of the forest we have inhabited for the previous four acts. "From the world" indeed seems to imply a level of monasticism from which Frederick might never be heard again, and one wonders whether Jaques will have any luck in speaking with him. As we will see, it also connects Frederick with sentiments expressed by Orlando before his wrestling match—an acceptance of death and renunciation of any worldly desires. What it is not is a conversion that opens up social relations, that is a prelude to gentleness or a sense of shared destiny, sympathy, or pity. Frederick does not come to ask for forgiveness; he merely restores the usurped crown and seized lands and exiles himself, imposes his "banishment," at last, on himself. And as Jaques uses this as an excuse likewise to swear off the dancing and celebration of the end of the play, it is hard not to wonder whether some of the searing criticism leveled at Jaques's self-indulgent melancholy-seeking (4.1.1–26) does not rub off on Frederick too, on this kind of antisocial and possibly misanthropic monasticism.

Duke Frederick is finally overthrown, then, by a few choice words that we never hear. But seeking the origins of that overthrow in the play leads us back to the literalized form of the word, in the wrestling match that introduces blank verse into the play and introduces Rosalind and Orlando to each other. In chapter 3 I wrote at some length about the religious overtones that Lodge lends to the scene: the way the Franklin whose sons are "massacred" by the king's champion takes on the quality of a martyr, and the way Rosader is drawn into combat through sympathy with that man, which is also felt by the assembled throng in a "mumur." I noted that, in sharp contrast to Shakespeare's play, Rosader's defeat of the champion seems a net positive for the usurping king, as it calms the simmering discontent of the crowd at the sight of estimable young men being crushed to death. Lodge uses the wrestling scene to ignite the passion between Rosader and Rosalind, and suggests that Rosalind's beauty has something to do with the force he musters to defeat the champion (although it is also initially a powerful distraction).[33] In Shakespeare, there are a couple of striking additions. One is that Orlando speaks with Rosalind and Celia before the match: they attempt

---

[33] See chapter 3, "Queer mythography: the Sirens."

to dissuade him, based on their assessment of his extreme youth. And in this dialogue Orlando expresses why he is comfortable with the risk he is taking. It is a speech that gathers resonance from our discussion of conversion and from the narrative of Duke Frederick's eventual conversion at the play's end. Despite reports from Oliver that Orlando is universally beloved (except by him) in the previous scene, Orlando describes himself here as friendless, one whose death or absence will go unremarked:

> if I be foiled there is but one shamed that was never gracious, if killed, but one dead that is willing to be so. I shall do my friends no wrong, for I have none to lament me; the world no injury, for in it I have nothing. Only in the world I fill up a place which may be better supplied when I have made it empty. (1.2.178–84)

This sounds like someone already converted "from the world," in that Orlando is able so clearly to picture the world without himself in it. And yet that appears a source of strength, in his mind—he is displaying the lack of "worldliness" associated with religious devotion, and which is the source of fearless strength for martyrs. And it deeply impresses both women, who instantly give up their efforts to dissuade him from what Celia calls his "enterprise" (170).

Orlando then shows in this scene signs of having recently been converted away from his worldly concerns, of trying to regain his stolen birthright from his older brother and to restore respect to himself. Emptied of desire, he is able to face his "trial" without fear. And yet from the same point, a different conversion has also been initiated, namely the beginning of the erotic conversion of Orlando and Rosalind to each other. This does not happen instantaneously. The speech quoted above is a key moment; Orlando's defeat of Charles is another; Orlando's revelation of his family identity—and loyalty to Rosalind's banished father—is a third. But as in Lodge, where the wrestling takes on the look of transferred erotic desire as Rosader beholds the saintly vision of Rosalind and then crushes another man's body beneath him, so here we move rapidly from Orlando's pseudo-conversion narrative to the erotic impression of this narrative on the two princesses to the overthrow and defeat of Charles, to Orlando and Rosalind soon afterward declaring themselves "overthrown" by Eros:

ROSALIND   Sir, you have wrestled well and overthrown
More than your enemies. (243–4)

ORLANDO   O poor Orlando, thou art overthrown! (248)

The play is fascinated with the image and the idea of overthrow and overthrowing: when it is a religious conversion it is words that convert one from one's worldly concerns and lead to the embrace of contemplation—a spiritual and intellectual shift that also leads to a self-initiated overthrow of a tyrant: either Duke Frederick is overthrown by religion or he overthrows himself. In similar manner, Orlando exhibits signs of the man converted from worldly concerns, which counterintuitively gives him fearlessness in combat and allows him to overthrow "his enemies." And then the play brings out the erotic and sexual implication of all of this: wrestling, men trying to master each other's bodies in sport (which in this case is blood sport: combat to the death) becomes metaphorical for sexual intercourse, as both Rosalind and Orlando are shown to be thinking of each other in bed as an extension or metamorphosis of the mortal combat they have just witnessed and participated in.

The component of mortality is a sticking point. Another version of "overthrow" in the play is the erotic "swoon." Rosalind in her famous speech disputes that any man ever died of love. The shepherdess Phoebe is introduced to us making a skeptical speech about power imputed to the eyes of the beloved by poetic lovers like Silvius:

> Now I do frown on thee with all my heart,
> And if mine eyes can wound, now let them kill thee.
> Now counterfeit to swoon—why now fall down!
> Or if thou canst not—O, for shame, for shame—
> Lie not, to say mine eyes are murderers.
>
> (3.5.15–19)

Here and elsewhere we are looking for physical evidence of the true faith of a lover. You claim that your life depends on my favor, that you will collapse under the force of my disdain: but look, now I frown at you, and you remain standing: so you must be lying about the strength of your love.

The link from this contemplation of conversion, overthrow, and swooning to translation is of course not looks but words. What are the words exchanged with the "old religious man" that are capable of instantly converting the tyrant duke? Can any narrative, any poetry survive the kind of skepticism applied by Phoebe and Rosalind to the representations of lovers? Can poetry achieve or aspire to the power to overthrow tyranny—not by force, but through eloquence, through aesthetic power? Can poetry create concord where there was murderous conflict? In this way the dynamics of translation and conversion converge in the play.

Sweet conversion / "in which hurtling"

The latter half of act 4, scene 3 proposes answers to all of those questions in compact and dramatic style, assembled through significant rearrangement of plot elements taken from Lodge. Rosalind in this scene suffers a swoon and is literally overthrown, as she finally receives a translation of the meaning of the bloody handkerchief carried by Oliver and, at the same moment of swooning, presented to her. It is not a frowning look, not murderous eyes, but Orlando's blood, sustained in his second wrestling match in the play, with a lioness. The moment calls into question her assumed male gender, as Oliver asks him to "counterfeit to be a man."

That is the comic and dramatic breaking point of the scene, but I will argue that its most significant revelations take place earlier, and the swoon is their culmination. Winding back the clock, we find the revelation of Oliver's identity, known to Rosalind and Celia as the brother that "so oft did contrive to kill" Orlando—a revelation that can also be experienced by audiences depending on how wildly clad and unshaven is the actor playing the exiled Oliver in the scene. This is a Shakespearean invention: making Oliver come to the women as a stranger, and only later reveal his identity, which, as he insists, is also not his identity. Because of course he has been converted, this time in a positive version of Laud's dream: he awakens from what he describes as a "miserable slumber," just at the moment of the "hurtling" which is the word he uses to describe Orlando's overthrow of the lioness and the commotion it creates. Far from alienation, Oliver awakens from what he now perceives as misery, an "unnatural" state plagued by violent desire and desire for violence. He "knows" that all of this was his prior life, but he also has absolute confidence that it is gone forever, and describes the feeling, and notably the "taste" in this way:

> 'Twas I; but 'tis not I. I do not shame
> To tell you what I was, since my conversion
> So sweetly tastes, being the thing I am.
>
> (134–6)

His conversion is so powerful, that is, that it cures shame, not in the sense that it makes him shameless, but that he has also attained a state of fearlessness, comparable to Orlando's before the wrestling match, but different in that it is lack of fear about his shameful past, a state of grace from an act of total penance, owning all that is shameful and letting it go.

We might consider that it is beholding his brother's near-mortal sacrifice on his behalf, risking his life to wrestle the lioness who would otherwise devour him, that propels Oliver into this state. But my sense is that the play is more invested in the unaccountable experience of conversion dreamt of by Laud and feared as much as desired by Elizabethans and early modern European Christians more generally. Indeed, I find a closer analogy to Oliver's description of himself in Demetrius's explanation at the end of *A Midsummer Night's Dream*. This is of course about erotic conversion, not religious, and the audience knows that these conversions are anything but spontaneous, and are in fact the result of applied and misapplied love potions. Still, the problem posed by Demetrius at the start of the play is not magical: it is that Demetrius had previously "made love to Nedar's daughter, Helena" (1.1.107), but his affections had unaccountably shifted, such that he arranged with Egeus to marry his daughter Hermia. We know that he is cured of that strayed affection through magical-chemical intervention. But Demetrius does not, and, searching for a way to describe his experience and his sense of himself, he also turns to taste, and his earlier self as one who "in sickness" is disgusted by ordinary and nourishing food. He has now come back to "my natural taste" (4.1.172).

But where Demetrius is describing the changes in his desire, the "sweetness" Oliver describes seems to apply to existence itself, continuous, and not dependent on erotic nourishment—or any other nourishment for that matter. As such, the word takes us back to the exiled duke's effort at translation that first introduces us to the forest of Arden: "hath not old custom made this life more sweet / Than that of painted pomp" (2.1.2–3) and, even more emphatically, "Sweet are the uses of adversity," picked up by Amiens as the "quiet" and "sweet" style from which the duke "can translate the stubbornness of fortune" (19).

In that sweetness then we see the convergence of the play's twin interests in translation and conversion. And in my view the most significant moment of such convergence has already happened before we get to Oliver's conversion narrative, the revelation of his new identity, and the revelation of the meaning of the bloody handkerchief and Rosalind's swoon. This moment is the one that directly follows the crisis of the tyrannical path that Rosalind has taken with respect to Phoebe and her letter. It is, once more, the archetypal situation of pastoral literature, the situation of Virgil's first eclogue, the meeting of strangers in the countryside, strangers who nonetheless immediately find sympathy through shared expression. I argue below that this moment actually translates Virgil, in the sense that Shakespeare had Virgil's pastorals in his ear as he wrote these lines. But my argument does not depend on that textual and prosodic correspondence. The moment also recapitulates and rewrites similar scenes from earlier in the play. There is, of course, the scene of "translation" I described above, where Orlando, ready for violence, finds an auditor who is ready to echo and riff on his request for sympathetic hearing. But this is subtler than that scene, as it is poetically in its own space: there is no review or updating of Elizabethan poetic styles—all three interlocutors express themselves with equal eloquence, in Latinate but entirely convincing English blank verse. But there is also a recapitulation of Duke Frederick's two impositions of blank verse on earlier scenes in the play: first when he stiffens his back and speaks formally to Orlando once he recognizes him as a potential enemy, and second when he interrupts Rosalind and Celia's discussion of love to banish her from the kingdom. In those moments, poetry functioned as an extension of social and political power, forcing itself upon interlocutors. Oliver likewise changes this scene from prose to blank verse, but in utterly different fashion. Finally, the scene recapitulates the moment when Orlando hailed Jaques in blank verse, and Jaques, out of some combination of ennui and unaccountable pique, dismisses him with "Nay then, God b'wi' you, an you talk in blank verse" and storms off the stage.

In the context of this moment, all of those look like failed or nightmare versions of what is achieved here. And it is achieved, I want to argue, instantaneously, with a dynamic that is informed by what we know and what the play shows us of conversion. It is achieved at the moment of greeting and recognition, and this is what it sounds like:

OLIVER   Good morrow, fair ones. Pray you, if you know,
    Where in the purlieus of this forest stands
    A sheepcote fenced about with olive-trees?
CELIA   West of this place, down in the neighbor bottom;
    The rank of osiers by the murmuring stream,
    Left on your right hand, brings you to the place.
    But at this hour the house doth keep itself—
    There's none within.

                    (4.3.74–81)

That's it: that's what it sounds like. I have left to an afterword the detailed discussion of Virgil's Latin that leads me to argue Shakespeare was hearing him here. But that technical analysis is ultimately circumstantial and less important than all of the other context that this chapter, and indeed this book as a whole, has been attempting to orchestrate, that everything about the power of what is happening is already reflected in the language and rhythm of Oliver's question and the answer it receives in equal eloquence. The quiet force for concord that the play presents us with, what Adorno calls "rustling," is all here. It is almost another footnote that the moment is also the inception of the rapidly developing love between Celia and Oliver. Shakespeare sweeps entirely away the elaborate courtship between the two included by Lodge. Here it is left to Oliver and Orlando to explain the rapid progress

of the relationship toward marriage a couple of scenes later. But it needs no
further explanation because we are being presented with a version of human
connection to which Eros is made to seem itself a footnote.

To the crescendoing protest of erotic and political tyranny, and of Christian Europe's hypocritical embrace of chastity and worship of beauty, to a
vision that tyranny and hypocrisy and self-pleasuring are all that we can
find on earth, the vision that finally informs the most ferocious stage in the
evolution of the Rosalind that had scorned "shepherds devise" in Spenser,
where love—and all human relations that pretend to something other than
self-interest—just makes you an instrument to play false strains upon you—
to all of that the answer that is worth hearing is this: a call and a response
both ancient and modern, sophisticated eloquence and effortless simplicity,
a music of sympathetic understanding. All of the cascading conversions and
revelations of the rest of the scene flow from this.

Technical afterword

In chapter 1, I gave a compact introduction to the *Eclogues* and some arguments for why these poems would have been revered and imitated in the
sixteenth century, along with some of the specific technical challenges of
translating this poetry and its virtues into English.[34] In many ways Shakespeare's blank verse in general is a response to this, but at a moment like
Hamlet's encounter with the players we can see a direct engagement with
Virgil's heroic verse.[35] That is harder to demonstrate here in part because
pastoral traffics in the ordinary. Nonetheless a close analysis reveals a few
things.

Principal among the qualities of the dialogue that to me match Virgil's
take on pastoral verse is the mix of plainness and mannerism. For plainness: "West of this place, down in the neighbor bottom"; for mannerism,
such a homely expression as "If that an eye may profit by a tongue." The effect in Virgil is one of luminous simplicity, effortless singing. What is clearly
of huge import is the rhythmic ease of Shakespeare's writing here, relative
to English pastoralists who have preceded him. So part of what is being
mobilized is Shakespeare's uncanny ability to write verse that sounds like
"natural" speech. But that doesn't tell the whole story.

I can submit a small collection of common materials—words and phrases
that seem to me together to build an association between Virgil's first eclogue

---

[34] See "Virgil Problems."
[35] See 2.2.395–558. The speech that Hamlet recalls from a play he saw seems to be original
to Shakespeare, resonating with Marlowe's *Dido, Queen of Carthage* (2.1) and principally with
Aeneas' narration of the close of the Trojan War in *Aeneid*, 2.506–58.

and this piece of dialogue. Celia's three lines of direction-giving especially concentrate these:

> West of this place, down in the neighbor bottom;
> The rank of osiers by the murmuring stream,
> Left on your right hand, brings you to the place.
>
> (77–9)

"Right hand" doesn't sound at all like specifically pastoral vocabulary, but it appears in Eclogue 1: "non umquam gravis aere domum mihi dextra red-ibat" (35), says Tityrus, while recounting his bad business luck in the time before he met Octavian: "never would my hand come home money-laden," translates the Loeb edition, but *dextra* is specifically "right hand," not just "hand." A more obvious place to look is at descriptions of places, as in this:

> fortunate senex, hic inter flumina nota
> et fontis sacros frigus captabis opacum.
> hinc tibi, quae semper, vicino ab limite saepes
> Hyblaeis apibus florem depasta salicti
> saepe levi somnum suadebit inire susurro.

> Happy old man! Here, amid familiar streams and sacred springs, you shall enjoy the cooling shade. On this side, as of old, on your neighbor's border, the hedge whose willow [osier] blossoms are sipped by Hybla's bees shall often with its gentle hum soothe you to slumber.[36]

"Hinc tibi, quae semper, vicino ab limite saepes" lines up especially well with "west of this place, down in the neighbor bottom." "Hinc" lines up with "this place," and "vicino ab limite" lines up with "down in the neighbor bottom."

"Neighbor bottom" demands a bit of explanation: "Bottom" here must mean "Low-lying land, a valley, a dell; an alluvial hollow,"[37] for which the OED supplies an apropos example, from W. Browne in *Britannia's Pastorals* (1616): "Past gloomy Bottomes, and high-wauing Woods" (2.2.2). Tempting as it is to read this as a piece of low-lying land that forms the limit of a neighbor's property, and thus lines up closely with "vicino ab limite," "neighbor" must instead mean "nearby."[38] However, this leads us into other interesting

---

[36] As in chapter 1, the Latin edition is *Eclogues, Georgics, Aeneid I–VI*, trans. H. Rushton Fairclough, vol. 63, Loeb Classical Library (Cambridge, MA: Harvard University Press, 1999), and in this case the prose translation is from the same source.
[37] OED, "bottom," 4.b.
[38] OED, 2.c.

pastoral territory, as the first example supplied by the *OED* for that meaning is nothing but *The Shepheardes Calender*, "June," "Whose Echo made the neyghbour groues to ring." As well, the previous meaning of neighbor, more specifically nearby towns or cities, cites first again Spenser's *Shepheardes Calender*, "Januarye," "I longed the neighbour towne to see," a line glossed, bizarrely, by E.K., in this way: "Neighbour towne) the next towne: expressing the Latine Vicina." The gloss was picked out by C. S. Lewis as an example of E.K.'s idiocy ("E.K. is a very ridiculous person," he writes, and then quotes this gloss[39]), but the alignment here suggests to me that "neighbor" as an adjective meaning nearby might have been odd enough in the late sixteenth century to sound like an echo of Latin usage.

In the same vicinity to that line, we have other more obviously pastoral materials: in one, the "rank of osiers"; in the other, the flower of the osier, "florem salicti." In one, the "murmuring stream"; in the other, plenty of moving water, "fontes" and "flumina," as well as "susurrus," though here of the bees sipping the osier flowers. As well, "murmuring stream" comes close to the dactylic gait of the end of every Virgilian hexameter. And the phrase is also as close to a Western linguistic topos for pastoral as one might ask for: its sound shows up in Theocritus's first Idyll and in numerous other European pastorals thereafter.

From elsewhere in Eclogue 1: "tugurium" (68), a specifically shepherd-appropriate dwelling that might be translated as "sheepcote." And finally as a sample of homely manner parallel to "if that an eye can profit from a tongue," there is Tityrus' effort to describe the vastness of Rome that begins thus: "sic canibus catulos similes, sic matribus haedos / noram, sic parvis componere magna solebam" (22–3). We can translate this as "that dogs are like to puppies, and mothers to kids / I knew; I knew the great to compare with small," but it is difficult to capture the proverbial compression of "sic canibus catulos."

A little reflection on the Virgilian scene in *Hamlet* might be our most sensible stopping point: that scene is characterized by its intense frustration—Hamlet remembers a play that was not a commercial success, but appreciated only by those with better judgments, and while his initial, halting recitation of the speech he longs for is greeted by praise from Polonius, the full speech carried on by the Player elicits boredom from him—and helpless fury from Hamlet. In contrast, this moment in *As You Like It*, so brief you could blink and miss it, is one where all speakers are enveloped equally, where the poetry's promise of concord is for a moment fulfilled.

---

[39] C. S. Lewis, *English Literature in the Sixteenth Century Excluding Drama*, Oxford History of English Literature (Oxford: Clarendon Press, 1954), 355. See also another translation of *vicina* to neighbor cited on 254.

5

Conclusion

Mary Wroth, Dora Jordan, and Katharine Hepburn

What is the place of Rosalind on the path to greater freedom and possibility for actual women? To explore this question I have selected three women from the 400 years of Rosalind's greater possible area of influence, that show off three very different possible effects or outgrowths of that influence. I begin with a woman writer contemporary to *As You Like It*, who could have seen the play or read it, and could have talked about it with Ben Jonson or her illustrious literary family. I mean Mary Sidney, Lady Wroth, the extraordinary literary figure of the early seventeenth century. I consider here her radical reimagination of the Petrarchan lyric in the context of Rosalind's more extreme readings of the poetry she encounters. Then I examine two women who came to Rosalind during spectacular careers on stage and screen, one, Dora Jordan, in the late eighteenth century and the other, Katharine Hepburn, in the first half of the twentieth. Both were conduits of immense erotic and social energies in their respective cultures, and in both cases, I consider less the nature of their specific performances of Rosalind, to which our access is anyway quite limited, and instead, as with Wroth, consider what their performance careers and lives as artists look like in the light of Rosalind.

Tyrannical Style: Mary Wroth (1587–1651)

About Mary Wroth, I want to argue that we might understand some of the ongoing difficulties readers have with her poetic style as related to the same forces of identity, translation, gender, and sexuality that we have seen swirling around Rosalind through the last decades of the sixteenth century. In particular, I want to link the scene of Rosalind's distorting, violent interpretation of Phoebe's love poem to what I suggest are aggressive, distorting

What Rosalind Likes. Paul J. Hecht, Oxford University Press.
© Paul J. Hecht (2022). DOI: 10.1093/oso/9780192857200.003.0005

effects in Wroth's lyric style. Wroth has been on the scene of anglophone literary criticism for almost a professional lifetime now, but in many respects her work is still arguably new, new in the sense that before the publication in 1983 of *The Poems of Lady Mary Wroth*, edited by Josephine Roberts, this poetry had for all intents and purposes ceased to exist.[1] The newness registers in a variety of ways, but one of them is in the way we refer to the author: Mary Wroth? Lady Mary Wroth in a kind of parallelism to Sir Philip Sidney? Or as Wroth's biography suggests in its title, *Mary Sidney, Lady Wroth*?[2] The lack of stability here reflects the fact that prior to 1983, hardly anyone was referring to Wroth by any name.

Newness also helps us to understand the dynamics of the reception of Wroth's works in the past few decades. Tensions around feminist literary criticism and the political and social movements connected to that criticism are very much here, and the tensions can be summarized around whether we are more interested in reading Wroth's poetry (as well as her prose and drama) for its political, historical, and social significance or for its literary or aesthetic significance. The historical significance is indisputable: Wroth was the first woman to publish in English a prose romance, the *Urania* (1621), and, in an addendum to that same work, the first woman to publish a sonnet sequence in English, *Pamphilia to Amphilanthus*. A second part of *Urania*, equal in size to the published portion, as well as a play, *Love's Victory*, survived in manuscript and both have now been edited and published.[3] The social and political significance follows fairly easily from this history. Recovering works by women in a time when it was so unusual for women to

---

[1] Lady Mary Wroth, *The Poems of Lady Mary Wroth*, ed. Josephine A. Roberts (Baton Rouge: Louisiana State University Press, 1983). This is the edition that came to be the standard for several decades; it was, however, preceded by Gary Waller's edition *Pamphilia to Amphilanthus* (Salzburg: Institut für Englische Sprache und Litertur, University of Salzburg, 1977).

[2] Margaret P. Hannay, *Mary Sidney, Lady Wroth* (Farnham, Surrey: Ashgate, 2010).

[3] The first published editions of the *Urania* were these: Lady Mary Wroth, *The First Part of The Countess of Montgomery's Urania*, ed. Josephine A. Roberts, Medieval and Renaissance Texts and Studies 140 (Binghamton: Center for Medieval and Early Renaissance Studies, State University of New York at Binghamton, 1995); Lady Mary Wroth, *The Second Part of the Countess of Montgomery's Urania*, ed. Josephine A. Roberts, Suzanne Gossett, and Janel Mueller (Tempe: Renaissance English Text Society in Conjunction with Arizona Center for Medieval and Renaissance Studies, 1999). Mary Ellen Lamb has subsequently edited an abridged version of the entire work: Mary Wroth, *The Countess of Montgomery's Urania (Abridged)*, ed. Mary Ellen Lamb (Tempe: Arizona Center for Medieval and Renaissance Studies, 2011). *Love's Victory* was first edited and published in S. P. Cerasano and Marion Wynne-Davies, eds., *Renaissance Drama by Women: Texts and Documents* (London and New York: Routledge, 1996), 91–126, and has been published in multiple locations since then.

write and be read helps more women write now: this is common sense, but it is also common sense backed up by a lot of research in social psychology.[4] But this very argument for editing and anthologizing and teaching and paying attention to Wroth also creates interpretive tension: because of the political and social significance, should contemporary readers treat her works differently from the way they would treat other (male) writers? And that tension is amplified by the difficulty of these works, particularly the prose romance—which is intimidatingly enormous—and the poems, which can be quite hard to understand, even as they also seem lacking in sophistication relative to the rest of the English sonnet tradition. In thirty-five years or so of interpretive history, just a couple of writers have gone so far as to explore the notion that the difficulty of the poems reflects artistic shortcomings in Wroth, but while those are nuanced and illuminating discussions, they are not the most memorable pushback that Wroth has received.[5] That would have to be a blog entry published in 2010 by Christopher Warley, still available on Stanford's *Arcade*, and still receiving comment as of this writing. The blog post is entitled "Un-canonizing Lady Mary Wroth?" and contains the memorable if blunt assertion that "the poems are terrible."[6] It goes on to recount the relief of Warley and his students when, in survey courses on seventeenth-century English lyric, Wroth was at last abandoned in favor of more poems by writers like Ben Jonson and Andrew Marvell.

I don't think the poems are terrible, but I do think we are still figuring out the most productive context in which to place them, as well as how to process some of their notable stylistic features—which are also the source of reading difficulty and frustration that could forgivably lead to a reader, even a reader of the sophistication and resource of Warley, to throw up her hands and give up. But Warley is also feeling a kind of fury that has been of interest to us in this study, and that takes us toward the scenes that were our starting point:

---

[4] This research has shown how subtle cues can actuate stereotypes that inhibit performance in a wide variety of areas. Though I have not yet seen other scholars of literature and literary history discuss this, the research adds a significant new dimension to the canon wars of the 1980s and 1990s, and indicates that the instincts of early feminist literary critics were correct and that there is even more at stake in these struggles than was previously recognized. For a cogent and rapid introduction to stereotype threat, see Claude M. Steele, *Whistling Vivaldi: How Stereotypes Affect Us and What We Can Do* (New York: W. W. Norton, 2010).

[5] The articles raising the possibility of Wroth's shortcomings are by Elizabeth Hanson, "Boredom and Whoredom: Reading Renaissance Women's Sonnet Sequences," *Yale Journal of Criticism* 10 (1997): 165–91; and Roger Kuin, "More I Still Undoe: Louise Labé, Mary Wroth, and the Petrarchan Discourse," *Comparative Literature Studies* 36 (1999): 146–61.

[6] Christopher Warley, "Un-Canonizing Lady Mary Wroth?," *Arcade: Literature, the Humanities, & the World* (blog), 2010, https://arcade.stanford.edu/blogs/un-canonizing-lady-mary-wroth.

Rosalind condemning "shepheardes devise," Rosalind pushing back against the misogynist dictum of women to be diamond-like and silent, Rosalind launching a verbal assault on Petrarchan poetics and sexual politics with Silvius and Phoebe, Rosalind reading Phoebe's love poem and tearing it to pieces. I want to suggest that the frustration Wroth generates with her lyrics resonates with all of these, even as the moment of their writing stands quite apart from the twenty years of poetic development in the biography of poetry we observed from 1579 to 1600. That is to say, attempting to carve out a space for a woman writer in a world where women were expected to be silent might partake in some of the dynamics of these Rosalinds, particularly the tense relationship of *As You Like It*'s Rosalind to the Petrarchan tradition that is so much in play when one writes a sonnet sequence in English in the years after 1600.

But there is another scene we have observed that seems relevant to Wroth's position as a writer, and that is the scene of "September," where a shepherd who is effeminized by brutal economic conditions searches for a style adequate to his sufferings, sufferings that include a metaphorical pregnancy as a result of rape.[7] In chapter 2 I argued that this shepherd's effeminized and marginalized position leads him to seek a style of expression that in various ways inverts and frustrates the expectations and ideals of Elizabethan poetry. It seeks "flat" expression, and in its critical zeal it does away with ornament and musical pleasure, attempting to dig to the bottom of the world's corruption. It does so with such locutions as "Badde is the best." I earlier also brought in another conceptual frame that might authorize such a reversal of presiding aesthetic values, and this is the late twentieth-century phenomenon of punk rock. In deliberate contrast with highly orchestrated and produced stadium rock of the 1970s, a countercultural music emerged where musicians were expected to avoid playing their instruments well.[8] This is to say, one way to read Mary Wroth's lyrics is as self-consciously "bad" if your idea of good is, for example, Philip Sidney's *Astrophil to Stella*. I have lately thought as well of other kinds of musical idioms forged in reaction to prevailing stylistic paradigms that might be relevant here. In the history of Black music in the United States we might find many examples, but one that

---

[7] See chapter 2, "Badde is the best."

[8] The point is well known enough not to require support, but it was interesting nonetheless to hear at a round table the drummer for Gang of Four, Hugh Burnham, finding himself in early rehearsals needing to unlearn some of the precision and proficiency that he brought to the band, this at a book launch event at the Seminary Coop Bookstore, Chicago, May 23, 2014, for Kevin J. H. Dettmar, *Entertainment!*, 33 1/2 (New York: Bloomsbury, 2014).

stands out is Thelonious Monk (1917–82), a pianist and composer who both in his piano technique and his compositional vocabulary defined himself by shearing away much of the nuance and complexity associated with piano and with jazz composition. Yet both components of his style have come to be recognized as distinctive, capacious, and durable as new generations of pianists incorporate aspects of his technique, and his compositions continue to be mined by new improvisers and taken in new directions. This example, or perhaps even such a comparatively easy example as that of Emily Dickinson (1830–86), might serve better than punk as a way of imagining how Wroth's distinctive style is being gradually processed by readers and interpreters into a more steady sense of enduring value.[9] Again: Wroth, despite being 400 years old, is still new.

But Rosalind, particularly Rosalind in her furious phase with respect to Silvius and Phoebe, is still a relevant comparison. I have in mind the divide that opens up between Phoebe's gentle love poem and Rosalind's furious interpretation of it. This creates a dissonance to me that is parallel to distortion, noise, which of course has been deliberately courted in the rock and roll tradition since before the advent of punk rock. In Wroth's lyrics, I find one of the central aspects of their difficulty to be a semantic distortion that is parallel to courting noise through overdriving guitar in amplifiers. Courting incoherence gives voice to anguish, produces a sense of rawness, and my reading of Wroth's facility as a poet makes me think that these are deliberate moves. The most relevant passage from Rosalind's history is of course the one that explicitly describes a style, although it is a style that has no relation to poetry it purports to describe. "Why, 'tis a boisterous and a cruel style. A style for challengers," she says, and as we discussed in chapter 4, assigns all manner of cultural others to join with that "challengers": class, gender, religion, and race all attributed to Phoebe's "Ethiope words."[10] It seems fitting then to take a Wroth poem focused on blackness—the blackness of night—as our primary example of her style.

---

[9] The history of criticism of Dickinson has been one of gradual appreciation and acceptance of her aesthetic decisions, or recognizing them as decisions, from early regularizing and "correction" of her poetry up to the contemporary understanding of many poems as existing in more than one form, and letting go the old editorial impulse always to seek singularity. Given that Dickinson's poems were only published and presented substantially free of those editorial impulses for the first time in 1998, in some ways Dickinson, like Wroth, is also new. See Emily Dickinson, *The Poems of Emily Dickinson*, ed. R. W. Franklin, 3 vols. (Cambridge, MA: Belknap Press of Harvard University Press, 1998).

[10] See chapter 4, "Mark how the tyrant writes."

Cloyed with the torments of a tedious night
I wish for day; which come, I hope for joy:
When cross I find new tortures to destroy
My woe-killed heart, first hurt by mischief's might,

Then cry for night, and once more day takes flight
And brightness gone; what rest should here enjoy
Usurped is; hate will her force employ;
Night cannot grief entomb though black as spite

My thoughts are sad; her face as sad doth seem:
My pains are long; her hours tedious are:
My grief is great, and endless is my care:
Her face, her force, and all of woes esteem:

Then welcome Night, and farewell flattering day
Which all hopes breed, and yet our joys delay.[11]

Various elements of the Wroth style are well represented here. The semantic distortion picks up in the second quatrain, where it becomes increasingly difficult to know who or what is the subject of the sentence that continues to unfold. If this is deliberate roughness as I believe it is, then it is making things harder for readers because, well, she just doesn't care. Likewise the stripped-down anti-*copia* vocabulary that focuses around words like "grief," and "sad," and "woe." And finally there is anti-musicality in such harsh phrases as "my woe-killed heart," and the stunningly ugly inversion, "Usurped is." Wroth doesn't always write with this level of intensive punk denial of the established pleasures of Elizabethan sonnets, but often enough she does, and as far as I can tell, she might as well be pulling a pistol on a room full of well-heeled connoisseurs and opening fire.[12]

---

[11] In Josephine Roberts's numbering system, this is P13. See Wroth, *Poems*, ed. Roberts. However, I have taken this modernized text from the admirable online edition that includes versions of the poems from the Folger manuscript, as well as the printed edition appended to the *Urania*. See Lady Mary Wroth, "Mary Wroth's Poetry: An Electronic Edition," ed. Paul Salzman, 2012, http://wroth.latrobe.edu.au/all-poems.html.

[12] The image is from the Sid Vicious/Sex Pistols cover of "My Way," released as a music video in 1978, but allowed a fuller, more obscene and violent version of the same footage in the film *The Great Rock 'n' Roll Swindle* (1980), now readily available on YouTube. In a college class in the 1990s on the contemporary British novel, Caryl Phillips showed us this video and told a story about its importance to him as a Black man born in St Kitts studying at Oxford in the late 1970s. After seeing this, he said, he felt things were going to be all right.

Our view of Wroth continues to evolve. When I first wrote about her sonnets in 2013, I was at the beginning of a shift in thinking that has been carried forward by other writers. Melissa E. Sanchez notes that "until recently" *Pamphilia to Amphilanthus* was "subject to critical protectionism" around a particular narrative of Wroth's life that led to a view that the poems depicted the speaker as an unrequited lover and social exile.[13] A combination of biographical research, textual scholarship, and new interpretive and methodological approaches to the poems have upended that earlier narrative.[14] And the view of her other writings is also evolving in ways that seem parallel to shifts in views of her lyrics. A notable recent example is Colleen Ruth Rosenfeld's recent study of the *Urania*. To the principal stylistic challenge to modern readers of that book, its labyrinthine involutions and etceterative exponential linguistic and narrative *copia*-seeking, Rosenfeld supplies a highly plausible explanation, built around the figure of periphrasis: "As an alternative to philosophy's direct grasp and the stylistic ideal of clarity that is a sign of this grasp, *periphrasis* defines fiction as the space of obscure ornamentation."[15] This does not set out for Wroth's prose style quite the level of aesthetic aggression that I see in the *Pamphilia* poems, but the sense of contrariness seems parallel.

The Romp: Dora Jordan (1761–1816)

There is of course another way of framing the connection I am suggesting between Rosalind and Wroth, and that is not that Wroth saw in Rosalind a way to envision a style for herself and her poetry that could succeed and satisfy her in the space of seventeenth-century British culture, but rather that it is *my* perception of Rosalind that allowed me to see something similar in Wroth, even as these views developed independently in me, or seemed to. In any case, I am now stepping away from speculative impacts of Rosalind on actual women of her time, in order to contemplate two women who were notable performers and embodiments of Rosalind. As I wrote at the start of this study, the popular sense of Rosalind doubtless owes as much or more to

[13] Melissa E. Sanchez, *Queer Faith: Reading Promiscuity and Race in the Secular Love Tradition*, Sexual Cultures (New York: New York University Press, 2019), 179.
[14] For biographical and textual scholarship, see esp. Margaret Hannay's biography, and Lady Mary Wroth, *"Pamphilia to Amphilanthus" in Manuscript and Print*, ed. Ilona Bell (Toronto: Iter Press, 2017), as well as Paul Salzman's electronic edition of the poems.
[15] See Colleen Ruth Rosenfeld, *Indecorous Thinking: Figures of Speech in Early Modern Poetics* (New York: Fordham University Press, 2018), 147.

these performances than the text itself, but in the limited space before me, I am not attempting to trace the influence of these performers' Rosalinds. Rather, I want to scrutinize a couple of wildly different versions of Rosalind and the lives of two women actors for whom the role was important. My attention is finally focused on the freedom and agency of their lives and their lives as performing artists. And while an homage like, say, Zadie Smith's to Katharine Hepburn is certainly suggestive, I am mostly going to refrain from speculating on how these performances of Rosalind might have led to more freedom and more agency for women writers and women simply leading their lives.[16]

The woman who has the most credible claim to being the greatest Rosalind in the stage history of the play began her career in unlikely circumstances in Dublin at the end of the eighteenth century. Claire Tomalin in her excellent biography of 1995 assembles a range of materials around how she got her start on the stage and what seemed to be the secret of her rapid triumph, but the matter remains mysterious. Her first stage success in Dublin came under the management of Richard Daly, who then impregnated her, either through a seduction or an assault. In any case, she fled with her mother and younger siblings to England and pursued another theatrical connection with Tate Wilkinson in Leeds. A meeting with Wilkinson began inauspiciously as he saw a pregnant woman of 20 with three dependent family members, no clothes for acting (which was expected of performers), and no money. Yet within an hour, once she had been convinced to recite a portion of *The Fair Penitent* (a source for *Clarissa*), the situation rapidly changed: "when he heard her voice he felt surprise and delight" and soon was negotiating terms to get her on the stage.[17] Three years on the road in northern England followed, learning huge amounts of repertoire, successfully battling the jealousy of other female performers, and mostly walking between cities when she wasn't performing. This period came to an end when she was offered a contract to perform at Drury Lane in London, and commenced her first season there in 1783.

---

[16] See Zadie Smith, "The Divine Ms H," *The Guardian*, July 1, 2003, https://www.theguardian.com/film/2003/jul/01/film.zadiesmith. Smith at one point notes that "the kind of woman she played, the kind of woman she was, is still the kind of woman I should like to be"—an observation parallel to Martha Nussbaum's about Rosalind noted in chapter 4, "Mark how the tyrant writes."

[17] Claire Tomalin, *Mrs Jordan's Profession: The Actress and the Prince* (New York: Alfred A. Knopf, 1995), 25. Subsequent page references will be made parenthetically in the text.

Thence began an astonishingly quick ascent to celebrity, powered especially by roles in which she wore men's attire. Shakespeare's cross-dressed heroines were here, along with many more contemporary plays. Among these, one of the most outstanding was a brief entertainment entitled *The Romp*. I want to look more closely at this one because it appears to have captured the public imagination especially powerfully, and we have an image of a scene from the play where Jordan, playing the title character, is standing "in a boxing attitude," frightening one of her suitors off the stage.[18] It is a moment that resonates with this study. It is hard to overstate her success in this season, in which she went from being unknown to attracting the attention and effusive praise of the senior lights of the theatrical scene, including Sarah Siddons who had seen her in the North and been initially unimpressed, but was won over by *The Romp*, as well as a substantial portion of the royal family including the King.[19] A benefit for her at the end of the first season raised £200, and she was separately offered £300 by a gentleman's club, just because.[20]

Claire Tomalin summarizes her meteoric rise in a memorable paragraph:

She was at once seen—and heard, for she had to sing—to be extraordinary: a perfect girl-boy in her young man's breeches that showed her slim waist and pretty legs. She was not shy, and she was not bawdy; she was easy and natural. Her face was finely expressive, her singing voice untrained, and all the more captivating for it. Either she had learnt her art quickly and without effort, or—as people preferred to think—she had simply been born with the gift for comedy. Her laugh bubbled up "from the heart," they said; and when she laughed the audience laughed back, helpless and delighted, like a whole house full of lovers, and her charm infused the theater from pit to upper gallery. (21)

Leigh Hunt looked back upon her career this way: "the reader will pardon me, but tears of pleasure and regret come into my eyes at the recollection, as

[18] The quotation is a stage direction from the text, Isaac Bickerstaff, *The Romp: A Musical Entertainment in Two Acts, Altered from "Love in the City"* (Dublin: Wilkinson et al., 1783), 32.
[19] The report of Mrs Siddons's change of opinion comes from observations made by Mary Tickell in correspondence with Elizabeth Sheridan and quoted by Tomalin, *Mrs Jordan's Profession*, 53.
[20] See Tomalin, *Mrs Jordan's Profession*, 55.

if she personified whatsoever was happy at that period of life, and which has gone like herself."[21]

Rosalind was one of the early vehicles for these collective emotions, but I want to concentrate on a phase of the "perfect girl-boy" that emphasizes the strangeness, if not the darkness, of Dora Jordan's seduction of late eighteenth-century Britain. And this is the tomboy character of *The Romp*, whose name is in fact Priscilla Tomboy. *The Romp* is a musical entertainment—a brief play, with songs—from the middle of the century, that was revived for her by Wilkinson before becoming a signature role. This is the kind of show that could be appended to a larger, more serious play—a Shakespeare play perhaps—as an extra joy to close out the evening, a kind of encore. But what seems most to have captured the imaginations and earned the laughter of English theatergoers are the scenes of violence or threatened violence, where Jordan's character's disregard of gender norms, her indecorous unfemininity, becomes physically dangerous for other people. The most iconic moment, as I have already alluded to, is the one that was captured in a stage sketch in 1785 (reproduced in Figure 5.1), when, as the stage directions

Fig. 5.1 Dora Jordan as Priscilla Tomboy. Attributed to R. Rushworth, 1785. Reproduced by permission
© The Trustees of the British Museum.

[21] Quoted by Tomalin, *Mrs Jordan's Profession*, 20.

describe it, "*Priscilla* puts herself in a boxing attitude and beats *Young Cockney* off"—that is, her would-be husband Walter Cockney.[22] That comes close to the end; her introduction to the audience is also accompanied by violence, when, working in a grocer's shop with Cockney's sister, the young man asks Priscilla for a stool so he can put it behind the counter, and she loses it: "There, take your stool, you nasty, ugly, conceited, ill-natured—— [*Throws it at him*" (6).

So, offering hatred, threatening to throw things and when asked to kiss, to offer to "spit in his face" (7) is a kind of Rosalind attitude toward unwanted sexual advances, and it is a surprising departure from gender norms as well as a revenge fantasy for many women, but the origins of these characteristics are presented in extraordinary terms in this play, and we hear about them right after the stool is thrown, as Young Cockney protests:

Look there now, did you ever see any thing so unmannerly? Miss Prissy, I wonder you are not ashamed of yourself; but this is the breeding you got in the plantations—— [...] I believe you think you have got among your blackamoors—But you are not among your blackamoors now, Miss. (6)

Thus after the introductory chorus had hailed London as the "noblest mart on earth ... whence riches, honors, arts, have birth" (5) we hear of the origin of the Romp's transgressive violence as the same as the principal origins of the age's wealth: the West Indies' outrageously profitable, slave-driven economy.[23] The play continues its focus on this going forward, sometimes fascinated, sometimes scandalized or perhaps horrified—it is hard to be sure. A character named Quasheba identified in the dramatis personae as "a Negro Girl," is also the subject of Priscilla's verbal abuse in the next scene. When Priscilla wants to confide in Cockney's sister Penelope about the true object of her affection, one Captain Sightly, she first orders Quasheba out and then bids her stay and threatens that if she lets out the secret she is about to divulge, "I will have you horse-whip'd 'till there is not a bit of flesh left on your bones" (9). We get an expression of repulsion at this treatment and

[22] Bickerstaff, *The Romp*, 32. Subsequent page references will be made parenthetically in the text.
[23] For a discussion of recent scholarship on this topic, see Fara Dabhoiwala, "Speech and Slavery in the West Indies," *New York Review of Books* 67, no. 13 (August 20, 2020), https://www.nybooks.com/articles/2020/08/20/speech-slavery-west-indies/.

threat from Penelope, "Oh poor creature!" (9), to which Priscilla offers this expatiation:

PRIS   Psha! What is she but a neger? If she was at home in our plantations,
she would find the difference; we make no account of them there at all: if
I had a fancy for one of their skins, I should not think much of taking it.
PEN   I suppose then you imagine they have no feeling?
PRIS   Oh! We never consider that there—But I say, Miss Penny ... (9–10)

And there the matter is closed.

The backstory is filled in a little more in other places, that men may be attracted to Priscilla by the promise of "a West Indian fortune" (17), and that Priscilla is threatened by her guardian with being sent back to Jamaica. Indeed, in addition to bragging about the ability to flay slaves at will at her plantation, she at one point, as part of a ruse to get Young Cockney to remove her from confinement, holds out this prospect: "if you go with me to Jamaica, I'll raise the negers for us—it's only beating them well, giving them a few yams, and they'll do any thing you bid them" (28).

Horrifying and entertaining words, "Ethiope words, blacker in their effect / Than in their countenance." To what extent is the perfect girl-boy in the noblest mart of earth standing atop the beaten and whipped corpses of the commerce of the centuries that stretch from Rosalind's words to these? How much is the violence she unleashes now not just that of Rosalind, furious at being pursued with "shepherds devise," or having to play the woman's part in a Petrarchan version of patriarchy, or of a character like Diggon, feminized and assaulted by economic "bulls" but now also the collective conscience, somewhere below the surface of the wide swath of English theatergoing society, that stretches from tradespeople to kings, that their comfort and wealth is built on enslavement and torture and death?

There is a painting from 1786 that depicts Jordan "as the Comic Muse supported by Euphrosyne, who represses the advances of a Satyr," a title supplied by the artist John Hoppner for the painting's display at the Royal Academy.[24] The painting is notable for the subtexts and subterranean forces it seems to unveil: here Jordan is not cross-dressed, is purely female, and her situation is fundamentally under erotic threat. The painting sets up the

---

[24] A detail of this painting, from 1786, appears on the dust jacket to this book. The painting currently hangs in Buckingham Palace, see https://www.rct.uk/collection/404611/mrs-jordan-1761-1816-as-the-comic-muse.

viewer to admire Jordan, and then attaches that admiration to the violent lust of the satyr lurking to one side. It is worth taking a moment to consider Jordan's personal life with respect to this depiction as well as the dynamic of gender transgression and un-repression of violence and guilt displayed in *The Romp*. I have already noted that Jordan was able to launch her career in the north of England in the wake of what might have been a sexual assault resulting in pregnancy, but in any case was a pregnancy in the context of an unwanted affair by a theater manager that tried to dominate and possess her, and from whom she escaped across the Irish Sea. Her early stage successes were during this pregnancy. In some ways, this pattern then continued for the rest of her career, albeit with major distinctions. There is much evidence of her love and affection for Richard Ford as well as her royal lover who was to become William IV. But both men contrived to live with her, and father children with her, without marrying her. This refusal by these two men to fully legitimate their relationship with her (and it is true that for William that may have been impossible under British law) had two powerful effects—on her life, and on her legacy. The effect on her life is obvious: William cut Jordan off when she took to the stage after his accession to the throne, this despite her having been the much greater earner during her professional life, and having actually paid his debts for much of it. She died in poverty and de facto exile. The effect on her legacy is also obvious and palpable: the project that Tomalin has undertaken, to restore to prominence an actress who was celebrated as one of the greatest of all time, is necessary because of the official ignorance and non-attention to Jordan by a royal family that for many years wished to pretend that the king had never had such a mistress and fathered numerous children with her. Thus the statue he had guiltily commissioned and intended for Westminster Abbey languished in a private collection instead (and it now adorns the back cover of Tomalin's book).

There seems always to have been a fight for possession of Jordan: what she gave to audiences, and what was thus collective and fundamentally shared was precisely what powerful men wanted to posses all for themselves. The greatest moment of jeopardy for Jordan's career seems to have revolved around these dynamics, in the wake of the scandal that she was having an affair with Prince William. Satirists attacked her and the prince with astonishing creativity and viciousness, reveling in the ability to bring the lofty and, in Jordan's case, the beloved down. The greatest charge in the public mind seems to have been that this was Jordan's plan all along, that her whole theatrical success was a grand seduction of the best possible bachelor, a woman who dared to perform herself into royalty. Jordan seems to have recognized this on December 10, 1791, when, returning to the Drury Lane stage for the first time since the scandal had broken, she was booed and hissed at. The report from her biographer James Boaden and others is that she calmly paused in her performance to address the audience, and that the sum of her remarks was that she belonged to them, that she had never ceased to "strive here to please you" and as a result considered herself "under the public protection," and these remarks produced a perfect reconciliation that was also a perfect moment of theatrical joy and forgiveness and mutual love: concord, that is to say.[25]

Jordan's theatrical power thus seems to have been a function of her vulnerability, and her abandon, her ability to give herself completely to performance, to audiences, while also always being possessed at some level by a satyr, in an illegitimate relationship of "keeping" in which for much of her career she was also pregnant, and always also caring for her children.

Morning Glory: Katharine Hepburn (1907–2003)

Katharine Hepburn had a tense relationship with Rosalind, and it is not clear that she was a Rosalind for the ages. Contemporary accounts suggest that things were overproduced, and that the show relied too heavily on her star power to draw audiences. Up until this point in her career, she had reason to be leery of the stage—a production of *The Lake* in 1933 had elicited harsh reviews and ended in early closure.[26] But I nonetheless want to argue that Rosalind was in her DNA, in a version of Shakespeare and Elizabethan lyric that is visible at the start of her career. Like Dora Jordan, Hepburn came to prominence on the force of some roles that were transgressive of gender norms, though transgressive in some pretty standard ways. But at Bryn Mawr, where she went as her mother and aunts before her had done, she partook in a female culture that included a great deal of cross-dressing, of extreme hazing rituals, of dances, and of thinly veiled lesbian affairs, and in her senior year, she was featured in the annual May Day festivities, which were, according to the dictates of the president, Carey Thomas, decidedly

[25] See James Boaden, *The Life of Mrs. Jordan*, 2nd edn., 2 vols., vol. 1 (London: Edward Bull, 1831), 212. Also see Tomalin, *Mrs Jordan's Profession*, 127.

[26] See Barbara Leaming, *Katharine Hepburn* (New York: Crown, 1995), 289.

Elizabethan in nature. As a senior in 1928, Hepburn played Pandora in Lyly's *The Woman in the Moon*.[27]

Hepburn got noticed by Hollywood people for her performance in *The Warrior's Husband*, in which she played an Amazon. Her role in Dorothy Arzner's *Christopher Strong* (1933) built on this tomboy part of her background. But other roles, as in her first film, *A Bill of Divorcement* (1932), and her third film, which also won her an Academy Award for best actress, *Morning Glory* (1933), were not obviously tomboy or cross-dressed. These roles do show off other aspects of her background, which had not included much theatrical training in the traditional sense. Largely on the strength of Barbara Leaming's biography, I am persuaded of the importance of several experiences from her childhood and aspects of her upbringing that seem to have had a powerful influence in preparing her for these roles. And while she may not have been one of the great Rosalinds, I want to argue that her sense of what it meant to have a truly successful career in acting and the arts was very much involved with Shakespeare and with Rosalind in particular. To play Rosalind well meant that Hepburn had lived up to the ideals of her parents, particularly her mother, and lived up to the ideals of culture and art that were so powerfully espoused at Bryn Mawr. It also meant that she had gotten over the embarrassment with Hollywood and the nature of being a film star, of finding an audience exponentially larger than any great stage actress of the last century, and yet wondering if the very size of that audience did not cheapen her achievement.[28]

My hypothesis is that Hepburn would have made a terrific Rosalind on screen or stage if the sense of the part and the play had been less influenced by a contemporary conception of the play as a "rustic revel," as the *New York Times* theater critic Brooks Atkinson put it in a review, which also claimed that Hepburn's "very sharply defined and electric personality" was wrong for the role and wrong for the play.[29] The production, which Hepburn had sought as a way to find new energy for the next phase of her film career, was extremely popular nonetheless, and we also know that her mother was pleased with the show, and that they spent time together reading reviews, good, bad, and indifferent, and laughing about them all.[30]

---

[27] See Leaming, *Katharine Hepburn*, 237. Leaming includes a photograph of Hepburn in the role in a plate between pp. 118 and 119.

[28] On Hepburn's mother's preference for Shaw and Shakespeare, see Leaming, *Katharine Hepburn*, 281.

[29] Brooks Atkinson, "Forest of Arden: Katharine Hepburn in *As You Like It*," *New York Times*, February 19, 1950, sec. 2.

[30] See Leaming, *Katharine Hepburn*, 439–40.

No footage of Hepburn in the part exists. But what we do have is *Morning Glory*, which not only displays with special intensity the relationship between film and theatrical success, but also imagines the height of greatness in Shakespeare and, indirectly, in Rosalind. With a plot that follows the general pattern of *A Star Is Born*, Hepburn plays an aspiring stage actress who comes to New York in search of work and fame. This kind of plot revels in the sense of ordinariness and limitless possibility in the person swept to stardom, and it also revels in the sexual ambiguity of the mentor relationship, where encouragement of dreams can merge with seduction, and where it can be difficult to tell who is seducing whom. In such a plot we always have one or more scenes where the aspiring star shows her stuff, and where we look at the faces of cynical, seasoned professionals and see that yes, this just might be the real thing. The scene like that in *Morning Glory* is at a party held by a theater manager, that includes various fictional playwrights and actors. Hepburn's character, Eva Lovelace (her stage name, as she keeps informing everyone), is brought by an older actor, who remembers the female stage luminaries of the recent past. Those luminaries are evoked twice earlier in the film, once when Eva asks the older man if he got to see Ellen Terry and Sarah Bernhardt, and he replies passionately in the affirmative, and once in the opening sequence of the film, where the shoddily dressed Eva wanders around the lobby of the theater, looking at portraits of famous actors, including Ethel Barrymore and, again, Sarah Bernhardt. That moment of connection is one of sexual ambiguity as well—Eva in this scene demands to be given lessons by the older actor, and we can't tell if in agreeing to do so, he is agreeing to help her or rather has sexual designs on her.

In the central party scene, the sexual ambiguity becomes less ambiguous, as an unscrupulous playwright actively works to get Eva drunk so that he can get her in bed. A younger man—a playwright with a name with plenty of eighteenth-century resonance, Joseph Sheridan—is clearly attracted to her, but is also trying to help her, in this case by getting her some food and saving her from the predations of the other playwright. And then there is the theater manager who is also attracted to her, and at the end of this scene has her carried from his lap on which she has fallen asleep to a bedroom—the next day we learn that he has later followed her there. So that's three generations of male lust focused on this young woman, each of them somewhere between curiosity about whether she really does have what it takes to achieve the success of those dominant actresses, and wondering whether they can or should control their desires or protect her, or what it would mean to protect her, and what it means to go to bed with her.

The point of giving Eva champagne is to take advantage of her sexually, but it ends up relieving her of her inhibitions so that she does something very different, and that is to seek to demonstrate her sense that she is capable of being "the greatest actress in the world." And to do that, she suddenly raises her voice, urges everyone in the room to be quiet, and proceeds to sit on a couch, taking on a brooding demeanor, and to launch into "To be or not to be." She gets everyone's attention, and gets as far as "there's the rub" before the unscrupulous and quite drunk would-be predator playwright interrupts, Polonius-like, that he heard Charlie Chaplin deliver this speech once, but never this funny. Eva is furious, and gets up to try another tack, this time grabbing a lace tablecloth, wrapping it around herself, calling for the lights to be turned out, and ascending a staircase that can serve as a balcony. Now she begins "Romeo, Romeo, wherefore art thou Romeo," and this time just about the entire room is enthralled, and when the time is right, the playwright Sheridan seamlessly offers "Shall I hear more, or shall I speak at this?" She ends the scene at "Take all myself," and wins the sustained applause of the room. The older actor explains to a confused partygoer what she was doing and says "She's playing Juliet and, my dear, she's *playing* it." Then to her as she descends the stairs he says by way of congratulation, "Beautiful. Childishly beautiful. Impossibly beautiful." The young playwright holds his head in pain. Why? Is he falling in love with her? Does he recognize her talent but fear that the world has no place for it? Does he recognize her talent but doubt whether this recognition is inflected by his love, or is it lust?

If the complexity of erotic observation here sounds beyond that of the male-dominated Hollywood studios of the 1930s, you are right, in that the screenplay to *Morning Glory* was based on a play by one of the few leading women of Hollywood production, Zoë Akins, who was also the screenwriter for *Christopher Strong*. *Morning Glory* was later revamped into a musical in the 1940s, but the play was never produced. A complete typescript is in the Zoë Akins Papers held by the Huntington Library, however, and it contains a revelation about the nature of this scene, and how close it comes to connecting not just with contemporary feeling about the relationship of stage and screen, not just with Katharine Hepburn's feelings about the relationship of Hollywood stardom to the kind of stardom commanded by Sarah Bernhardt and Ellen Terry, but finally with the relationship of all of this to Rosalind. And that is because in the play, the first attempt of Eva Lovelace to demonstrate she is the world's greatest actress is not with the world's most famous soliloquy, but rather with a spontaneous transformation in which she partially disrobes, grabs a cane, and declares, as Rosalind, "So this is the forest of Arden." As in the film, what Eva has achieved here (the stage directions call it a "certain air") is disrupted by an inebriated guest, and when, as the stage directions note, "the interruption has broken the spell for the moment," Eva resets herself with a shawl and a staircase and moonlight let in through a window to perform the *Romeo and Juliet* balcony scene. And while she begins the scene later than in the film, it ends in much the same way, except that the theater manager's intentions toward her are made more clear, that he has allowed himself to be seduced, or decided to seduce her.[31]

The scene in the film is powerful, and Hepburn moves without cuts between inebriation and sexual vulnerability into intense concentration, and sells us on the notion that her feeling for the words is such that, while she is saying them, her alcoholic haze is burned away. Why could the film not work with Rosalind? It seems most likely that Arden just wasn't famous enough, and that instead the mass audience of cinema required the two most famous scenes in all Shakespeare to generate a proximate effect. But what are we to make of the sense in the play that with Zoë Akins, her first thought for the way for a young woman to demonstrate she was the greatest actress in the world was to get cross-dressed, or at least to disrobe and modify her clothes to allow a "certain air" of cross-dress, to grab a cane-sword, and announce herself as Rosalind?

What is the nature of the power of this moment? It is read as comic by the women, but not the men—is that because the men are more conscious of what she is doing (there are some indications that the women are either too drunk or not familiar enough with Shakespeare to get the reference)? Or are the men impressed by the vision of the "perfect girl-boy" that Eva has become? Or is it that theatrical power for women comes from assuming the attributes of men, some of the force of tyranny and patriarchy? Or is it that theatrical power is also seductive power, and they do as the other men have been doing—feel caught between desire and desire to protect and nurture, uncertain how to proceed, "a whole house full of lovers" as Tomalin called Jordan's audiences?

---

[31] The pagination of the typescript is not continuous; this scene takes place in act 2, marked p. 28, in "The Morning Glory," typewritten carbon copy play script, ca. 1930, mssZA 1–7330, Zoë Akins Papers, Box 21, Huntington Library, San Marino, California. Another significant shift from the play to the film is the specific genealogy of stage acting that is being conjured. In the play Ellen Terry is there, but instead of Sarah Bernhardt, famous for her Hamlet, the play cites Eleonora Duse. I haven't been able to find evidence that Duse was more associated with Rosalind than Bernhardt, but it seems clear that Bernhardt was more associated with Hamlet, and thus the film's decision makes sense in that light. Both actresses were equally renowned, and both had toured the US extensively in the recent past: Duse died while on a US tour in 1924, and Bernhardt died in 1923.

Katharine Hepburn's early-film successes were intensely personal achievements in ways that her audiences and her collaborators could not likely have known—Leaming's biography makes a strong case for this. She learned gender transgressiveness as well as love and awe toward classical theater from her experience at Bryn Mawr. She had a powerful example of a tomboy in her aunt Edith, who also had early acting ambition, and was one of the first female medical students at Johns Hopkins and a no-holds-barred fighter for woman's suffrage. She learned political engagement and leadership from her mother who was a national suffrage leader. It seems pretty clear that she learned to be dramatically comfortable with her body and sexuality through her parents as well, who were notably open about their satisfying sex life. Her father, a doctor and surgeon, was known to spend time naked in his house and greet guests in varying states of undress.

And her early films also connected with the darkest side of her background, the history of suicide in her family. Hepburn's family, like many upper middle-class white families in New England at the time, was progressive in their support for women's rights, but also deeply influenced by eugenics and concern for heritable traits, madness being one of the most feared of these. (The Bryn Mawr president Carey Thomas's views supporting eugenics attached explicitly to white supremacy have been a cause of a recent reckoning about that woman's in many ways extraordinary and exemplary legacy with the college.) Hepburn's parents were stunningly open about sexuality, but utterly closed about this. Her mother thought she could never speak about the suicide in her mother's family, and her father likewise viewed silence as the only response to suicide of his brother. And Hepburn herself, at age 14, walked into her older brother's attic bedroom at a house they were staying at in New York to find him dead by hanging, a particularly horrific hanging which required extreme resolve on his part as he could not get high enough to have his feet off the ground. The family denied that this had been a suicide and then never spoke of it. Then, a family history of madness is the central plot point in Hepburn's first film, *A Bill of Divorcement*, in which the daughter of a mad father ultimately swears off marriage in favor of remaining childless and devoting herself to his care. *Christopher Strong*, as I already mentioned, has Hepburn's character commit suicide in flight over her sexual guilt from an affair with the married title character.

In these early films, Hepburn was able successfully to use this personal history to her advantage, and draw power from it. But in my view, *Morning Glory* shows her taking on a different kind of technique to answer the doubts about the nature of cinema versus stage acting, and more fundamentally, art versus political action (in the case of her mother) or devotion to service (her father). Shakespeare seems to be a nexus for these energies: the place to connect with an artistic seam of such historic power and ongoing value as to justify a life in art. It was Hamlet and Juliet, as well as a remarkable final scene built around the character's first real stage success (which we do not see), that brought Hepburn a first Academy Award and a measure of legitimacy with her parents.[32] It was the Rosalind she played in the 1950s that seems to have completed the job.

How does Hepburn seem next to the example of the early trailblazer for women's writing, Wroth, or the pansexual power of Jordan? It is extraordinary looking back from 2022 to think that people acting in film in the 1930s could have doubted whether their achievements could be comparable to those of the previous generation of stage actors, but of course that generation has the advantage of no record but recollection, whereas we can take in a performance by Hepburn as many times as we like, albeit from the same angle, and without the unique truth of a live audience and moment that can never be reproduced but through memory.

The early part of Hepburn's career looks a little like Jordan's as various men seek to possess her—including a poet who was for a brief time a darling of critics and hope for American poetry, who seems to have seen her as a kind of goddess.[33] Hepburn too ended up in a non-marital relationship, first with John Ford, and then, for an extended period, with Spencer Tracy. These were not fully satisfying relationships, but she bore no children, and when Tracy died she did not die in obscurity, but reinvented herself, and kept doing so through Rosalind in the 1950s and beyond up into the 1980s. She died, at 96, possessed of herself, and one can only conclude that the richness and fulfillment of her career and life was the product of the long struggle in which Rosalind had played a role, in which Hepburn's aunt and mother had played vital roles, and which through her own imaginative and performative life she also played vitally, making space for women, establishing freedom and possibility that will not be withdrawn or retracted however much men and ideology attempt to withdraw it or retract it.

---

[32] The film in this way seems to avoid the hazards of attempts in the same era to "capture" stage performances in the cinema, especially performances of Shakespeare. For an account of the failings of one such attempt, with Elisabeth Bergner's famous Rosalind, see Russell Jackson, "Remembering Bergner's Rosalind: *As You Like It* on Film in 1936," in *Shakespeare, Memory and Performance*, ed. Peter Holland (Cambridge: Cambridge University Press, 2006), 237–55.

[33] The poet is H. Phelps Putnam (1894–1948), and the poem is "The Daughters of the Sun," which appears in *The Five Seasons* (New York: Scribner, 1931); see Leaming, *Katharine Hepburn*, 254.

Bibliography

Adelman, Janet. *Suffocating Mothers: Fantasies of Maternal Origin in Shakespeare's Plays, "Hamlet" to "The Tempest."* New York: Routledge, 1992.

Adorno, Theodor W. "In Memory of Eichendorff." In *Notes to Literature*, edited by Rolf Tiedemann, translated by Shierry Weber Nicholsen, 1:55–79. New York: Columbia University Press, 1992.

Adorno, Theodor W. "Stefan George." In *Notes To Literature*, edited by Rolf Tiedemann, translated by Shierry Weber Nicholsen, 2:178–92. New York: Columbia University Press, 1992.

Akins, Zoë. "Morning Glory." Play typescript. mssZA 1-7330, Zoë Akins Papers, Box 21, The Huntington Library, San Marino, CA, ca 1930.

Alpers, Paul. *What Is Pastoral?* Chicago: University of Chicago Press, 1996.

Anker, Elizabeth S., and Rita Felski. "Introduction." In *Critique and Postcritique*, edited by Elizabeth S. Anker and Rita Felski, 1–28. Durham, NC and London: Duke University Press, 2017.

Atkinson, Brooks. "Forest of Arden: Katharine Hepburn in *As You Like It*." *New York Times*. February 19, 1950, sect. 2.

Attridge, Derek. *Well-Weighed Syllables: Elizabethan Verse in Classical Metres*. Cambridge: Cambridge University Press, 1974.

Augustine. *Confessions*. Translated by Garry Wills. New York: Penguin, 2008.

Barish, Jonas A. "Mixed Prose-Verse Scenes in Shakespearean Tragedy." In *Shakespeare and Dramatic Tradition: Essays in Honor of S. F. Johnson*, edited by W. R. Elton and William B. Long, 32–46. Newark: University of Delaware Press, 1989.

Barish, Jonas A. "Mixed Verse and Prose in Shakespearean Comedy." In *English Comedy*, edited by Michael Cordner, Peter Holland, and John Kerrigan, 55–67. Cambridge: Cambridge University Press, 1994.

Barkan, Leonard. *Transuming Passion: Ganymede and the Erotics of Humanism*. Stanford, CA: Stanford University Press, 1991.

Berger, Jr., Harry. *Revisionary Play: Studies in the Spenserian Dynamics*. Berkeley and Los Angeles: University of California Press, 1988.

Bickerstaff, Isaac. *The Romp: A Musical Entertainment in Two Acts, Altered from "Love in the City."* Dublin: Wilkinson et al., 1783.

Boaden, James. *The Life of Mrs. Jordan*. 2nd edn. 2 vols. London: Edward Bull, 1831.

Borris, Kenneth. *Visionary Spenser and the Poetics of Early Modern Platonism*. Oxford: Oxford University Press, 2017.

Britton, Dennis Austin. *Becoming Christian: Race, Reformation, and Early Modern English Romance*. New York: Fordham University Press, 2014.

Brogan, T. V. F., A. T. Cole, and L. Blumenfeld. "Classical Prosody." In *The Princeton Encyclopedia of Poetry and Poetics*, edited by Roland Greene, Stephen Cushman,

Clare Cavanagh, Jahan Ramazani, and Paul Rouzer, 4th edn., 260–2. Princeton: Princeton University Press, 2012.

Burrow, Colin. *Shakespeare and Classical Antiquity*. Oxford Shakespeare Topics. Oxford: Oxford University Press, 2013.

Callaghan, Dympna. *Shakespeare Without Women: Representing Gender and Race on the Renaissance Stage*. London: Routledge, 2000.

Cerasano, S. P., and Marion Wynne-Davies, eds. *Renaissance Drama by Women: Texts and Documents*. London and New York: Routledge, 1996.

Chambers, E. K. *The Elizabethan Stage*. 4 vols. Oxford: Clarendon Press, 1923.

Clausen, Wendell. *A Commentary on Virgil Eclogues*. Oxford: Oxford University Press, 1994.

Coles, Kimberly Anne. *Religion, Reform, and Women's Writing in Early Modern England*. Cambridge: Cambridge University Press, 2008.

Curtius, Ernst Robert. *European Literature and the Latin Middle Ages*. Translated by Willard R. Trask. Princeton: Princeton University Press, 1953.

Dabhoiwala, Fara. "Speech and Slavery in the West Indies." *New York Review of Books* 67, no. 13 (August 20, 2020). https://www.nybooks.com/articles/2020/08/20/speech-slavery-west-indies/.

Deleuze, Gilles. "Letter to a Harsh Critic." In *Negotiations, 1972–1990*, translated by Martin Joughin, 3–12. New York: Columbia University Press, 1995.

Dettmar, Kevin J. H. *Entertainment!* 33 1/2. New York: Bloomsbury, 2014.

Dickinson, Emily. *The Poems of Emily Dickinson*. Edited by R. W. Franklin. 3 vols. Cambridge, MA: Belknap Press of Harvard University Press, 1998.

DiGangi, Mario. *The Homoerotics of Early Modern Drama*. Cambridge Studies in Renaissance Literature and Culture. Cambridge: Cambridge University Press, 1997.

Dolven, Jeff. "The Method of Spenser's Stanza." *Spenser Studies* 19 (2004): 17–25.

Dolven, Jeff. "Spenser's Metrics." In *The Oxford Handbook of Edmund Spenser*, edited by Richard A. McCabe, 385–402. Oxford: Oxford University Press, 2010.

Eliot, T. S. *The Waste Land: A Facsimile and Transcript of the Original Drafts*. Edited by Valerie Eliot. New York: Harcourt, Brace & Co., 1971.

Engle, Lars. *Shakespearean Pragmatism: Market of His Time*. Chicago: University of Chicago Press, 1993.

Felski, Rita. *The Limits of Critique*. Chicago: University of Chicago Press, 2015.

Fisher, Will. *Materializing Gender in Early Modern English Literature and Culture*. Cambridge: Cambridge University Press, 2006.

Goldberg, Jonathan. *Sodometries: Renaissance Texts, Modern Sexualities*. Stanford, CA: Stanford University Press, 1992.

Gosson, Stephen. *The Schoole of Abuse and A Short Apologie of the Schoole of Abuse*. English Reprints. London: Thomas Woodcocke, 1579.

Gross, Kenneth. "Shapes of Time: On the Spenserian Stanza." *Spenser Studies* 19 (2004): 27–35.

Guy-Bray, Stephen. *Homoerotic Space: The Poetics of Loss in Renaissance Literature*. Toronto: University of Toronto Press, 2002.

Guy-Bray, Stephen. *Loving in Verse: Poetic Influence as Erotic*. Toronto: University of Toronto Press, 2006.

Hannay, Margaret P. *Mary Sidney, Lady Wroth*. Farnham, Surrey: Ashgate, 2010.

Hanson, Elizabeth. "Boredom and Whoredom: Reading Renaissance Women's Sonnet Sequences." *Yale Journal of Criticism* 10 (1997): 165–91.

Harvey, Elizabeth D. *Ventriloquized Voices: Feminist Theory and English Renaissance Texts.* London and New York: Routledge, 1992.

Henderson, Diana E. "The Theater and Domestic Culture." In *A New History of Early English Drama*, edited by John D. Cox and David Scott Kastan, 173–194. New York: Columbia University Press, 1997.

Huffer, Lynne. *Are the Lips a Grave? A Queer Feminist on the Ethics of Sex.* New York: Columbia University Press, 2013.

Jackson, Russell. "Remembering Bergner's Rosalind: *As You Like It* on Film in 1936." In *Shakespeare, Memory and Performance*, edited by Peter Holland, 237–55. Cambridge: Cambridge University Press, 2006.

Jarvis, Simon. *Adorno: A Critical Introduction.* New York: Routledge, 1998.

Jonson, Ben. *Every Man In His Humour, Quarto Version.* In *The Cambridge Edition of the Works of Ben Jonson*, edited by David Bevington, 1:111–227. Cambridge: Cambridge University Press, 2012.

King, John N. *Spenser's Poetry and the Reformation Tradition.* Princeton: Princeton University Press, 1990.

Kinney, Clare R. "Feigning Female Faining: Spenser, Lodge, Shakespeare, and Rosalind." *Modern Philology* 95 (February 1998): 291–315.

Kuin, Roger. "More I Still Undoe: Louise Labé, Mary Wroth, and the Petrarchan Discourse." *Comparative Literature Studies* 36 (1999): 146–61.

Leaming, Barbara. *Katharine Hepburn.* New York: Crown, 1995.

Lewalski, Barbara Kiefer. *Writing Women in Jacobean England.* Cambridge, MA: Harvard University Press, 1993.

Lewis, C. S. *English Literature in the Sixteenth Century Excluding Drama.* Oxford History of English Literature. Oxford: Clarendon Press, 1954.

Lodge, Thomas. "A Reply to Stephen Gosson's Schoole of Abuse in Defence of Poetry, Musick, and Stage Plays." In *Elizabethan and Jacobean Pamphlets*, edited by George Saintsbury, 1–42. New York: Macmillan, 1892.

Lodge, Thomas. *Lodge's "Rosalynde" Being the Original of Shakespeare's "As You Like It."* Edited by W. W. Greg. New York: Duffield & Co., 1907.

Lyly, John. *Euphues: The Anatomy of Wit, Euphues & His England.* Edited by Morris Croll and Harry Clemons. London: Routledge, 1916.

Mantuanus, Baptista. *Adulescentia.* Translated by Lee Piepho. New York: Garland Publishing, 1989.

Masten, Jeffrey. *Queer Philologies: Sex, Language, and Affect in Shakespeare's Time.* Philadelphia: University of Pennsylvania Press, 2016.

McKay, Adam, dir. *The Big Short.* 2015.

Medovoi, Leerom. "Dogma-Line Racism: Islamaphobia and the Second Axis of Race." *Social Text* 30, no. 2 (2012): 43–74.

Montrose, Louis Adrian. "'The Place of a Brother' in *As You Like It*: Social Process and Comic Form." *Shakespeare Quarterly* 32 (1981): 28–54.

Musser, Amber Jamilla. *Sensational Flesh: Race, Power, and Masochism.* Sexual Cultures. New York: New York University Press, 2014.

Musser, Amber Jamilla. *Sensual Excess: Queer Femininity and Brown Jouissance.* Sexual Cultures. New York: New York University Press, 2018.

Nicholsen, Shierry Weber. *Exact Imagination, Late Work: On Adorno's Aesthetics.* Cambridge, MA: MIT Press, 1997.

Nicholson, Catherine. *Uncommon Tongues: Eloquence and Eccentricity in the English Renaissance.* Philadelphia: University of Pennsylvania Press, 2014.

Nicholson, Helen. *The Knights Hospitaller.* Woodbridge: Boydell Press, 2001.

Orgel, Stephen. *Impersonations: The Performance of Gender in Shakespeare's England.* Cambridge: Cambridge University Press, 1996.

Ovid. *Amores, Medicamina Faciei Feminae, Ars Amatoria, Remedia Amoris.* Edited by E. J. Kenney. Oxford: Clarendon Press, 1995.

Panofsky, Erwin. *Meaning in the Visual Arts.* Chicago: University of Chicago Press, 1955.

Prescott, Anne Lake. *French Poets and the English Renaissance: Studies in Fame and Transformation.* New Haven: Yale University Press, 1978.

Pugh, Syrithe. *Spenser and Ovid.* Burlington, VT: Ashgate, 2005.

Putnam, H. Phelps. *The Five Seasons.* New York: Scribner, 1931.

Rackin, Phyllis. *Shakespeare and Women.* Oxford Shakespeare Topics. Oxford: Oxford University Press, 2005.

Rackin, Phyllis. "Dated and Outdated: The Present Tense of Feminist Shakespeare Criticism." In *Presentism, Gender, and Sexuality in Shakespeare,* edited by Evelyn Gajowski, 49–60. New York: Palgrave Macmillan, 2009.

Rambuss, Richard. *Spenser's Secret Career.* Cambridge Studies in Renaissance Literature and Culture. Cambridge: Cambridge University Press, 1993.

Rambuss, Richard. "The Straightest Story Ever Told." *GLQ: A Journal of Gay and Lesbian Studies* 17, no. 4 (2011): 543–73.

Rancière, Jacques. *Dissensus: On Politics and Aesthetics.* Translated by Steven Corcoran. New York: Continuum, 2010.

Reamer, Owen J. "Spenser's Debt to Marot—Re-Examined." *Texas Studies in Literature and Language* 10 (Winter 1969): 504–27.

Rodriguez, Juana Maria. *Sexual Futures, Queer Gestures, and Other Latina Longings.* Sexual Cultures. New York: New York University Press, 2014.

Rosenfeld, Colleen Ruth. *Indecorous Thinking: Figures of Speech in Early Modern Poetics.* New York: Fordham University Press, 2018.

Ross, Alex. *The Rest Is Noise: Listening to the Twentieth Century.* New York: Farrar, Straus and Giroux, 2007.

Sanchez, Melissa E. *Erotic Subjects: The Sexuality of Politics in Early Modern Literature.* New York: Oxford University Press, 2011.

Sanchez, Melissa E. *Queer Faith: Reading Promiscuity and Race in the Secular Love Tradition.* Sexual Cultures. New York: New York University Press, 2019.

Sanchez, Melissa E. "'To Giue Faire Colour': Sexuality, Courtesy, and Whiteness in *The Faerie Queene.*" *Spenser Studies* 35 (2021): 245–84.

Schwarz, Kathryn. *What You Will: Gender, Contract, and Shakespearean Social Space.* Philadelphia: University of Pennsylvania Press, 2011.

Servius. *Servii Grammatici Qui Feruntur in Vergilii Carmina Commentarii.* Edited by Georg Thilo and Hermann Hagen. Vol. III. Leipzig: Teubner, 1881.

Shakespeare, William. *As You Like It*. Edited by Richard Knowles. New Variorum Edition. New York: Modern Language Association of America, 1977.

Shakespeare, William. *As You Like It*. Edited by Juliet Dusinberre. London: Arden Shakespeare, 2006.

Shakespeare, William. *The Norton Shakespeare*. Edited by Stephn Greenblatt, Walter Cohen, Suzanne Gossett, Jean E. Howard, Katharine Eisaman Maus, and Gordon McMullan. 3rd ed. New York: Norton, 2016.

Shannon, Laurie. *The Accommodated Animal: Cosmopolity in Shakespearean Locales*. Chicago: University of Chicago Press, 2013.

Shapin, Steven. *A Social History of Truth: Civility and Science in Seventeenth-Century England*. Chicago: University of Chicago Press, 1994.

Sherman, Lowell, dir. *Morning Glory*. 1933.

Sidney, Sir Philip. *Sir Philip Sidney*. Edited by Katherine Duncan-Jones. The Oxford Authors. Oxford: Oxford University Press, 1989.

Smith, Bruce R. *Homosexual Desire in Shakespeare's England: A Cultural Poetics*. Chicago: University of Chicago Press, 1991.

Smith, Bruce R. *Phenomenal Shakespeare*. Blackwell Manifestos. Chichester, UK: Wiley-Blackwell, 2010.

Smith, Zadie. "The Divine Ms H." *The Guardian*. July 1, 2003. https://www.theguardian.com/film/2003/jul/01/film.zadiesmith.

Sontag, Susan. *Against Interpretation and Other Essays*. New York: Farrar, Straus and Giroux, 1966.

Spenser, Edmund. *The Faerie Queene*. Edited by A. C. Hamilton, Hiroshi Yamashita, and Toshiyuki Suzuki. 2nd edn. Harlow, England: Longman, 2001.

Spenser, Edmund. *The Shorter Poems*. Edited by Richard A. McCabe. London: Penguin, 1999.

Spenser, Edmund. *The Yale Edition of the Shorter Poems of Edmund Spenser*. Edited by William A. Oram, Einar Bjorvand, Ronald Bond, Thomas H. Cain, Alexander Dunlop, and Richard Schell. New Haven: Yale University Press, 1989.

Steele, Claude M. *Whistling Vivaldi: How Stereotypes Affect Us and What We Can Do*. New York: W. W. Norton, 2010.

Temple, Julien, dir. *The Great Rock 'n' Roll Swindle*. 1980.

Terry, Ellen. *Four Lectures on Shakespeare*. Edited by Christopher St. John. Reprint of 1932 edn. New York: B. Blom, 1969.

Tomalin, Claire. *Mrs Jordan's Profession: The Actress and the Prince*. New York: Alfred A. Knopf, 1995.

Traub, Valerie. *The Renaissance of Lesbianism in Early Modern England*. Cambridge Studies in Renaissance Literature and Culture. Cambridge: Cambridge University Press, 2002.

Virgil. *Eclogues, Georgics, Aeneid I–VI*. Translated by H. Rushton Fairclough. Vol. 63. Loeb Classical Library. Cambridge, MA: Harvard University Press, 1999.

Warley, Christopher. "Un-Canonizing Lady Mary Wroth?" *Arcade: Literature, the Humanities, & the World* (blog), 2010. https://arcade.stanford.edu/blogs/un-canonizing-lady-mary-wroth.

West, William N. *As If: Essays in "As You Like It"*. Earth: Dead Letter Office, BABEL Working Group, 2016.

Wilkinson, L. P. *Golden Latin Artistry*. Cambridge: Cambridge University Press, 1963.

Wilson-Okamura, David Scott. *Spenser's International Style*. Cambridge: Cambridge University Press, 2013.

Wilson-Okamura, David Scott. *Virgil in the Renaissance*. Cambridge: Cambridge University Press, 2010.

Wroth, Lady Mary. *Pamphilia to Amphilanthus*. Edited by Gary Waller. Salzburg: Institut für Englische Sprache und Litertur, University of Salzburg, 1977.

Wroth, Lady Mary. *The Poems of Lady Mary Wroth*. Edited by Josephine A. Roberts. Baton Rouge: Louisiana State University Press, 1983.

Wroth, Lady Mary. *The First Part of The Countess of Montgomery's Urania*. Edited by Josephine A. Roberts. Medieval and Renaissance Texts and Studies 140. Binghamton: Center for Medieval and Early Renaissance Studies, State University of New York at Binghamton, 1995.

Wroth, Lady Mary. *The Second Part of the Countess of Montgomery's Urania*. Edited by Josephine A. Roberts, Suzanne Gossett, and Janel Mueller. Tempe: Renaissance English Text Society in Conjunction with Arizona Center for Medieval and Renaissance Studies, 1999.

Wroth, Mary. *The Countess of Montgomery's Urania (Abridged)*. Edited by Mary Ellen Lamb. Tempe: Arizona Center for Medieval and Renaissance Studies, 2011.

Wroth, Lady Mary. "Mary Wroth's Poetry: An Electronic Edition." Edited by Paul Salzman, 2012. http://wroth.latrobe.edu.au/all-poems.html.

Wroth, Lady Mary. *"Pamphilia to Amphilanthus" in Manuscript and Print*. Edited by Ilona Bell. Toronto: Iter Press, 2017.

Index